LIFEBOATS
TO
ARARAT

Also by Sheldon Campbell

SNAKES OF THE AMERICAN WEST
(with Charles E. Shaw)

LIFEBOATS
TO
ARARAT

Sheldon Campbell

NYT
Times
BOOKS

*All photographs in this book
appear courtesy of the San Diego Zoo,
with the exception of the killer whale photograph,
which was provided by Sea World, Inc.*

Published by TIMES BOOKS, a division
of Quadrangle/The New York Times Book Co., Inc.
Three Park Avenue, New York, N.Y. 10016

Published simultaneously in Canada by
Fitzhenry & Whiteside, Ltd., Toronto.

Library of Congress Cataloging in Publication Data

Campbell, Sheldon.
   Lifeboats to Ararat.

   Includes index.
   1. San Diego, Calif. Zoological Garden.
2. Zoological gardens.   3. Wildlife conservation.
I. Title.
QL76.5.U62S262   639'.9   78-53301
ISBN 0-8129-0767-1

Manufactured in the United States of America.
Illustration by Howard Berelson
Designed by Beth Tondreau

For my wife, Florence
Fellow trudger over many zoos

And the ark rested in the seventh month, on the seventeenth day of the month, upon the mountains of Ararat.

(GEN. 8:5)

And God spake unto Noah, saying . . . Bring forth with thee every living thing that is with thee, of all flesh, both of fowl, and of cattle, and of every creeping thing that creepeth upon the earth; that they may breed abundantly in the earth, and be fruitful, and multiply upon the earth.

(GEN. 8:15, 17)

And the fear of you and the dread of you shall be upon every beast of the earth, and upon every fowl of the air, upon all that moveth upon the earth, and upon all the fishes of the sea; into your hands are they delivered.

(GEN. 9:2)

Let us feel a little shame that such a conference should be necessary at all.

GERALD DURRELL at the opening of the First Conference on "Breeding Endangered Species in Captivity," on the Island of Jersey, 1972.

Contents

Acknowledgements

Writers of books like this need much good will and help, and I have received both beyond measure.

If willing cooperation and conscientious assistance could be transmuted into gold, it would require a Midas to repay Marvin L. Jones, an incredible man with a computer mind programed for instant recall with encyclopedic knowledge of the world's zoos, their directors, staffs, and animals. To him I owe much.

Much encouragement to write this book came from Edwin and Gloria Self, publisher-editors of *San Diego Magazine*, which printed some of my earliest zoo stories.

Obviously, I am indebted to the trustees and staff of the San Diego Zoo and San Diego Wild Animal Park, specifically, to J. Dallas Clark, president of the Zoological Society of San Diego, Charles L. Bieler, the director, Kurt Benirschke, M.D., director of research, and Kenhelm Stott, Jr., research associate, all of whom read the book in manuscript and offered both encouragement and advice. Many others also contributed: James P. Bacon, Jr., Ph.D.; Richard L. Binford; Ernest B. Chew; Frederick Childress; William B. Crytser; James M. Dolan, Jr., Ph.D.; Joan Embery; Charles Faust; Katharine Garstka; George Gillespie; Lynn A. Griner, D.V.M.; Robert H. Grams; Pegi Harvey; Clyde A. Hill; Bill Lasley, Ph.D.; Kenton C. Lint; N. Kendall Marvin; Charles A. McLaughlin, Ph.D.; Jane E. Meir, D.V.M.; John W. Muth, Jr.; Mark S. Rich; Arthur Crane Risser, Ph.D.; Phillip T. Robinson, D.V.M.; Charles R. Schroeder, D.V.M.; Thomas Schultz; Kirstie Shaw; Marjorie Shaw; JoAnn Thomas; Carole Towne; Kenneth Willingham; and Jay Wilson.

Thanks also to Devra Kleiman, Ph.D., of the National Zoo, Charles J. Sedgwick, D.V.M., University of California at Davis, Michael Soule, Ph.D., University of California at San Diego, Gerald N. Esra, D.V.M., of the Los Angeles Zoo, and William Seaton of Sea World, Inc., for providing ideas and material used in this book.

Maureen Robison was a conscientious and hard-working typist who somehow managed to wend her way through the illegibilities of my original manuscript—for which I am grateful.

Finally, this book could not have been written had I not been able to visit many great zoos and talk with their directors and assistants. Countless thanks go to Director Walter van den Bergh of the Antwerp Zoo and Planckendael, Harald Jes of the Cologne Aquarium, Wolfdietrich Kümhe of the Cologne Zoo, Director Dr. Lothar Dittrich and Dr. Wolf Everts of the Hanover Zoo, Director Wolf Brehm of Walsrode, Dr. Hans Frädrich of West Berlin Zoo, Dr. Werner Schröder of the Berlin Aquarium, Dr. Wolfgang Grummt of the Tierpark in Berlin (East), Dr. Christoph Scherpner of the Frankfurt Zoo, Director Dr. Wilfird Neugebauer and Dr. Anton Brotzler of the Stuttgart Zoo, Director Dr. Ernst Lang of the Basle Zoo, Director Dr. Peter Weileman and Dr. Christian Schmidt of the Zurich Zoo, Prof. Jacques Nouvel, former director of the Paris Zoo at Vincennes and the menagerie in the Jardin des Plantes, Director Ir D. van Dam of Rotterdam, Hon. Director Gerald Durrell and Director Jeremy Mallinson of the Jersey Wildlife Trust, Director C.G.C. Rawlins of the London Zoo and its wild animal park at Whipsnade, Director John Knowles of Marwell Zoo, Director Geoffrey Greed of Bristol Zoo, and Dr. Janet Keir of Slimbridge Wildfowl Trust. In the United States I had much help from Director William Conway of the New York (Bronx) Zoo, Ronald Reuther, formerly of the Philadelphia Zoo, Director Dr. Theodore Reed of the National Zoo and its breeding reserve at Front Royal, Virginia, Director Warren Iliff of the Portland Zoo, Director Saul Kitchener of the San Francisco Zoo, and Director Dr. Warren Thomas of the Los Angeles Zoo.

Preface

Zoos are among mankind's oldest institutions, dating back at least 4,500 years, and probably more. Across the world they have brought together and displayed live wild animals for people to look at and over the years hundreds of millions have. Any institution with so long a history and so universally attended must reach something in people deeper than idle curiosity. Since it is fashionable to speak of roots today, it might be suggested that zoos allow us to stay in touch with our most primitive roots in a primeval world where human survival depended on knowing the shapes and habits of wild animals. So important were wild creatures to our distant ancestors that they were the most frequent subjects of paintings on cave walls, formed the basis for virtually all early religions, and were in numerous instances worshiped as gods.

Now our survival is threatened more by what we ourselves have wrought, and by the stresses of living among these creations, than it is by wild animals to whom we relegate less and less living space with each passing year. In this world the need for good zoological gardens is urgent. The exponential growth of human population and the ever-increasing sprawl of cities does more than rob land from wildlife: it pushes the animals farther away from city dwellers. People live in brick, concrete, and glass environments where they lose all touch with wilderness; children grow up who have never tried to catch a frog, never seen a hawk soar or a deer step daintily into a forest clearing—let alone watched a herd of elephants amble across the savannah or a pride of lions stalk prey.

People who have the time and money can take an occasional trip to the remaining wilderness and find, in places where wild animals still live, the renewal of spirit that comes from prolonged visits to wild country. For millions of others who are unable to leave the cities or can't afford to, good zoos laid out among plants and trees can bring what conservationist Ian Player calls "a taste of wilderness." Perhaps more important in the long run, zoos can help give deprived people an awareness that we share the world with many other animals and should have a decent regard for their worth and right to live. If zoos did no more than accomplish these two ends, they would serve a noble purpose.

As it happens, however, today's zoos can do far more. They can become breeding centers for those wild species whose continued existence has become precarious. The term "captive breeding" has been used to describe this new role of zoos, and this book describes the effort—the most important task that zoos have yet undertaken.

Behind the stories of zoos and captive breeding lies the assumption that we who are lords of the earth and challenge the heavens must do all in our power to keep our fellow creatures alive on this planet—for it may be our last chance. Arguments for saving wild animals from extinction can be set forth at great length. In short, they go something like this: First, whenever we humans cause a sharp decline in any wild animal population, we may be doing something to the environment that also threatens us. Second, life on a barren planet largely denuded of wildlife would be worse than dreadful; it would very likely cause irreparable damage to the human psyche. Third, our willful destruction of animal species is immoral—unless we accept the Hobbesian notion that the true state of nature is one of general war in which the possession of power, and that alone, determines what is right or wrong. Finally, though, the arguments vanish and we are left with intuition. In the words of Henry David Thoreau, "Every creature is better alive than dead, men and moose and pine trees, and he who understands it aright will rather preserve its life than destroy it."

All this may sound quite stuffy and serious, or even worse, philosophical. Fortunately, much of what goes on in zoos is funny, at least in retrospect, and for those who feel as I do that the world has enough sadness, any vein of humor is worth mining. I have, I hope, mined a rich lode here.

One should always write about what one knows best; so much of the material in this book is drawn from my forty-three years of intimate experience with the San Diego Zoo and later, the San Diego Wild Animal Park. Because these two institutions get frequent mention I should differentiate them. Both are managed by the nonprofit Zoological Society of San Diego (of which I am one of twelve trustees). The zoo, set on nearly 100 wooded acres of Balboa Park in the heart of San Diego, was founded in 1916. The Wild Animal Park, opened in 1972, is a breeding reserve open to the public that is situated on 1,800 acres of foothills along the San Pasqual Valley some thirty miles north of San Diego. The zoo's exhibits are built on traditional lines, with extensive use of open moated enclosures. The Park on the other hand emphasizes open space, with enclosures that average 80 acres each where animals live in mixed groups as they would in the wild (except for their natural predators). Visitors walk or ride buses around the zoo, but see the Park from a ground monorail that travels for five miles among the exhibits.

There are many fine zoos in the world, and a few other wild animal parks. Each has as much to offer in the way of anecdotes and stories as the ones I know best. Some (and I could wish more) that appear in this book I gathered in trips to many of the world's zoos, quite a few of which are moving seriously into the exciting realm of captive breeding.

Let no one think this book is an apology for zoos. For every good zoo in the world there are bad ones that no defense can justify, and they get none here. With proper care and good environments wild animals thrive in captivity. Improperly kept under poor conditions they languish in misery and boredom. This situation should never be, and any zoo or parts of zoos where animals are impoverished should be changed or abolished. The zoo of the future, to borrow a phrase from Dr. Heinrich Dathe, director of the Tierpark in Berlin, should be a paradise for animals.

SHELDON CAMPBELL
San Diego, California
March 20, 1978

LIFEBOATS
TO
ARARAT

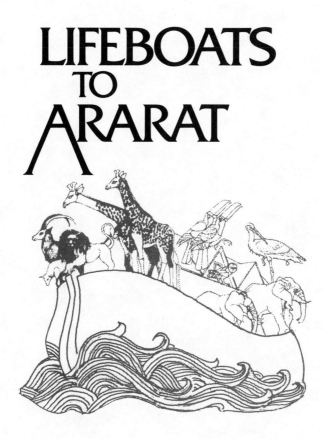

The Bear and the
Unicorn

Venturing out of the forests near the Ocean Cape Coast
Guard Station (LORAN) on the Yakutat Peninsula of
Alaska, Blue Bear (or Blue Barry as he later became
known) put himself on the welfare rolls. It became his habit several nights a week during that summer of 1972 to collect garbage,
and anything else edible he could get his paws on, whether the
men and their families stationed at Ocean Cape wanted it collected
or not.

As the people at the station became increasingly aware of Blue
Bear's assumption that any food left outside of double-locked and
bolted doors constituted a handout they became concerned not so
much about the stolen food and the incredible mess that Blue Bear
created, but at the possibility that someone, perhaps a child, might
meet the animal during one of his raids and be mauled. This concern became more urgent when Blue Bear took to breaking and
entering. One night, motivated no doubt by the delicious smells
wafting from half a case of Banana Dream cupcakes, he smashed a
window in the station's main Quonset hut, moved in and devastated
the kitchen, cupcakes included. The point was that two men were
present, though certainly not sleeping, in quarters next to the
kitchen. Their room was large enough for two men but definitely
not for two men and one bear.

No town meeting was called, but the decision was arrived at
nonetheless that Blue Bear must be disposed of. In matters like this
people use words like dispose or destroy, or in the case of the
United States Department of Agriculture, depopulate, when what
they really mean is kill. Blue Bear it was thought and generally
agreed would have to be killed.

3

Killing the bear posed no problem. Trophy hunters would scramble from all points of the globe where men hunt for sport to get a shot at a genuine blue or glacier bear, a subspecies of the American black bear (*Ursus americanus*) that lives only on the Yakutat Peninsula. The American black bear is not always black, being cinnamon colored over parts of its range, blue, and even white on Princess Royal and Gribble islands off the coast of British Columbia. The blue phase doesn't show up very often. Most of the Yakutat bears are black, though presumably many carry the genes that turn some a gun-barrel blue and makes them the immediate and much sought-after target of trophy hunters. In fact, at the time of Blue Bear's depredations there was a notice posted on bulletin boards in nearby Yakutat that offered $1,000 from a wealthy Los Angeles hunter for information that would enable him to kill a blue bear.

Blue Bear's doom now appeared certain, for even as the softhearted at Ocean Cape vacillated, he not only continued his raids, he extended them into the nearby town of Yakutat. Had he been human and able to predict the reaction to this bold move he would have known it was suicidal. It was now open season on bears, and away from the Coast Guard Station he would no longer have the protection that being on federal land ironically gave him.

There were still people at the station who felt that Blue Bear should be saved—removed from the area, they agreed, but saved so that blue bears would continue to exist. Alaskan game laws do not distinguish blue from black but blue bears, being such prized trophies, seldom live to see the second half of life, and as a result do not breed as many young as their black brothers and sisters. It seemed a shame, argued the conservationists at the Ocean Cape station, to let this fine specimen be cut down in his early bearhood.

Several of the Ocean Cape personnel had been stationed at the Coast Guard Station in San Diego. One of them, Jim Jensen, a member of the coterie that wanted to save the bear, recalled the many hours he had spent in the San Diego Zoo. Perhaps, he suggested to his companions, the zoo might be interested in capturing a blue bear.

Clyde A. Hill, Curator of Conservation for the San Diego Zoo was spending the evening watching his youngest son idly flip through TV stations when the phone rang. Hill answered.

"Mr. Hill? My name is Jim Jensen. I'm calling from Yakutat, Alaska. Have you heard of the blue bears that live around here?" Hill allowed that he had. Jensen continued. "Well we have one here that can easily be taken if the San Diego Zoo is interested—and I hope you are because otherwise the animal is going to be shot."

"We're definitely interested," Hill replied. "Let me call you back."

That simple exchange triggered an incredible series of events that led ultimately to an expedition that few zoos have been involved in to obtain animals since the late nineteenth or early twentieth century.

At the outset Hill, a tough-minded former paratrooper with a respect for the proper order of things, recognized that he personally could not authorize an expedition of such possible magnitude. In many zoos curators have a small budgetary leeway in spending money to buy animals, but this expedition would not only greatly exceed any budget, it would affect the zoo's public posture. If, for example, word got out prematurely that the San Diego Zoo was trying to capture a rare blue bear it would almost certainly arouse ultra conservationists who might well mount a campaign to "Keep the Blue Bear Free." They would not want the animal shot either, but if the threat of capture were immediate they would tackle that problem first and deal with the shooting later. In the meantime Blue Bear was raiding even farther afield, increasing the odds that someone with a gun would quite legally bring him down.

Hill reported his conversation to the zoo's director, then Donald J. Kintner, a man unfamiliar with animals but well aware of the effect of publicity on both institutions and individuals. Kintner was delighted with the prospect of going after Blue Bear, but certain that the Zoo's Exhibit Committee and the trustees would not want to spend funds substantially in excess of the already established budget. Perhaps there was another way. Might not the military like to help? The president of the San Diego Society at that time was Lt. Gen. Victor H. Krulak, U.S.M.C., ret. Possibly through his connections . . .

As it turned out the United States Navy, particularly in the person of Comdr. Marchel Tevelson, acted as catalyst to an operation that eventually included brass as high as an Assistant Secretary of Defense, the California Air National Guard, Alaska Airlines, and the Alaskan Department of Fish and Game. Kintner had given the first push by talking at a review that same day to Capt. Ralph DiCori, Commanding, United States Naval Training Center in San Diego. Capt. DiCori saw the opportunity to bring in a Navy program called Project Handclasp, designed to spread goodwill among humanitarian, service, educational, and religious organizations under which the zoo fortunately qualified. DiCori in turn passed the idea to Comdr. Tevelson, the chief handclasper.

Hill in the meantime was clearing a different set of channels. After first confirming with Lt. (j.g.) Barry Benson, commander at Ocean Cape, that there was a problem bear, he telephoned Frank Jones of the Alaska Fish and Game department who agreed to issue a permit for the capture of Blue Bear, in effect appointing the San Diego Zoo an agent of Alaska Fish and Game to set up a propagating bank for the color phase (provided of course that mates for Blue Bear could be found).

Return now to Tevelson, who would qualify for anybody's book of records as champion long-distance caller since the telephone was invented. Outfitted with a switchboard that provided direct connections with military installations throughout the world, Tevelson put Hill on the line and began a marathon series of calls that would have done credit to a mission design to rescue a marooned astronaut, let alone a marauding bear. It was Friday afternoon. From 3:00 P.M. to 5:30, then again from 6:30 until midnight, both Hill and Tevelson had their ears pressed to the phone. At midnight an exhausted Hill fell into bed while the indefatigable Tevelson carried on alone until 2:30 A.M. In their first call they exacted a promise from Lt. Benson that no attempt would be made, by the Coast Guard people at least, to kill Blue Bear during the next two days, which was all the time Benson felt he could risk. Now what they needed was more than promises of cooperation, plenty of which they got, but the authority to turn the capture attempt into a full-scale military mission.

By Saturday morning some 75 calls had been made and the Coast Guard, Air Force, Navy, Air National Guards of Alaska and California, and Alaska Airlines were wired in on the proposed mission. But still no authorization had been received. Shortly after

8:00 A.M. Saturday morning Hill and Tevelson finally got through to an Assistant Secretary of Defense who, at the time their call came, was on a ladder painting his house. The Assistant Secretary was hesitant at first—"A blue what?"—but kindly promised to research the subject and call back. Twenty-three hours after the first call had been placed—and with one day left of Lt. Benson's promise not to harm the bear—permission was granted for full military participation in the San Diego's Zoo's effort to capture an animal.

Since the California Air National Guard trained on weekends anyway, it was directed to handle the mission. At the zoo a capture team composed of Hill, Charles J. Sedgwick, D.V.M. (expert on the use of capture guns), and Ron Garrison, photographer, was directed to stand by. With the orders cut, the military wasted no time. At 5:00 P.M. that same day the zoo personnel, who had barely enough time to gather warm clothing and their supplies, including a crate for Blue Bear, were picked up and started on their way to Yakutat. The aircraft was one used to fly California's governor. Not only was it a bit more comfortable than the normal Guard equipment, it was flown by a senior pilot Col. Jerome N. Hoberg, seconded by Capt. Chris Pantos, a former Pan Am jet pilot turned Sacramento schoolteacher. Even so, on early Sunday morning at Tacoma, Washington the first hitch developed. Weather conditions between Tacoma and Juneau were sour with heavy icing and turbulent air. It was weather that a jet could fly above, but the Guard plane was a C-54, military version of the DC-4, and if it flew at all, which was inadvisable, it would have to fly through. This being Sunday, less than a day remained of Blue Bear's reprieve.

For two days while everyone fretted about what was happening to the bear the C-54 was grounded. At this juncture Alaska Airlines stepped in. They couldn't take the crate, but the regular jet to Yakutat had room at their expense for the three zoo people. Col. Hoberg promised to bring the crate as soon as the weather cleared. The mission was on again.

When Hill and his cohorts arrived at Ocean Cape, Lt. Benson informed them that the race to save Blue Bear had narrowed. Several hunters, including professionals, had taken to the field hoping to kill the animal. Benson had in fact found and removed some moose meat bait and a hunting platform that eager hunters had set up on government land. With the guns out it was simply a question of who got Blue Bear first.

Benson assigned the zoo men rooms with a clear view of the base's main garbage rack, a focal point of Blue Bear's raids, which had continued unabated. Nevertheless, Hill found that the bear had not exhausted his goodwill. Many of the people on the base, informed that the rescue team was coming, had taken to leaving out scraps of hamburger, buns, and even the beloved cupcakes in order to keep the bear near the base and away from the hunter-ridden forests near Yakutat.

Because the zoo team was determined to start its hunt that very night, Dr. Sedgwick immediately had to tackle a critical problem. One does not go around shooting drug-filled darts into an animal without knowing as much as possible about that animal. Drugs are chancy at best. Their effects are changed by such variables as the animal's age, general health, and, most critical of all, weight. The descriptions of Blue Bear's pelage and the very fact that he was a live blue bear, not yet a rug, indicated his youth. The amounts and types of food he regularly ate were only too well known since the people at the base were his principal purveyors. They assured Sedgwick that he had to be a healthy bear—a very healthy bear.

His weight was another matter. Jensen in his first call to Hill had said that Blue Bear tipped 300 pounds, but weights under such circumstances tend to become exaggerated, particularly if the animal is potentially dangerous and has a thick fur coat. Sedgwick needed to know the weight with some precision since the amount of drug needed for a 300-pound animal might kill a 200 pounder. To arrive at the correct dosage Sedgwick took a fix. There were no photos of Blue Bear, but several witnesses had caught glimpses of him during his raids. By asking the witnesses to compare Blue Bear with everything from a gorilla to a 55-gallon oil drum, Sedgwick finally settled on 200 or fewer pounds and dosed the dart accordingly.

The capture team also spent some time discussing a second problem. The drugs used in capture darts don't take effect immediately; like a sleeping pill they allow several moments before slumber comes. The zoo men were perfectly aware that in these moments the bear, stung by the dart, could cover a lot of ground. The

forests around Yakutat, which gets over 133 inches of rain a year, are dark and lush, providing many places for a bear to hide among immense Sitka spruce and western hemlock. The prospect of chasing their quarry across sphagnum moss and pine needles that could conceal many natural booby traps—sharp stumps, rocks, deep holes, small streams—was not pleasant. Their greatest fear, though, was for the bear. If they lost sight of him after the hit he would find a concealing thicket somewhere, lie down, fall asleep, and die. Reconaissance was the only answer, so as the fall evening waned they used the remaining light to scout the probable lines of Blue Bear's retreat from the garbage racks, searching out and noting any obstacles that might impede the chase.

It turned cold that night. The first snows were due at any time, and they were grateful during their vigil over the garbage cans that they (or their wives) had packed warm clothing. As the night wore on without any sign of the bear, the adrenaline flow of the past few days, the keyed-up feeling, was dulled and fatigue began to weigh heavily. And with fatigue strange thoughts, begun as little jokes to pass the time, began to be taken half seriously by numbed minds. It was Dr. Sedgwick who came up with the direst thought. Suppose, he suggested, that they and the San Diego Zoo were victims of the world's most elaborate snipe hunt? Each of them at one time or another during their youth had waited somewhere at night with an open bag for a snipe that never came, and then found amid the laughter of comrades next morning that it had been a hoax, one of the oldest known rites of initiation into adulthood. Sedgwick, speaking in low tones, went on to elaborate his suspicion. Men at isolated military bases were noted for the practical jokes they played to relieve the monotony of their lives. Perhaps Blue Bear didn't exist at all. Perhaps he was just an updated version of the snipe, and when next morning came all the men at Ocean Cape would join in the laughter, not only at them, the chief victims, but at the California Air National Guard, Alaska Airlines, all the others. . . .

A ringing telephone dispelled the gloom. It was Jensen. The bear was even now visiting his house trailer. "Come on the double!" The injunction proved impossible to obey, since they had to awaken a chief who could provide a truck and driver to cover the considerable distance to Jensen's place, but in spite of the slowness, or possibly because of it, they had a reward. As they moved down the dirt road toward Jensen's trailer they saw for one clear instant in the beams of the truck's headlights Blue Bear himself, or as Hill later put it, "A blue bear, a magnificent blue bear, a pluperfect blue bear, far superior to any museum specimen I had ever seen . . ."

That momentary sight of Blue Bear removed any thoughts of hoax and reawakened confidence that their mission would be a success. But as day after day passed while the bear was reported infuriatingly at the places they weren't, confidence began to wane again. Striving to change their luck they even tried an aerial reconnaissance. Jim Boulette, who worked in the local airport control tower, flew them over hundreds of square miles around the base as he gave instructions to a student flier. The only bear they saw and photographed was a Yakutat grizzly running across a grassy swale to escape the low-flying plane.

On Friday, one week after the adventure had begun, they had about reached the end of their hopes. The weather now was turning colder every day, and the first snows were surely not far off with their signal for Blue Bear to begin his hibernation. It would be bad enough, they realized, to return empty handed in any event, doubly bad if they strung an eventually unsuccessful hunt out much farther. Failure in the mission would probably cause the zoo's trustees to look coldly upon suggestions for any similar expeditions, which would be a pity, for both Hill and Sedgwick were convinced that the future would increasingly require zoo efforts to capture animals whose existence in the wild was threatened. With their spirits at lowest ebb they decided that Saturday would have to be the last full day.

Then came a break. They received a report that on Thursday night a bear had robbed the garbage can at the home of Ken Mitchell, state forester in the district. Arriving with all speed at the Mitchell home they interviewed the family. Only the children, barely more than toddlers, had actually seen the bear, and they reported it to be a grizzly. Yet with the clarity that children often put into their language the Mitchell kids described the bear as "sparkly all over." From this statement, knowing that they were grasping at straws, the zoo men inferred that the children had actually seen Blue Bear whose coat would glint in a "sparkly" way

when light struck the blue hairs. The tide of hope began to rise again.

That night they staked out three sites. Dr. Sedgwick sat shivering in an unheated toolshed that gave him a good view of the Mitchell house and garbage cans. (As he later put it, never had so few spent so much time with their eyes glued on garbage cans.) Ron Garrison sat shivering in a jeep that overlooked a spot near the airport where he swore he had once seen the bear while driving by himself. Hill sat shivering in a truck on another part of the base where Blue Bear had previously raided. The shivering was all. Nothing else occurred that night.

On Saturday morning Hill made reservations for the return flight. Then, much in the mood of mourners about to leave a wake, they paid their respects to the people who had helped in the hunt. This would be their last night. With little thought of success they decided to vary the previous night's plan only slightly. Sedgwick would again stake out the Mitchell house while Hill and Garrison patrolled the other likely spots in a jeep.

Sometime after 8:00 P.M. while there was still light from the Aurora Borealis to see by, though dimly, Sedgwick, clad in multilayered clothing, his teeth chattering, saw through the partially open door of the toolshed the clear outline of a bear's head poked warily around the corner of the Mitchell house. He brought his capture rifle to a ready position. The bear was within close range, so close that a well-aimed shot—and Sedgwick had used the capture gun many times at the zoo—could scarcely miss. He began to exult quietly to himself, "We're going to get him. We're going to get him!"

But the script, as anyone versed in suspense stories knows, called for one final complication. It came in the form of a truck, a truck Sedgwick swore that had to be carrying loose horseshoes and other odd bits of iron, as it chugged and clattered and banged its way up to the Mitchell house. A man got out, slammed the door as though he were mad at it, stomped over to the Mitchell's door and knocked loudly, meantime shouting, "Hey, is anybody home?" Someone was and he was let in. Sedgwick could hear him asking to borrow an air mattress. During the conversation one of the children announced that Sedgwick was on stakeout in the toolshed. In a few minutes the man came out, but instead of returning to the truck he came over to the toolshed to ask Sedgwick how it was going. "It would go a lot better if you got out of here," Sedgwick whispered. "The bear is within a few yards of us right now." With an incredulous look the man stood for a moment, then walked on obvious tiptoe back to the truck, started it up and clattered off into the night.

In the long vigil that followed Sedgwick again began to lose hope. Surely the bear had been scared off by the noisy truck. For a brief moment, in fact, he felt he was hallucinating when the bear reappeared at the same spot as before. It sniffed the air, moved its head in several directions, listened for unusual sounds, then came around the corner of the house and headed for the garbage can. The light was now so dim that Sedgwick could see only the shape and not the color. It seemed large enough to be a grizzly, and a grizzly might not as readily succumb to the amount of drug in the dart. Yet this was what the whole adventure was about, to get the bear. He couldn't risk scaring it off in an effort to identify it. Deciding to go ahead, he raised the dart gun to his shoulder. The movement caused his jacket to rustle, not loudly but distinctly. Before he could take aim the bear coughed, clicked its teeth in an ominous manner, and charged.

Sedgwick believed his end had come. In his mind's eye he saw his widow and children getting the news that a bear had mauled him to death. It was the last fate he would have contemplated for himself. But like many animals who charge, the bear was bluffing. A yard from Sedgwick it swerved off. Then it scrambled up a small pine tree that grew near the toolshed. The vision of his grieving wife vanished from Sedgwick's mind. Now he would have his chance. Leaping from the toolshed, he shouted, "Get up that tree, damn you! Go on, bear, get up that tree!" The bear scrambled even higher. At this point Sedgwick was in the ideal position for a man with a dart gun. When the bear was hit it would be unable to run. He raised the rifle to his shoulder, took aim as carefully as the darkness would permit, and fired. He could hear the soft plop as the dart hit the bear, but the animal made no further move. In three minutes it began to have trouble holding onto the tree. It kept trying to tighten its grip, but an effort of will could not overcome the effects of muscle-relaxing drugs, and inch by inch the animal began to slide toward the ground. Four minutes

later the end came. Like one of the creatures in a Disney cartoon the bear slid down the trunk and collapsed gently at the foot of the tree. Sedgwick made a cautious approach and looked down. It was a blue bear.

For a time at least, Yakutat Barry did not enjoy a life of complete fulfillment in his large moated enclosure at the San Diego Zoo. For one thing were were no garbage cans to raid, and who knows what Hemingwayesque moment-centered joy, what danger-sharpened perceptions a bear may get out of risking its life to get a meal. Nor were there now in Barry's existence an abundance of Banana Dream cupcakes. There were, in fact, none at all. His zoo diet was carefully prescribed to give him a proper balance of fats, carbohydrates, and proteins with an occasional naturally sweetened goody thrown in.

Barry's principal deprivation, however, was of a bear companion, a mate to share his exile. No one wanted to deprive him. Almost from the day Barry arrived via the California Air National Guard plane, Curator Hill started looking for a suitable consort. At first, suitable for Hill meant a blue female, a tall order since the infrequent reports of blue bears (sex unknown) on the Yakutat Peninsula inevitably came from places that would be accessible only by helicopter or parachute, which would pose serious problems of transport even if a team was successful in finding and then darting a bear that might not really be there in the first place. One doesn't parachute away from places, and taking out a crated bear would require a larger helicopter than any available at Yakutat. Hill also racked his and his fellow curators' brains, to say nothing of consulting a computer readout from the Minneapolis-based International Species Inventory System (ISIS) which maintains records on all animals in major United States and some European zoos. He didn't expect to locate a true blue bear; other than Barry none existed in zoos. What he sought was black bears that had come from the Yakutat Peninsula. It turned out that the Portland Zoo had one, but it was an older animal. Hill continued to think he might get a blue from the wild, and besides there was some uncertainty as to which of two females in the same enclosure at Portland had actually come from Yakutat.

The worst solution in Hill's eyes would be to take a plain Jane black bear from anywhere, U.S.A. Not that Barry would mind;

he was programed to avoid mating with grizzlies, polar bears, and the like, but blue, cinnamon, black, or white (any *Ursus americanus*) would be acceptable. What made this solution unacceptable was Hill's (and the Zoo's) desire to perpetuate the blue subspecies. It was best therefore to find a female who carried blue genes.

Bluegenes, as she became named—for the people at San Diego will stop at nothing in a punning approach to animal names—came a year or so after Barry. A frightened black cub, she had been found alone in the forest near Yakutat and turned over to Alaska Fish and Game. They had been keeping Barry in mind so they notified Hill. Shipping her was easy. Hill had foresightedly sent knocked-down crates to Yakutat against the possibility that another bear might be captured. Aside from her color the only drawback was the cub's age. She was too young to be placed immediately in the enclosure with Barry. But if the recessive genes are in her, she and Barry should produce one blue bear out of four cubs —provided, of course, that they remain compatible and sexually competent. If she lacks the blue genes then, unless the Zoo can get another bear, they will have to breed back a daughter to Barry, for the daughter will have the right genes.

It might appear to some that in the rescue of the blue bear the San Diego Zoo and its military escort functioned something like a fire department going up a tree to save the old lady's kitten. For many the concern over Blue Barry did not extend beyond his personality. Like neighbors gathered to watch the firemen, they cheered as the ladder was placed against the tree and cheered even louder as the kitten was brought safely to the ground. During the entire episode the focus was on a particular animal. It was in trouble and needed rescuing; then it was saved and that was a happy end to the whole affair.

There were also the cynics. They viewed the salvation of Blue Barry as a zoo-engendered publicity stunt that got a lot of newspaper and TV coverage to pull more people through the turnstiles, particularly after Barry went on exhibit. That's all the zoo really wanted, that and another rarity to add to its collection along with koalas, okapi, douc langurs, and other unusual animals that were to the zoo what rare and beautiful stamps are to the stamp collector.

Barry makes a good display when he isn't dozing in the Southern

California sunshine, for zoo visitors like to see active animals. But the undoubted pride in having the only blue-colored blue bear outside of Alaska was only part of what zoo professionals like Hill and Sedgwick felt. They knew, if the public didn't, that according to the world's principal conservation organization, the International Union for the Conservation of Nature (IUCN), which keeps the accounts, there are only about 500 blue bears left in the world. That population is presently considered to be stable and well-managed by the Alaska Department of Fish and Game. But when a wild population is that small—and for many wild species the numbers are even fewer—then it should be backed up by a scientific captive breeding program. The real importance of Blue Bear and Bluegenes will lie in their becoming the forerunners in a serious attempt to preserve the organism itself, the particular chromosomic code that decrees which *Ursus americanus* will become blue bears. This is the true rescue operation, and it is infinitely more complex and difficult than saving the old lady's kitten.

The idea that zoos can become true animal preserves is still not widely accepted nor understood, even among the people who manage zoos. Conservation as a word has long been part of the zoo lexicon; virtually every zoo in the world claims conservation as one of its missions. To say otherwise would be to admit to the accusations made by conservationists that zoos are net users of wild animals, a continual and unnecessary drain on the wilderness. Yet the only conservation in most zoos has been the care of particular animals that perhaps might have died sooner in the wild. They might have produced young, most of which would be sold or traded with other zoos. Conservation was also used in conjunction with education. Traditionally, zoos had educated by showing what an elephant, giraffe, leopard, oryx, or secretary bird was and telling a little about them; but as times changed conservation education meant telling people why certain animals should be saved for posterity. In very few places was there any serious attempt to conserve through the sustained and scientifically conducted propagation of captive wild animals in the same way that race horses are bred, with due attention to genealogy and using all the artifices of a good husbandman.

What the San Diego Zoo had done in going after animals like Blue Bear and what Gerald Durrell and others at his zoo on the

Channel Island of Jersey have since done in capturing and breeding animals of endangered species had one particularly notable precedent. Toward the end of the fifth decade in this century there lived in the searing wastes of the Rub'al Khali, the bleak empty quarter where Aden, Yemen, and Saudi Arabia join, the few remaining specimens of the Arabian oryx (*Oryx leucoryx*), an animal which was once numerous in desert wildernesses from the Sinai Peninsula through Arabia. A member of the antelope family, the Arabian oryx is closely related to the scimitar-horned oryx of North Africa, the Beisa oryx of East Africa, and the gemsbok of South Africa. It is a lovely, graceful animal, so lightly colored as to be almost pure white except for the black markings around its eyes that help protect them from the intense desert sun.

When the Fauna Preservation Society of Britain undertook to finance an expedition to save the Arabian oryx they knew that they were trying to preserve not only an animal but a legend. Of several animals, including, improbably, rhinoceroses that have been seen as the source of the unicorn legend, the Arabian oryx probably has the chief claim (unless there really *was* a unicorn). Long, straight horns stick up almost vertically from the top of the animal's head. From the side these appear as one horn. However, since any movement of the animal or any other viewing angle would immediately reveal that the oryx has two horns, it is difficult to swallow the idea that the legend of the unicorn, which has lasted over a thousand years, got its start because somebody once saw an oryx sideways. A Carmelite friar, Vincenzo Maria, who visited Muscat in 1656, both confirmed the Arabian oryx as the source of the unicorn story and pointed to the folly of it. He described wondrous animals: "as large as stags, similar to them in the shape of head and body, except that they are purest white . . . with coat the same all over silken and so clean that nothing more graceful was ever seen. They all have two horns, two or three cubits high at the root about as thick as the circumference of a crown, at the tip extremely thin, straight, even and black, divided into equal nodes, as though they were screw turned. I myself believe these creatures to be those which some writers describe as the Unicorn, some of which, it is said, were to be found in olden days in Mecca, but as a matter of fact they are not Unicorns."

The most likely source of the early relationship between oryx

and the unicorn was one of the writers to whom Father Vincenzo referred. Aristotle had stated flatly that the oryx was a one-horned animal,[1] and perhaps the one he saw or heard about actually was, since in Egypt where oryx were often kept in private zoos, the breeders apparently knew how to bind the sprouting horns of a young oryx so that they would grow together becoming a single horn—a unicorn.

By 1960 the remaining wild oryx—and one report even held that none remained—were in serious trouble. Like the quagga, a zebralike animal of Southern Africa that is now extinct, and the legendary passenger pigeon of the United States, the last of which, Martha, died in the Cincinnati Zoo in 1914, the Arabian oryx was a victim of overhunting. Hunting is not the most frequent cause of extinction to animals, although to the quagga and passenger pigeons many others like the dodo and great auk can be added. More serious is the destruction of an animal's habitat, which removes its chief sources of food and shelter. But the Arabian oryx, which could live in deserts where few men went willingly, had been hunted nearly to death. Oryx hunts had long been a tradition among the Bedouin, for by hunting and killing an oryx a man could truly prove his mettle. If one can imagine riding a camel to the limits of its endurance across barren sand or plains intersected by rocky, sparsely-vegetated washes called wadis that could fill within minutes in a sudden rain—and all this in furnace heat, save for a sometimes chilling night wind, then one can envision what the Bedouin hunter went through. At the end, if he got his wary game he did it with bow and arrow or muzzle-loading rifle. And the animal could be dangerous. One story is told of an Arab who sought a brother overdue from an oryx hunt. He found the brother alive but impaled through the thigh and held fast by an oryx horn. All the man could do was hold on with both hands to the animal's back. Afraid to shoot lest he kill his brother, the rescuer tossed a knife to the impaled hunter who was able to kill the oryx and free himself.

When in the old days the Bedouin at last got his oryx, nothing of the animal went to waste. Fat, blood, and water, all reputedly

[1] From Aristotle, the Roman writer Pliny the Elder copied the idea in his Natural History.

good for snakebite, were kept wrapped in part of the dead animal's intestine. In addition the fat, either rubbed on or burnt and inhaled, was a supposed cure for rheumatic pains. Gastric juices from the oryx's stomach were used to extend water supplies and any undigested solid matter was fed to camels. Flesh was prized not only as meat to be eaten but for its use in exorcising devils. The skin was a fine leather much prized for rifle butts, and the famous horns became plaintive pipes for Arab shepherd boys.

The decline of the oryx began in earnest when modern rifles came into vogue among Arab hunters. The herds were pushed back from the Sinai, Israel, and Jordan into two major areas, one in northern Arabia, the other in the Rub'al Khali. Those in the north fell first under the guns. Then rapid depletion of the southern herd began. Trucks, jeeps, and motorcars replaced camels, and often the hunters used submachine guns instead of rifles. The Arabs, who were at least responding to a tradition, were joined in hunts by employees of oil companies who simply wanted to gun down animals. By 1960 the end was near, hastened when ruling members of the Qatari tribe crossed 500 miles of open desert in a specially equipped motor caravan, found a large part of the southern herd and shot down twenty-eight oryx. In two further raids during the next two years the Qataris slaughtered all but a remnant of the remaining animals.

At this point the Fauna Preservation Society decided to act. The Arabian oryx was near the point of no return. It was evident that the only way the species could be saved was to take a breeding group out of Arabia. Without knowing where the animals could be put (it was vaguely thought that a reserve near Isiolo in Kenya might do), a capture team was assembled at Al Mukalla in what was then the Aden Protectorate. The group was to be led by Maj. Ian Grimwood, at that time Chief Game Warden in Kenya. It included several British old school scientific types, one of whom, the deputy leader Michael Crouch, was an "old girl," for he along with three other men had graduated from an exclusive girl's school in Limuru, Kenya, an honor that entitled him to have the school choir sing at his wedding.

The expedition was well equipped with a specially designed and custom-built capture car, a Piper Cub for aerial scouting, proper tents, numerous Arab bearers, and whiskey, gin, and beer that the

British Army had thoughtfully helped smuggle into this Muslim country where the use of alcohol was forbidden. The most serious deficiency, wrote Anthony Shepherd who recorded the adventure,[2] was a genuine virgin. Didn't the legend have it that only a virgin could capture a unicorn? At a cocktail party discussion of the matter someone was unkind enough to suggest that both virgins and unicorns were declining in numbers at about the same rate.

Without a virgin the expedition left Al Mukalla in the company of units from the Hadhrami Bedouin Legion, a British-officered military force that had previously set out to rescue the oryx, had caught two and seen them both die, one from old gunshot wounds, the other from complications arising from a pregnancy. A serious setback came within a few days when the capture car, which had an ailing gear box, finally came completely unglued and wouldn't budge in any gear. It was left beside the road and the capture team pressed on though now jammed together in dirty land rovers and trucks that reeked of gas and oil fumes in the stifling desert heat.

The plan was to establish a base camp at Sanau, a fort guarding the only water hole for the next 150 miles. From Sanau they would work toward the border of Muscat and Oman steppe country with its sparse grass and brush to which the oryx came looking for food and shade when the summer sun made life unbearable even for them on the sandy wastes of Ar Riml where they wintered. Further misfortune dogged the expedition, principally equipment failures like that of the beacon, which was to provide guidance for the pilot of the Piper Cub in this unmapped land where countless plateaus, hills, and wadis had a confusing sameness when looked down upon from the air.

Yet all of the discomfort, mitigated only by the camaraderie, the pint of water allowed for washing each day, and the short rations of Allsopps beer or scotch and water each evening, disappeared when their Arab tracker Tomatum (so named because his father had favored tomatoes) informed them that he had seen the week-old tracks of two oryx. So there were some left after the Qatari massacres. There were twenty men in the hunting party including the seven Englishmen, game experts, a veterinarian, biologists, most of whom had taken vacation or leave from their regular

[2] In a book *The Flight of the Unicorns* (New York: Abelard-Schuman, 1966).

jobs to join the expedition. These men had thus far been sustained only by vague hopes and the less than inspiring rationalization that even an unsuccessful hunt would advance human knowledge. With the finding of the tracks they experienced a rebirth of purpose. As they went out on their daily hunts perceptions were heightened so that the surrounding landscape seemed to stand out more clearly, and they did not mind endlessly scrutinizing each of many small outcroppings of white gypsum to determine whether they were really gypsum or the white body of a resting oryx. They knew now that the oryx were there.

The country of their search, land of the Mahra people who were ruled by the Sultans of Socota, covered six thousand square miles, larger than all but a few of the world's national parks, and mostly unexplored except by Bedouin hunters, searchers after oil, and a locust control task force. With so much territory to cover, Maj. Grimwood and his team worked from a grid, determined to cover the small squares one by one starting with those that contained the favorite foods and shady spots of the oryx in summer. In this barren, rocky land it was said that rain would fall on any particular spot only once every fourteen years. Yet when rain did fall it often came down in torrents, filling up the wadis, sometimes flooding even the sandy wastes, and providing enough water to keep the thrifty desert plants green for many years. One such spot where rain had fallen a scant two years before was Wadi Mitan, and it was there they conducted their first hunts.

The party went out in several trucks and land rovers, including a new capture car—a pickup truck hastily modified—without the powerful engine, sharp turning radius, and more sophisticated gearbox of the capture vehicle that had broken down. It would be the driver's job to avoid the largest rocks and potholes, to keep from flipping the truck on hills or plunging off cliffs, while at the same time maintaining the same single-minded tenacity in chasing the game that a wolf or Cape hunting dog pack would. Bounced around in the back of the truck were the men who manned the two capture poles, lengths of aluminum tubing which, when they were bolted together, reached out thirteen-and-a-half feet. Counterweighted at the butt for easier handling, they had a noose at the tip, which from a jolting, skidding, turning truck the pole handler was supposed to drop over the horns and head of a running, twist-

ing, swerving oryx. Drug-darting would not have been much easier, and in 1962 when the hunt took place, darting had not been refined enough to be a usable technique.

At midday in this place the temperature reached 120 degrees in the shade. Consequently, most hunting was done at first light or in the evening, periods when the oryx, who wisely lay up in the shade during the heat, would most likely be moving about. The first few days were fruitless except for finding old tracks, all of single animals, an indication of the havoc wrought by the Qatari raids. One morning they finally found fresh signs, oryx droppings that had been made only a few hours before. They picked up the track of a single oryx and started following it, moving slowly because their guides told them the animal was looking for shade. Shortly before 10:00 A.M. the animal jumped up from a bush some 250 yards away and ran off. The country, fortunately, was relatively flat. Within moments the capture truck was brought alongside and after one or two false drops the pole handler succeeded in noosing the oryx. They had made their catch. It was a bull.

At the base camp in Sanau stalls had been prepared, so when it was determined the oryx had not been damaged or overtaxed by the capture they put it in one of the crates they had brought with them and dispatched a truck to Sanau. The bull arrived without incident and within a day or so was eating well.

A few days later at about one-thirty in the afternoon, hot, tired and having found no more fresh tracks, they were discussing whether or not to suspend hunting until evening when three oryx broke cover nearby. The capture team chased after them through an almost impossible terrain of spurs, gullies, ravines, soft sand, and hard rock, devilishly varied to create the unexpected. The oryx used this terrain well, running in and out of gullies and ravines, changing direction rapidly, finally scattering in three different directions. The capture team selected one animal and continued the chase. It was impossible to anticipate every jolt and bounce. The men in back were thrown up and down against the sides, cab, and guardrails of the truck. One particularly severe jolt threw Maj. Grimwood against the side of the truck's cab with enough force to break several ribs. He shouted that the hunt should continue.

Once they thought they had lost their quarry, which had run into a ravine, but the Arab guides spotted the animal again lying down, trying to catch its breath. When they approached it got slowly to its feet, obviously distressed, its sides expanding and contracting as it gasped in the air it needed to continue running. It took only a few more jolts and bumps for them to catch and noose the animal, which sank to its knees almost as though it were relieved. They had chased the animal because they were sure it was a female. It turned out to be another bull.

In spite of the pain from his broken ribs Maj. Grimwood determined that they would not miss the opportunity to capture at least one of the remaining two oryx they had seen. Driving slowly back to the place where the animals had dispersed, they soon found the spoor of one. They hadn't tracked it far before it was sighted well ahead of them. At first they thought they would never be able to catch up with it, for they were crossing a corrugated area full of gorges and rocks which was, if anything, worse than the terrain they had covered in the first chase. But then the oryx made the mistake of moving into flat country. Soon they were able to come alongside. Maj. Grimwood himself noosed the animal. After the other members of the team had jumped out, wrestled the oryx to the ground, blindfolded it and given it an injection to minimize shock they were able to make their examination. This time they had caught a cow. The future of the oryx seemed a little more secure.

Their jubilation was short lived, for when they returned to camp they found that the second male, the one they had just caught, had died, probably from the effects of the hard chase, for a subsequent autopsy showed a ruptured liver. It also revealed a .303 bullet in one of the animal's hind legs put there probably during the Qatari hunts. For this bull oryx, life had been hard.

Maj. Grimwood himself drove the truck that took the female back to Sanau, for his ribs needed medical attention and proper binding. For several days the other members of the team searched the area for the third oryx and a possible fourth, for when they had flushed the three animals one of the Arabs thought he saw a fourth animal, but it was too far off to identify, and since gazelle were fairly numerous it might have been one of them. The hunts proved fruitless.

When Maj. Grimwood returned, bound so he found it difficult to move, they decided that the best chance in the short time they

had left and considering the broken down state of their vehicles, was to penetrate the area called The Sands. Their hope lay in the possibility that some oryx had not left for the summer pastures. As they traversed the enormous dunes with occasional fertile spots scattered among them that provided the meager grasses and plants the oryx and a few other animals ate, they came upon the scene of one Qatari hunt. It was a desolate place where the wide tracks of many balloon tires remained fresh, indicating that the Qatari hunters had moved abreast like an invading army, covering a wide area, driving the animals before them, converging occasionally to make a kill, then moving on again.

The desolation of this place was made more intense by the capture team's knowledge that somewhere in these dunes was reputed to be the ruins of Uber, once the capital of a tribe called the Ad and now covered with sand, legend had it, because the Ad people continued to worship many gods after they had been clearly instructed that there was only one, true God, Allah. It had been a great city, said to be "rich in treasure, with date gardens and a fort of red silver." They were awed therefore when on one hunt the guide Tomatum pointed out the remains of a road and identified it as the road to Uber.

But theirs was not an archaeological expedition, though they wished they could follow the tracks Tomatum showed them, tracks few westerners had seen. They were after oryx and for a change good luck came swiftly. They ran across tracks of a single animal, another remnant of the once sizable herd. The spoor, fortunately, was on a graveled plain, for tracking would be impossible in the sand. They followed the prints for several hours, once with sinking hearts because the oryx had veered toward the sand. But then it had changed direction and made its way up a wadi with steep cliffs on either side where they came upon it. The chase was short, causing little stress to the animal, for it had trapped itself, being able to travel in only one direction because of the cliffs. The oryx, in splendid condition, was another male.

It was to prove the last one taken. The capture truck had all but collapsed in a heap of fatigued metal, and several of the other vehicles were being kept together with gum and bailing wire. They left The Sands and returned to Sanau. All three of the animals were in excellent health, a highly desirable factor if they were

to become the progenitors of what was called, somewhat gran-
diosely at first, the world herd. They were also the last taken from
the wild. A few other animals survived but only for a few years.
When an expedition in October, 1972, tried to ascertain the status
of the wild oryx its members came up with worse than zero. In
high expectation they followed some fresh tracks, the only ones
found, and discovered at the end the carcasses of three oryx, probably the last. Over those same lands the oryx had roamed with the
people of Ad, and had met the same fate—but not from the wrath
of God.

With their world herd of three oryx, Maj. Grimwood and his
team had next to get the animals out of Arabia without overtaxing
them. As with the expedition to capture Blue Bear, the military
came to the rescue. The RAF commandant at Al Mulhalla dispatched an old Beverly bomber to Sanau. The crated animals were
loaded aboard and flown to Al Mulhalla. From there after refuel-
ing it was supposed to take them straight to Nairobi. However,
the Beverly, true to the tradition of mechanical breakdown that
had dogged the expedition from the start, developed engine trouble. A shrewd man who knew the condition of his equipment, the
commandant had anticipated possible breakdown and held over a
plane that otherwise would have left for Nairobi before the Beverly
returned from Sanau. Within a few minutes the oryx were transferred and their flight resumed.

Nairobi proved to be rather inhospitable. There had been an
outbreak of hoof-and-mouth disease at their destination, so the
animals were kept near Nairobi in a climate that didn't agree with
them. The Fauna Preservation Society finally decided that the
best spot on earth to start the breeding program would be the
Phoenix, Arizona, Zoo, in a climate like that of their native land.
Once again the problem of transport was critical since a long ocean
voyage might place too much strain on the animals. This time the
military couldn't help, but in what was seen by many as a supreme irony considering that overhunting had brought the Arabian
oryx to their depleted state, a prominent United States hunting
organization, the Shikar-Safari Club, not only undertook to fly the
animals from Nairobi to Phoenix but raised the money to build the
barns and enclosures at their new home. In the process the club's
president, Maurice A. Machris, who like many of its affluent mem-

bers had bagged all of the big five African game animals [3] and many more besides, became so obsessed with the preservation of the Arabian oryx that he was appointed one of the first trustees of the world herd.

Fortunately, the herd was enlarged at Phoenix through the acquisition of six animals that had been in captivity. The London Zoo sent a female as did Sheikh Jabir Abdullah al Sabah of Kuwait. Best of all, perhaps as a kind of atonement for a situation he really couldn't control, King Saud of Arabia sent two males and two females from a small private herd.[4] Yet in spite of the fact that they now had four males and five females no one connected with the project breathed easily. The first five youngsters born to the herd were all males.

The arrival of the first female calf, "Annie," on September 8, 1966, seemed to be the signal that a corner had been turned. From then on the herd built in size until it had 36 members. The trustees, who met once or twice a year to review the situation and make decisions about the oryx's future, then determined that the herd should be split. One of the dark dreams that causes animal breeders to wake suddenly in the dead of night is of the unstoppable virus or rapidly multiplying bacilli that race through their breeding unit with the speed of a sneeze, leaving behind dead and dying animals. The best way to avoid this disaster is to divide the animals and keep them at widely separated places, served preferably by different groups of keepers, veterinarians, and managers or if by the same group, under hospital-like requirements of sanitation so that diseases cannot be transferred from one unit to the other. The Zoological Society of San Diego agreed in November, 1972, to take Section II of the world herd at its 1,800 acre Wild Animal Park near the town of Escondido, California.

When the trustees met in the spring of 1977, the herd had increased to 60 animals and a most critical decision could be made to complete the circle. The future of the Arabian oryx seemed secure enough that a small experimental group of animals could be

---

[3] Leopard, lion, Cape buffalo, rhinoceros, elephant. Such hunting is now largely a thing of the past because the old hunting grounds in Kenya and Tanzania have been closed down by governmental decree.

[4] He later sold a bull and two cows to the Los Angeles Zoo, which now has a herd.

returned to their original range at a new reserve, Shaumari, eight miles from the great oasis of Azraq in Jordan. The trustees knew they were setting up a test. The last game around Azraq was killed off in the late 1950s. The question now is: Have the men who live there changed enough in their habits and attitudes to let the restored game survive?

It became a cliché of the older zoo world to cite Père David's deer (which had been preserved in zoos for over 3,000 years), the European bison (wisent), and Przewalski's wild horses as animal species that owe their continued existence on earth to zoos. Critics of zoos agree, but complain they are pitifully few in number when set against the four millennia that zoos have existed and the thousands of species, including many now extinct, that have been kept. Now perhaps the Arabian oryx can be added to the list of the saved. But the new breed of zoo managers would say the significance of Operation Oryx was not in the animals being preserved any more than the significance of the Blue Bear capture was the same as saving the old lady's cat. For the first time a leading conservation organization saw captive propagation as the best and probably the only way an animal species could be kept from extinction. For the first time an expedition was mounted with the express purpose of capturing free-roaming animals so they could be confined in a zoo for reasons better than appealing to people's craving for novelty, or to help satisfy their curiosity about the natural world. For the first time zoos were called upon to be something more than collections of animals. Zoos were being challenged to be the lifeboats to Ararat.

Send Birds of Paradise, but Color Them Magpie

The idea that zoos can become preserves for some endangered species, while talked about a good deal, has not been firmly grasped by all those who managed zoos. What zoo managers do have a firm grasp of is the terrifying fact that wild animals, without which they cannot continue to operate zoos, are becoming increasingly hard to acquire. Some animal species that have been exhibited in zoos for centuries have been reduced in numbers to a few hundred or less in the wild. The Indian one-horned rhinoceros is one. For over a thousand years it has been featured in zoos or traveling menageries. It was exhibited in Pompeii in 61 B.C. The T'sien-han-shu Annals of 300 A.D. show that the King of Hwanchi near what is now Madras, India, sent a one-horned rhino to Ping Wang-mang in China. Rhinos then numbered in the tens of thousands. Now the remaining wild one-horned rhinos in India and Nepal are no more than a thousand.

A further problem facing zoos in acquiring animals has been the mounting restraint on the trade in wildlife. Influenced by various interests, particularly conservation groups, governments have passed laws restricting the capture and shipment of many species from their native habitats—a praiseworthy effort that does not always take sufficiently into account the economic and social pressures that continue to erode or destroy those habitats.

Throughout their history zoos have obtained most of their animals from dealers, businessmen whose profits come from capturing or buying animals in their native lands, shipping them, and then selling them at a profit to zoos or others such as pet dealers and research centers. As legislation closed down these traditional pipelines some zoo managers were brought to a state of near panic. Visitors to zoos came to see exotic animals, traditional favorites like the apes, monkeys, big cats, bears, giraffes, zebras, elephants, rhinos, giant snakes, and birds with strange bills and colorful plumage. As one concerned zoo director observed, the public is not likely to be attracted to zoos if cages that once held tigers are filled with domestic cats or the zebra pens are turned over to goats.

Not least of the worries that beset zoo operators was the continued bull market in animal prices, the rise of which paralleled that of many other scarce commodities. A nice portfolio of scarlet tanagers, birds no bigger than sparrows, could have been bought ten years ago at around $10 each. Had these been somehow tucked away where they couldn't age, on today's market they would bring nearly $150 per bird, a much better performance than that of the stock market. The more expensive Indian rhinoceros has gone up from $15,000 to $45,000 in the same period.

The increased prices for some animals were further boosted by their use as a source for other desired commodities. Ivory went up in price at the same rate as gold, with the forecastable result that the killing of elephants, whether or not they were in protected areas, increased accordingly. The year 1975 saw the tusks of 300,000 elephants pass through the ivory exchanges of Hong Kong. In the first nine months of 1976 that figure was exceeded. The price of powdered rhino horn, a favorite aphrodisiac in Asia,[1] shot up, and so were an increasing number of rhinos. Nor were the lesser known creatures neglected. There are four particular scales on a pangolin that are useful in warding off ghosts, so with a burgeoning population in China the price of pangolins rose as more people in that communist state required protection against evil spirits. The meat from snakes and civets is used in China to bring up body heat during winter, and pickled bear paws, a delicacy, can still be bought in communist department stores. In Europe particularly, women continue to demand fur coats made from the skins of spotted cats so the skin trade even in endangered species like the snow leopard has continued.

[1] In what had to be an interesting scientific experiment for the participants it was shown conclusively that powdered rhino horn has no effect on sexual desire—no more than powdered human fingernails, which are made of the same material, keratin.

As the supply of animals decreased and the need to keep zoo exhibits filled continued, zoo managers pursued two different courses of action, sometimes unknowingly within the same zoo. One was the course of desperation, of getting the animals at any cost whether or not the methods used were questionable or downright illegal. The second course, initially more expensive because it required more space and extensive research, involved the establishment of breeding programs to make zoos self-sufficient.

The illegal approach was most tellingly exposed in a letter sent by A. Yoshikawa of the Ise-Shima Zoo in Kobe, Japan, to the director of the Jakarta Zoo in Indonesia. Mr. Yoshikawa, reported the conservation journal *Oryx*, made no bones about it, he was after some Birds of Paradise, traffic in which is illegal. But Mr. Yoshikawa had thought his way around mere legalities. He suggested "that the name of the item . . . be specified just 'magpie' instead of 'Bird of Paradise' on all necessary documents and when shipped, the tail of the birds to be pulled out and birds to be painted [with] watercolor so that our sincere desire to get the birds can realize by any means." Calling it a "monstrous request" the Jakarta Zoo director refused, and was therefore surprised several weeks later when he received from Yoshikawa a price list of 500 animals he was willing to sell, including lowland gorilla, orangutan, sable antelope, okapi, Malayan tapir, snow leopard, and great red kangaroos, many of them banned for sale under international convention. Mr. Yoshikawa was not modest about his prices either. He asked a mere $158,000 each for the okapi, which hail originally from the jungles of Zaire. Since at the time he didn't have any okapi he was willing to make what stock traders call a short sale, probably in the hope that he could pick some animals up in Zaire, where they reputedly could be had for $100,000 a pair and turn a tidy profit of $216,000 in the process.

In the United States the course of desperation reached its nadir with the incredible tale of the Philadelphia Reptile Exchange, a story international in scope, both ludicrous and appalling, replete with its own small version of Watergate, and with a multiple death that had it happened to people instead of snakes and lizards would have been considered a most monstrous and reprehensible crime.

It might come as a surprise to some people that reptile houses are popular attractions in zoos. The number of true snake and lizard (to say nothing of turtle and crocodile) fanciers for every thousand people in Western Europe and the United States is extremely small, so when people are asked through generalized surveys and questionnaires about their animal preferences reptiles do not score high. But what counts at a zoo is where the people are—what exhibits they go to in large numbers and here the reptile house is a center of interest. Snakes are probably the biggest draw. Alligators and crocodiles lie inert most of the time; water turtles swim a little, but more frequently cluster around a rock or log, while land tortoises when they move at all do so in a glacial manner. Lizards are better because they sometimes scurry, and the big ones like Komodo dragons provide a good topic of misinformed conversation. But snakes have the most going for them—bizarre colors and patterns, psychic associations ranging from folk medicine to belly dancing (with its obvious phallic overtones), and a long history of creating the fear in people of being crushed, swallowed, or fatally poisoned. Their devotees come to the reptile house to exclaim over the form, pattern, and colors; most others come out of curiosity or simply because they can experience feelings of fascination and revulsion in safety.

The key to a successful reptile house is in keeping it well stocked, particularly with the most exotic, largest, or most venomous forms of snakes. This used to be fairly easy to do. Snakes were cheap in comparison with most mammals, and they are probably the easiest animals in the world to transport. They can go for months without food, requiring only some water and protection against extremes of hot and cold. Giant snakes like the pythons, boas, and anacondas and dreaded poisonous serpents like the king cobra, death adder, bushmaster, spitting cobra, and Gaboon viper came through dealers in their native lands to dealers in Europe and the United States, who then sold them to zoos, university researchers, and private fanciers. A shocking number of people, including apartment dwellers in most large cities, have pet snakes, not a few of them deadly, and some of which pop up in neighbors' bathrooms every now and then.[2]

---

[2] Not long ago the San Diego Zoo accepted as gifts one seven-foot spitting cobra and two six-foot bushmasters from a young man who was reluctant to part with them, but had to, he explained, because his new bride didn't want them in their apartment.

For many years the trade in reptiles was free and easy. There were virtually no restrictions on what could be imported and shipments were, if anything, speeded up when freight handlers found out what kind of freight they were handling. The largest dealer in the United States was Mr. Henry Molt, proprietor of the Philadelphia Reptile Exchange, which by 1976 was handling three-fourths of the live reptiles being imported into the country.

Starting in 1973 the trade began to be hampered by new restrictions that applied to all animals. In part these came from laws to protect endangered species. Stimulated by an international conference held in Washington, D.C. in 1973, many nations enacted legislation to protect their own wildlife. The United States not only passed its own Endangered Species Act, it also agreed to respect the laws restricting exportation of animals passed by other nations. Thus if Australia placed severe restrictions on the export of Australian fauna, the United States agreed to ban the import of the same fauna. In the United States there was also a tightening of an old law, the Lacey Act, which had originally been designed to protect American livestock from being infected with diseases brought in by exotic animals, but was now broadened in light of greater sophistication about ecology to prevent alien animals like the mongoose or king cobra from being loosed upon the land to disrupt local ecosystems or threaten the lives of United States citizens.[3]

Under one or another of the new laws traffic in most venomous snakes and in all Australian snakes (which are mostly venomous) was forbidden even to zoos, except by permit. Patently, the constant need to draw up permit applications and not know whether or not they would be granted was at least irksome and at most a costly burden to both zoos and dealers. It was tempting for those who needed animals to circumvent the regulations, quite easily managed with reptiles but not with conspicuous animals like gi-

---

[3] Florida provides the best example of the damage that can come when exotic animals like the walking catfish are introduced into a ecosystem that has made no provision for them. Hawaii is a close second with the mongoose, brought in originally to control rats. Being diurnal where rats are nocturnal, the mongoose found its best living off Hawaiian birds. The rats continue to flourish, but many of the birds are gone.

raffes nor with any animal that requires daily attention while being shipped.

The scandal of the Philadelphia Reptile Exchange grew from small beginnings and burgeoned like one of those crystal flowers that grow from a single pill in a glass of water. It began with three expeditions to Fiji, Australia, and New Guinea, ostensibly sponsored by the Exchange in 1972 to 1974. Molt had found that there were a few profit-minded reptile enthusiasts, some from wealthy families, to whom the reptile garnering expeditions promised to be a moneymaking lark. They joined as partners in a venture which eventually collected some 350 snakes, lizards (including the rare and beautiful Fiji iguana), and crocodiles. Most were purchased from local dealers and just plain folks, with the object being to buy cheap and sell high. A Boelen's python, much sought after by the curators of zoo reptile houses, might be bought in Australia or New Guinea for $25 and later sold for $500. Even allowing for shipping costs, care, and a few deaths, these profit margins would be envied by most businessmen.

One must now envision again how easy it is to ship snakes and lizards. They can be placed in cotton bags and carried in trunks or suitcases disguised as clothing, since they require only enough oxygen to sustain slow metabolic processes. It was in fact disguised as luggage that most of the reptiles were taken to Zurich, Switzerland. There, after they had gone through Swiss customs, they were crated and shipped through John F. Kennedy Airport in New York under labels that indicated they were the kinds of reptiles that could be legally imported into the United States—labels that harried customs men with their limited knowledge of the difference, say, between a reticulated and amethystine python would not be likely to question. And snakes are the hot coals of the animal trade. Everybody wants to pass them along quickly to the next person.

And so they came, mostly in good order and alive, to the Philadelphia Reptile Exchange. For 75 of the new arrivals, however, the long trip culminated in a mass burial in an unmarked grave in the New Jersey countryside. During one cold November night they were left out and simply froze to death.[4] Since the corpses of

[4] This is a record ophiocide. Carl Hagenbeck, the famous German zoo director and animal dealer, tells of 65 giant snakes, boas, and pythons, that

snakes and lizards are difficult to conceal in one's garbage or from ragpickers on the city dump, prudence dictated the mass burial. From the grave the dead were to rise to haunt the gravediggers.

The distribution of the surviving reptiles—and some others that had been illegally brought in by a few zoos and sold to the Exchange—took place over the months after they had arrived. Because many of the deals with customers were concluded on the telephone, somebody at the Exchange ordered that all calls be tape-recorded without bothering to notify the callers. Not realizing that they were being recorded (which is illegal under Pennsylvania law), many callers were less formal in their talk—and less cautious —than they might otherwise have been. Verbal repartee that took on a buddy-to-buddy quality often revealed a caller's underlying convictions, or lack of them, about the legalities involved in buying the smuggled reptiles. Boiled down and stripped of expletives, the gist of some statements made by a small number of zoo curators was "Never mind the law, send me the snakes." At the time few people in the zoo world were convinced that enforcement of the new laws would be rigorously applied to snakes. Unfortunately, there were also a few who didn't know the new laws existed.

Having the advantage of national example set by the White House of what can happen when one tape-records everyday conversations, it is surprising that the Philadelphia Reptile Exchange not only continued the practice, but failed to heed the greatest lesson of all. No one destroyed the tapes before government agents could impound them. It was Watergate with snakes and lizards.

The first agents from United States Customs were attracted to the Exchange because of another oversight by Molt and his associates. Like most animal dealers, the Exchange regularly published a flyer that showed its current inventory and prices. Not too long after the reptiles had been smuggled in, an alert customs official got his hands on one of the most recent inventory-price lists. While he was not a herpetologist he was good at remembering values shown on customs declarations, and between the high prices on the flyer and the low valuations he remembered, there was an oceanic gap.

And so an investigation was launched with its simple beginnings

---

froze to death on a North Sea packet while on the way to his place near Hamburg in March of 1883.

in a disparity between declared and actual value that made Uncle Sam think he had been had. Undreamed of by the agents who started the case, which looked as if it would proceed down a simple, short corridor, was the complicated maze that they would get into when they first opened the door. Or to put it another way, the federal agents, thinking they were about to climb a molehill, had actually started up a mountain.

It may have been a disaffected investor, one of those young people who had helped Molt finance the collecting expeditions but who had not received the promised profits, or it might have been another source that led the federal agents to the mass grave. In any event they found it and exhumed the 75 carcasses buried there. Like any dead animals, reptiles decompose, but their tough skins are the last to go, and it is from patterns and scale counts that accurate scientific identifications can be made. These dug-up animals were still in a remarkable state of preservation. Trained herpetologists had little difficulty in assigning each carcass its proper name. The names did not square with those on the customs declarations, and many were of reptiles forbidden importation without permit under the Endangered Species Act of 1973 and modifications to the Lacey Act. Since no permits had been obtained, the possible violations by the Philadelphia Reptile Exchange (and by customers who had bought the smuggled reptiles) were somewhat more serious than understated valuations, for the case now came under laws administered by the United States Department of the Interior. The enlarged government team, including some biologists to keep track of the species, began to dig deeply into the smuggling operation. More was involved, they found, than the Philadelphia Reptile Exchange and its 350 snakes, lizards, and crocodiles. Over a thousand reptiles had been smuggled into the United States through what the government alleged in its indictments was an international network of animal dealers who cooperated in the smuggling because they were playing for stakes worth millions. When the case came out of the Federal Grand Jury in August, 1977, indictments were handed out to the principal violators in the United States like Henry Molt, Jr., and to dealers who were citizens of several nations including Christopher Wee and Y.L. Kow of Singapore; Walter Zinniker of Basel, Switzerland; Maurice Van Derhaege of Metz, France; and, besmirching a famous name, Jonathan Leakey, second son of L.S.B. and Mary Leakey and brother of Richard Leakey. Jonathan runs a snake farm near Lake Baringo, Kenya.

Even after the first indictments were handed down the zoo people who were customers continued to twitch nervously. The Philadelphia, St. Louis, Memphis, Knoxville, Sacramento, Dallas, Rochester, and National Zoos had been named as those that had purchased smuggled reptiles. In most cases, the government prosecutor thought, the zoo people had been innocent of intentional wrongdoing. They had simply not been careful enough in requiring proof that the reptiles had been legally brought into the United States. Moreover it was clear that in many instances curators had obtained reptiles without informing their superiors. Ignorance did not, of course, absolve the superiors of responsibility. To some zoo directors the whole affair was doubly embarrassing. Not only did it expose cracks in their organizational structures, it left them lamely trying to explain the actions of subordinates which ran directly counter to the directors' firmly held and publicly expressed convictions.[5] Thus Dr. Theodore Reed, director of the National Zoo, an international leader in the serious effort to breed endangered animals in captivity, found himself explaining to a reporter from *Newsweek*, "There has been a long tradition of relying on United States Customs. If an animal was brought in through a fairly reputable dealer, you assumed that customs had satisfied themselves that it was a legal shipment."

"A fairly reputable dealer." That was the weak peg upon which a defense had to be built, a defense made weaker because the qualifying adverb fairly had to be used. For many years zoos had dealt with Molt and others like him, trusting, as Dr. Reed had, in the essential honesty of the dealer or if not trusting then looking the other way in the smug conviction that no government would interfere in such a trivial matter as the importation of a few snakes. Yet the Philadelphia Reptile Exchange's reputation had been questioned long before the government cracked down. A red flag should have been raised when the Exchange dropped its membership in the American Association of Zoological Parks and Aquariums (AAZPA), the national professional and self-policing

---

[5] Most directors stood by their subordinates. The same cannot be said of one zoo's city administration, which required that the director of its zoo hire and pay for his own legal counsel.

organization for zoos and aquariums. Put in simple terms, the Philadelphia Reptile Exchange was not a member of AAZPA and most reputable dealers are. Since the AAZPA discourages traffic by member zoos with nonmember dealers, the zoo people who bought reptiles from the Exchange were courting trouble. Yet in a world of declining wildlife and increasing laws zoos that wanted to do business as usual were willing to take the risk.

What was business as usual? For most zoos until the 1970s it was the continued reflexive response to two unwritten and seldom talked about rules of operation that had governed the zoo world for years. First, display as many animals of as many different species and subspecies as possible, even if you have only one of a kind; and second, try to have some rarities—giant pandas, koalas, pygmy chimpanzees, okapi, bongo—that few other zoos have or can get. The older generation of zoo directors and curators often derived their greatest satisfaction from outdoing one another in kinds of animals and lavishness of exhibits. The most virulent strain of this competitive bug caused some zoo managers to be more concerned about the opinion of their peers than they were about the reactions of the public that supported them or the health and happiness of the animals they displayed.

Only a few zoos ran counter to the trend. In the United States William Conway of New York assumed a leadership role during the 1960s. Taking note of what was happening to wildlife he began to change the collection in the Bronx Zoo to emphasize breeding groups rather than singletons or pairs.

Even in its name Roland Lindemann's Catskill Game Farm in upstate New York emphasized breeding with large groups of mostly hoofed stock. Lindemann was also the first by more than ten years to establish breeding groups away from the public's view. Dr. Reed in Washington began to change the makeup of the National Zoo; and Dr. Charles R. Schroeder, director of the San Diego Zoo, began plans that culminated in the opening in 1972 of the San Diego Wild Animal Park at San Pasqual as a breeding reserve. Both Dr. Warren Thomas of the Los Angeles Zoo and Louis DiSabato of San Antonio started effective captive breeding programs, particularly with antelope species.

In Europe a prototype for captive breeding was established by one of the great leaders of conservation, Sir Peter Scott, at Slim-

bridge, England, where the Wildfowl Trust began propagating threatened and endangered species of water birds like the all-but-extinct Hawaiian goose, now restored in significant numbers to the wild. Another clearly outstanding leader was Gerald Durrell, who in the early 1960s founded the Jersey Zoo on the Channel island of Jersey on the premise that zoos would have to become, in his words, "the stationary ark." [6] Also in the forefront were Walter van den Bergh, director of the Antwerp Zoo and its wild animal park at Planckendael; Dr. Heinrich Dathe of the East Berlin Zoo; Dr. Bernhard Grzimek of the Frankfurt Zoo; and Dr. Ernst Lang of the Basel Zoo. A few zoos by specializing had kept themselves apart from the general competition for more species and rare animals. Most notable of these is the Arizona-Sonora Desert Museum at Tucson, Arizona, which, combining museum and zoo techniques, displayed only those animals found in the Sonora Desert, among them fortunately some of the public favorites like jaguars, ocelots, mountain lions, bears, and otters.

A first hint of the great change that was about to come over the zoo world appeared in a voluntary boycott established by members of the AAZPA in 1962, who agreed that they would not traffic in certain animal species without first getting permission from the organization's Conservation Committee. An original list of three endangered animals, the monkey-eating eagle, orangutan, and gorilla, was broadened during the next few years to include the Galapagos tortoise, Komodo dragon, golden lion marmoset, Zanzibar red colobus, Javan rhinoceros, Sumatran rhinoceros, and mountain zebra. High-minded as the boycott might sound, not all members took it seriously, and the AAZPA, lacking legal authority, could do no more than censure one member who legally imported some animals on the list without obtaining permission through AAZPA.

While the International Union of Zoo Directors subscribed to the self-imposed boycott the European zoos in general paid little heed, continuing on their old competitive ways, getting animals by whatever means they could. The most criticized acquisition during the period was made by the Cologne Zoo when it obtained two

[6] Which is the title of his latest book published in the United States by Simon and Schuster, 1977.

young female mountain gorillas, rarest of the three gorilla subspecies. The manner of this acquisition illustrates another flaw in
the organization of some zoos, their occasional dominance by a
generally well-intentioned amateur who is in a position of power
above the zoo's professional staff. At Cologne, where the Lord
Mayor himself took a personal interest in the zoo, the honorable
gentleman thought it would be exceedingly nice if his zoo (as he
liked to think of it) were to have some animals that no other German zoo had. His chance came when he heard through a friend
that Cologne might be able to get some mountain gorillas from the
government of Rwanda. Many zoos exhibit the lowland gorilla
(*Gorilla gorilla gorilla*), but the impressive subspecies from the
mountains of central Africa (*G.g. beringei*) is a rarity. A deal was
made, all perfectly legal of course since no one could question the
right of a sovereign government to give away its own animals even
if they were from a supposedly inviolate national park. Because
they were from a national park and because the hunters used the
old method of killing the mothers to get the babies, who were
both females, howls of pious outrage were raised in Europe, particularly by Drs. Bernhard Grzimek and Ernst Lang[7] when they
heard about the capture from Dian Fossey, who had to hand raise
the youngsters at her research station before they were sent to
Cologne. An unfortunate side effect of the opprobrium heaped on
Cologne has been that zoo's inability to get a male mountain gorilla, the numbers of which continue to dwindle as Rwandese
farmers cut and slash new fields on the slopes of the Virunga vol-
canoes where the gorillas live.

   The shift that is now underway from zoos that stripped the wild
to get their animals and zoos that breed their own—and thereby
help to preserve animal species for posterity—is the first major
change in the ways of acquiring animals since zoos first began
thousands of years ago. The underlying biological or social reasons why men want to keep other animals, except as food, are diffi-

---

[7] Detractors among zoo directors joked cynically that Grzimek and Lang
were jealous because they hadn't gotten the animals for their zoos. It had
been charged that both men stoutly opposed putting any animals on the
endangered list until their zoos had some; then they couldn't wait until
the animals were declared endangered so no one else could get them. There
are many jealous people in the world of zoos.

cult to assess. Curiosity, companionship, ego gratification (both by dominating the animals and by showing off to the neighbors), relief from boredom, the collector's compulsion, aesthetic satisfaction—all of these singly or intermingled must enter. The line between keeping pets and keeping a zoo is of course a narrow one, since both domesticated and wild animals can be pets. The first man who caught and kept alive animals of more than one species had effectively started the first zoo.

Zoos as we now think of them—substantial collections of wild animals—have existed for at least 4,500 years. The earliest zoos on record were apparently private animal breeding farms near Saqqara, Egypt. These date back to 2500 B.C. According to the records on nearby tombs the owner of one zoo kept two species of gazelle, ibex, addax, and oryx, most likely the Arabian oryx. A second zoo in the area kept even more meticulous records. It had 5,358 cattle of three different breeds, 1,305 oryxes, 1,135 gazelles, and 1,244 other antelope, numbers which indicate that the zoo's owner was more than a hobbyist and was perhaps striving to domesticate wild animals. The records further indicate that the animals were captured through two common methods that are still used. They were netted or driven with a herd into a natural cul-de-sac or stockade. Most of the animals, it is likely, came from lower Egypt or the Sudan, for up until the time of Chinese Gordon, Lord Kitchener, and the war with the Mahdi and his dervishes in the 1890s, the plains and river banks of the Nile valley teemed with large groups of most African hoofed animals, rhinos, hippos, elephants and the attendant predators.[8]

The development of zoos in Egypt probably culminated in the great collection at Alexandria established by Ptolemy II (283–246 B.C.). It was this Ptolemy who opened up Ethiopia as a source for animals, introduced the chimpanzee for the first time to the civilized world, and responded to thrill seekers by exhibiting, historians claim, a 45-foot python brought from the Sud region of the upper Nile. One must suspect the historians in this case of the kind of

[8] Carl Hagenbeck noted the before and after situations in the Sudan. Before Kitchener's campaign, which like other military adventures in Africa saw the soldiers fed off the land, most of Hagenbeck's imports came from the Sudan. After the war few animals remained in the areas ravaged by the armies.

exaggeration about the length of snakes that became commonplace thereafter, for the African rock python (*Python sebae*) seldom exceeds 20 feet and the record through fairly reliable measurement is 32 feet.[9]

By the time of Ptolemy II the chief problem in operating a zoo involved the frequent introduction of novelty by finding attractive new animals (or in the case of snakes attractively repugnant) and maintaining a continued supply of all animals. From this time on the demand for wild animals seldom lessens and for several periods greatly increases. In Greece animals were kept in traveling shows—which included trained animal acts—and in private menageries. Because of Alexander the Great's penetration into India, westerners for the first time saw such exotics as parrots, peafowl, and tigers—and a new source of animals for European zoos was opened up. By introducing games in which animal was pitted against animal and men against animals in various combinations that usually ended with the animals being slaughtered, the Romans presented a great problem for animal suppliers. People apparently became jaded with the same old acts. What, another bear hunt? Why don't they try something new? Newness came with exotics like rhinos, hippos, giraffes, elephants, oryx, cheetahs, and leopards—and of course lions. The enormous demand for animals is revealed by the passage of a law that is a forerunner to the Lacey Act. Around 170 B.C. the Roman Senate made it illegal to import African beasts into Italy. Their major reason was the possibility that wild beasts might get loose in the Roman countryside and harm the citizens, but a more plausible reason was political. The Senators, mostly aristocrats, were trying to put down a rising group of plebeian politicians who were appealing to the common folk by sponsoring the popular circus games. The new law came too late. The games had become so popular that it was almost immediately overridden by a

---

[9] Exaggerating the length of a snake reached dizzying heights in a 1948 Brazilian newspaper story. The account soberly reported that a detachment of soldiers had been sent to a town to subdue an anaconda that had wreaked havoc there by knocking down buildings and strewing cars about through its lashing. And no wonder. When the monster was killed and measured, the reporter solemnly wrote, it proved to be 156 feet long! No doubt Ptolemy II spun in his tomb with shame for his stubby snake. The fact is that while anacondas, members of the same family as boas and pythons, may grow to more than thirty feet, most are smaller.

law which expressely permitted the importation of African wild-life.

The Roman games exhibited what was probably their worst example of cruelty to animals around 55 B.C. in an event which stimulated one of the first expressions of a view that has become quite familiar, if not pervasive, today. The particular affair, a series of games in which animals were killed in the arena over a period of several days, was sponsored by the Roman General Pompey. Among numerous other animals Pompey had brought from Egypt were 21 elephants, shipped after Pompey's assurances that they would not be harmed. For several days the elephants were exhibited. Then, on the last day of the games, Pompey ordered a final spectacle. All the elephants were to be killed by javelin throwers. One animal, it was reported, astonished the onlookers by fighting on its knees after its legs had been so badly wounded it could no longer stand. It even managed to flail aside with its trunk the shields of several tormentors before it finally succumbed. The trumpeting of the great beasts and their frantic efforts to escape caused an upwelling of humane feelings in the crowd "so that the spectators rose and cursed Pompey for his cruelty." Most significant was a statement made afterward in a letter by the great orator and statesman Cicero. The killing of those elephants, he said, had aroused in him more than pity; he experienced the feeling that the elephant "is somehow allied with humankind."

Elephants attract many people who see them as extraordinary creatures, so perhaps Cicero's feeling of alliance with them would not apply to other animals. Certainly, his recognition of a unity between man and beast was a precursor to much of today's thought about the animal world, which has seen a declaration of the rights of animals and resulted in strenuous human effort to save dolphins from tuna fishermen and whales from whalers. But through most of history these thoughts have been few and far between. Whatever ethical principles men applied in their own relationships they paid little heed to any responsibility to animals, even to treating them humanely. Humane societies didn't come into existence until the nineteenth century. Animals might get decent treatment from decent individuals but virtually nothing in law and little in western religions offered them much protection. They were on earth to be hunted, exploited, used for their feathers and skins, displayed in zoos and circuses, or kept as pets. Perhaps the saddest commentary on the relationship between men and animals is that men made little effort to understand the animals. To identify them, yes. To establish the relationship of one species to another, yes. To learn about their internal structure, yes. But not to know them from the inside out as creatures with their own motivations, desires, behaviors, and, in some instances, intelligence superior to that of a few of the people that gawked at them. One wonders if Noah would have taken the animals aboard the ark unless God had told him to.

To satisfy the enormous demand for exotic animals in Rome pleas were constantly sent to provincial administrators to supply more. Surprisingly, to capture some—elephants for example—licenses were required, and during one period the killing, though not the capture, of lions was prohibited unless the killer was defending himself, his family, or his livestock. Provincial administrators were apparently most plagued by rich friends or sponsors of games who wanted them to commission the capture of specific animals. When the same Cicero who wrote the comment about the slain elephants became governor of Cilicia in Southern Asia Minor he was bombarded (if one can use bombard to describe missives that traveled on galleys) with letters from a friend, M. Caelius Rufus, who had been elected aedile and by convention had to sponsor some games. Caelius wanted some "Greek" leopards[10] and was not at all hesitant about using every persuasive technique from cajolery to threats. "In nearly all my letters to you," he wrote, "I have mentioned the subject of leopards. It will be a disgrace to you if, when Patiscus has sent ten to Curio, you don't get many more. Curio has made me a present of these ten, and of another ten from Africa . . . Do please see that you attend to this. You like taking trouble . . . In this affair the trouble for you is only to talk—I mean to issue orders officially and give commissions. For as soon as the leopards are caught, you have my people . . . to look after the animals' keep and bring them to Rome."

In a later letter Caelius was downright petulant. "It will be a disgrace to you if I don't have any Greek leopards." But on this matter as on others Cicero was a model of rectitude, commenting

---

[10] Probably one of three subspecies of the leopard (*Panthera pardus*) found in Persia and Asia Minor. Of these the most striking is *P. p. saxicolor*, still extant but rare.

to a friend about Caelius's request, "I replied that it was not consistent with my reputation that the Cibyrates would hold a municipal hunt on official orders from me."

Nevertheless the flow of animals to Rome went on for hundreds of years. To capture the vast numbers and different species, including carnivores, various methods were devised or more often adapted from hunting techniques that men had developed during millennia of hunting. Nor have the methods changed much since then; most are still employed with of course refinements wrought by modern technology. In fact the only completely new technique is the drug-filled dart fired by pistol, rifle, or blowgun.

A single picture of about 300 A.D. found in a Roman villa at Bona in Algeria depicts two methods of capturing animals. The particular hunt seems to be concentrated on carnivores—cheetah, lions, and leopards—which have been driven toward a stockade of netting reinforced on the inside by thorn bushes. There are two types of beaters: blacks mounted on horses protected by breastplates of wood or leather, and Roman hunters, possibly soldiers, moving in close formation on foot each carrying a shield and brandishing a torch. Other animals also being captured are ostriches, oryx, hartebeest, aoudad, and a wild ass which, to introduce a second capture method, is being lassoed by one horseman. Transport for the carnivores is standing by. There are wooden crates with guillotine doors and sides reinforced by iron bands. These wait on carts drawn by horses (which, one suspects, had been previously conditioned to accept the smell and sound of enraged big cats without bolting).

The Romans also employed several other methods of capturing animals. Nooses were set in a frame and attached to a log so that an animal that was unfortunate enough to get its foot caught would have to drag the log around until the trapper came. Leopards and lions were caught in covered pits or boxes that dropped when a trigger was struck or pulled. Bait was either rotten meat or a live goat, calf, or dog so cruelly restrained that it advertised its presence to the neighborhood carnivores by bleating, bawling, or yelping. Nets were also dropped from trees, carried by beaters, or raised to ensnare frightened birds as they first took wing to escape from a line of beaters. Hoofed animals and ostriches were sometimes driven in front of a long rope bedecked with brightly colored ribbons and bells. In this way they would be directed toward an open corral that was quickly closed when there were enough inside.

Perhaps the most unusual way of capturing leopards was described in a Roman poem. According to the poet Oppian, water holes were drugged with strong wine. When the unsuspecting leopards came to drink they imbibed enough alcohol to make them tiddly. One can envision the drunken animal, its feet wobbly, striving to focus its eyes, staggering off a few steps, belching loudly, then stupefied, lying down to sleep it off. Next day it would awaken in a packing crate already on its way to one of the Roman arenas, experiencing no doubt a raging thirst and aching head. Unlikely is the best word to apply to Oppian's method.[11] He had probably just received his poetic license.

Although mortality rates are not much discussed, they must have been high. At the time of capture terrified animals would break their legs or dash themselves against corral fences. Some would die of weakness or starvation, for the method of pacifying the trapped creatures was to deprive them of food for a few days. Elephants, for example, which were normally captured in natural cul-de-sacs made into stockades, were given diluted barley water for five or six days until they were tractable or weak enough to handle. After the traumas of capture and conditioning came long journeys on foot or in wooden crates and cages pulled on carts, most often by plodding bullocks. At North African and Asian ports shipments of animals would frequently have to wait several weeks until they could be taken aboard slow-moving ships to Ostia or other Roman ports. Long delays before shipment became such a rule that finally an imperial edict was issued that animals were to be kept no more than seven days in one municipality. The concern, be it noted, was not for the animals but for the citizens of port towns who had to bear the expense of keeping the animals while they waited for shipment. In the animals' arduous journey from point of capture to destination death must have come to many. For each one that arrived safely the way must have been strewn with five or six others left for the carrion eaters.

For most arrivals the remaining days in imperial or municipal

---

[11] Although South American monkeys are sometimes captured by trappers who use rum-soaked bananas. Gorged—and drunk—the animals either fall asleep or tumble from the trees. In either event they are readily captured.

menageries were numbered and their last sight of life was of shouting spectators and the bloodied sands of an arena. Not all animals, however, were used in games. There were some permanent menageries and even some open-air deer parks not unlike modern wild animal parks. Most of these were the private preserves of wealthy aristocrats who kept them for their own pleasure. Probably the largest private zoo, mainly of birds, was established by Marcus Terentius Varro (116–27 B.C.) at his great country estate near what is now Monte Cassino. Varro, an enthusiastic scholar of zoology, was one of the first in a long line of wealthy men whose passion for animals leads them to establish private zoos[12] a group which in fairly recent times has included men like the Duke of Bedford, Jean Delacour, John Aspinal, and John Knowles.

During the medieval period the demand for wild animals slackened. The killing games of the Roman period were no longer fashionable,[13] although one early Renaissance nobleman held what could be called a revival of the Roman games. Around 1544 Augustus the First, Elector of Dresden, inaugurated fights involving lions, tigers, bulls, bears, and boars which were carried on periodically until 1719, when for reasons not stated one of his successors, Augustus II, ended the practice by personally killing off the remaining animals with ball shot. The lot of animals was often poor under kings whose power, they were assured, came from divine right. What motivated Augustus II to slaughter his animals is uncertain but he had a precedent. On January 20, 1583, Henry III of France woke up after dreaming that the animals in his zoo were bent on eating him, thought about the situation for a moment, then took up his harquebus and removed the possibility of being eaten by slaying every creature in the collection.

Several good-sized menageries were operated for medieval kings and noblemen. During the eighth century Charlemagne established

[12] Before charitable trusts or non-profit corporations were invented, the death of a wealthy animal collector often meant the end of his zoo. Heirs, generally less enthusiastic about keeping animals, disposed of collections, often with unfortunate results. When the Earl of Derby died in the middle of the 19th century, his heirs sold a collection that contained breeding groups of quaggas and passenger pigeons, both now extinct.

[13] Although bull fighting, which had its origins at least as far back as the Minoans, and games of animal torture like bearbaiting continued.

three zoos, one of which included an elephant sent to him by Haroun al Raschid. The elephant provided a living symbol of the great king's power when it was paraded before the populace. William the Conqueror founded a zoo at the Tower of London that was greatly enlarged by his son King Henry I of England. Perhaps the greatest collection of the medieval period was that of the Holy Roman Emperor Frederick II, naturalist and author of one of the first books on ornithology. Frederick actually had three zoos and kept a traveling menagerie that contained lions, leopards, cheetah, camels, elephants, and monkeys. None of these European zoos rivaled the one established by Kublai Khan in China, nor for that matter the great zoo kept by Montezuma in Mexico.

The raids upon the wilderness to supply zoo animals slackened for several hundred years during which science and all other aspects of thought were dominated by Aristotle. The principal source of knowledge about animals, if one did not have them to look at, were Aristotle's Natural History and the completely erroneous (and for modern readers frequently hilarious) Bestiaries, stories about real or imagined animals from basilisks to unicorns that were written for moral uplift.

During the Renaissance and its revival of the scientific spirit the demand for wild animals increased, stimulated also by ocean voyagers like Columbus and Vasco da Gama who brought back with them animals that were new to Europe. Nobles and municipalities began to establish collections that set the stage for the menagerie-zoos that dominated the zoo world during the nineteenth and early twentieth century. In a few instances collections were used for important research. Linnaeus (Carl von Linné) turned to the royal Swedish zoo for some of the research that led to the publication of his famous treatise on the classification of animals, the *System of Nature*.

The oldest extant menagerie-zoo of modern history was established in Vienna, Austria, in 1752, at Schönbrunn Palace. It drew many of its original animals from a private zoo at Neugebäu of the Emperor Maxmilian II. By this time there were already animal dealers established in Europe, and in the ensuing years both they and the number of new zoos they supplied began to proliferate—at Madrid, Paris, London, Dublin, Bristol, Berlin, Frankfurt, Hanover, Hamburg, and in many other cities. During its formative years

the United States had been served mostly by traveling menageries, circuses that carried such common exotic animals as lions and tigers and occasionally uncommon ones like Indian rhinos, from place to place on wagons, or put them on display at such famous institutions as P.T. Barnum's museum in New York. The first American zoos, founded just over a hundred years ago, were New York's Central Park Zoo, first to open, and the Philadelphia Zoo, first to be operated by a zoological society.

Supplying an increasing number of zoos, which paid little or no attention to breeding their own animals, made a constant drain on the wilderness sources through a network of dealers, the middlemen who supplied not only zoos but a growing number of pet dealers, circuses, and in later years research organizations that wanted animals for medical experiments.

One of the largest animal dealers of the late nineteenth and early twentieth century was Carl Hagenbeck, who with his family introduced a new type of open-enclosure zoo at Hamburg, Germany, and supplied animals for many other zoos, mostly outside Germany, since his fellow zoo directors in other German cities tended to be jealous and objected to buying animals from Hagenbeck. In reading Hagenbeck's description of an expedition to the Sudan to capture African animals one can detect little improvement either in methods of capture or of transportation over those that had prevailed in Roman times. To avoid building the stockades required for rounding up large numbers of herd animals, the collectors hit upon the simple method of chasing wild herds on horseback until the young and weak animals became exhausted and fell behind. With many of the antelope species the next step was simple—the young animals were hog-tied and carried back to jerry-built pens at a base camp. But animals like elephants and rhinos would stop running and stand by their exhausted young, creating hazards for the collector. This too was dealt with quite simply. As Hagenbeck put it with that offhand insensitivity that has most often characterized human attitudes toward his fellow animals, "the [young elephants or rhinos] cannot as a rule be secured without first killing the old ones." In the Sudan, lacking modern high-powered elephant guns, the tribesmen of the Taka who were assisting Hagenbeck displayed their specialized hunting skills in killing the old ones. Several Taka horsemen, all but one riding dark horses and that one a gray, set out to make their kill with sharp cutting swords. It was the responsibility of the rider on the gray horse to draw the doomed animal's charge and then stay tantalizingly just out of reach so the charge would be prolonged. The other riders would then move in behind to cut the hamstrings on one leg of the charging animal. Hurt and infuriated, the elephant would turn to ward off these tormentors. The man on the gray then dropped from his horse and ran in to cut the second hamstring. The immobilized animal was then powerless to prevent the hunters from cutting its leg arteries so it would bleed to death. But the battle did not always go to the hunters. Few Taka men, it was reported, ever died in bed.

In Hagenbeck's time almost no improvement had been made in the transport of captured animals. As in the Roman era they moved slowly a few miles each day from the area of capture to a port from which they could be shipped. "The larger animals," Hagenbeck wrote, "are driven along by one or more attendants—a giraffe taking three persons, an elephant from two to four, an antelope two, and ostrich, if large, also two. The smaller animals, such as young lions, panthers, baboons, pigs or birds, are carried in cages . . . placed on the backs of camels. Right in the midst of our procession there marches a group of camels harnessed in pairs. Over the pack saddles of each pair are laid two stout poles, and from these poles . . . hangs a large cage, made of strong rods bound together with strips of hide. Each cage contains a young hippopotamus, who, in spite of his youth, weighs with his cage well over a quarter of a ton. Each [hippo] requires a large party to wait upon him; for, in addition to the two camels which convey him along, six or eight others are required for carrying the water which he demands continuously throughout the journey, as also for the bath—made of tanned ox-hide—which he enjoys every day during the halt. Hundreds of head of sheep and goats are driven along with the procession; the nanny goats providing a constant supply of milk for the young animals, and the remainder being used as food for the carnivores."

From the animals' point of view little had changed in the 20 centuries since the Romans first began to capture and transport animals for their games. Assuming the wild creature survived the trauma of capture, it would have to withstand the rigors of a long,

This rare blue bear was going to be shot for his raids on Alaskan garbage cans until an epic rescue was mounted.

Male Galapagos tortoise sticking his neck out proved to be one of only three remaining males of his species.

Borneo orangutan, "Bob."

Whenever two or more orangutans got their heads together, zoo officials feared they were plotting another break.

Age-old instincts came into play when captive-bred Przewalski's wild horses at the Marwell Zoo confronted a pack of foxhounds.

Cheetahs may exist finally only in places like the San Diego Wild Animal Park, where these cheetah kittens were born.

A Houdini of spectacled bears, he constantly appeared where he wasn't expected, until he found himself face to face with a Bengal tiger.

A container of semen from this male pygmy chimpanzee, "Kakowet," posed a problem for airport security on its way from San Diego to Antwerp.

"Kakowet" and "Linda" produced one female offspring a year until male "Kalind" was born, assuring better prospects for the survival of this species.

At the San Diego Zoo the Komodo dragons can't breed because the nine foot male single-mindedly chases a female who constantly eludes him.

A question at the San Diego Wild Animal Park was whether or not the mighty lowland gorilla "Trib" would know his own son.

slow, journey, speeded somewhat by steamships and railroads, but not enough to reduce the enormous rate of attrition that even in 1966, according to Ian Grimwood, saw three to six animals die to provide one healthy animal for circus, zoo, or pet dealer. The advent of large airplanes, particularly jets, marked the first real break for the animals. All but the very largest (or tallest in the case of giraffes) could be flown from a holding area or quarantine station near the point of capture directly to their destination. Given tender loving care immediately after capture and upon arrival at their new home, many more animals survived because of the speed of their journey. On a flight from Singapore to Los Angeles it is not necessary to bring along a herd of sheep and goats to provide milk for the young and meat for the carnivores.

Modern zoos have generally acquired most of their animals through dealers; some by trading or selling animals to one another, and a few through their own expeditions into the field for the express purpose of capturing animals. This method is what zoo curators dream about, but the economic realities of running a zoo preclude outfitting expeditions to the wilderness—unless angels can be found. And angels, it seems, are hard to come by. These days most of them own professional baseball and football teams but there were once well-read wealthy men with the romantic vision of themselves in safari jackets, boots, and Aussie hats moving through animal-dotted savannahs or down jungle trails. The breed is not entirely extinct, but now they tend to take 21-day packaged tours to East Africa, where for a time they can imagine themselves living the kind of life that was written about by a Robert Ruark, Ernest Hemingway, or Isak Dinesen.

Their value to zoos was, and still could be, in financing trips to collect animals. One such angel during the 1930s was G. Allan Hancock, who had come into a fortune because his family had homesteaded a patch of earth called Rancho La Brea near Los Angeles that proved rich in two resources, oil and fossils. The fossils, in the famous La Brea tar pits, Mr. Hancock gave to the County of Los Angeles. The oil he and his family sold.

Possibly inspired by the discoveries of sabertooths and mastodons at his tar pit, Hancock developed a dilettante's interest in natural sciences. He also had a yacht in the grand old style of a J.P. Morgan: If you had to ask how much it cost, you couldn't afford it.

His ship, the 195-foot Valero III, was superbly outfitted for luxury, safety, and scientific study. In its staterooms hung curtains so valuable that those aboard were asked not to smoke in these cabins. But the ship, capable of cruising 10,000 miles, was designed, the press releases said, for "scientists to scan new frontiers of knowledge." One of the frontiers in those days was the Galapagos Islands, which lie in the Pacific Ocean 600 miles from Ecuador like "five and twenty heaps of cinders dumped here and there in an outside city lot."[14]

Then as now the Islands were noted for their curious animals. To study them and collect some for the San Diego Zoo, Hancock took the Valero III on two expeditions in 1932 and 1933. Aboard were a number of scientists, including one who would make anybody's list of most unforgettable characters.

C.B. "Si" Perkins was then Curator of Reptiles for the San Diego Zoo. A Naval aviator during World War I, he had gone to Princeton, dutifully entered investment banking, and then for some unrevealed reason decided to chuck the respectable life of a banker and take up the study of reptiles. A tall, slender, slightly stooped man with a neatly trimmed mustache and a habit of peering owlishly over his reading glasses, he was one of the earliest and most respected staff members of the San Diego Zoo, where he compiled a still unequaled record of eccentricities. He was particularly hard on any zoo visitors who rapped their knuckles against the windows of snake cages to stir up some action. Even when he was inside the reptile house and the glass knockers were outside where they couldn't hear him he nonetheless bawled them out. Unfortunately, because of the beatific smile fixed on his face many recipients of his blasts thought he was merely being pleasant. One nun at whom he had smilingly shouted, "Keep your God damned hands off the glass, sister," was so impressed by his nice expression that she actually raised her hand in what she thought was a return benediction.

Perkins kept diaries, and the unpublished record of his trips aboard the Valero III to the Galapagos helps preserve an era when men were innocent despoilers, perfectly willing to disrupt nature in the name of science. His main purpose in being aboard the

[14] Herman Melville's description in his account of the Galapagos, "The Encantadas."

Valero III was to capture and bring back penguins, fur seals, sea lions, boobies, and other wild creatures that lived there. He was most interested, of course, in the reptiles for which the islands are famed, the large land iguanas, marine iguanas, and giant tortoises that so impressed early visitors.[15]

Life aboard the Valero III was not rigorous, but for Perkins it had its shortcomings. To begin with he had a tendency to be seasick. This, however, did not cause him quite so much discomfort as the fact that Captain Hancock, as he liked to be called, believed in upholding the social tradition of dressing for dinner, whether or not they were on zoological expeditions. Since Perkins had already demonstrated his contempt for these traditions by shifting from stocks and bonds to snakes, he was not above putting a strain on dinner conversation by showing up fairly frequently without a coat and tie. But his greatest hardship grew out of Captain Hancock's reluctance to serve cocktails before dinner. Under any but the most stringent standards Perkins was no alcoholic, but it was understood by his friends and associates that he savored a few ounces of whiskey each evening nearly as much as he liked the strong Mexican cigarettes called *Campiones*. In his diaries of the first voyage appears a daily lament, "No cocktails tonight." The second voyage saw a marked change. Captain Hancock for some reason decided to serve cocktails nearly every evening and even relented on the dress code when the ship was in the tropics. To Perkins' delight he could record "Cocktails are such a regular thing that I won't mention them unless they are absent."

Since Perkins was antireligious, well-read, and a firm believer in evolution it is surprising to find no reference in the extensive diaries to Charles Darwin's visit to the Galapagos aboard the *Beagle*. There is in fact little introspection in the diaries, nor is there, as one might expect, a sense of awe for a place that is to the theory of evolution what Mecca is for Muhammadanism. But Perkins was a man of his times, and for the natural scientists of the period the emphasis was upon finding and classifying animals, not upon their evolutionary status, ecology, or behavior. Tampering with nature

[15] First called Islas Encantadas, or Enchanted Islands, they were later referred to as the Galapagos, or Tortoise islands. Officially, however, their name is Archipiélago de Colón—to honor Columbus, who of course never saw them.

was not considered a sin, probably because there was still so much nature to be tampered with. It is, for example, easy for Perkins to agree with Captain Hancock's suggestion that they capture forty of the land iguanas from South Seymour Island and "plant them" on North Seymour, where none were to be found, and "in a few years come down and see if anything has happened. A good idea, I believe." The idea seemed so good that they translocated twenty more of the South Seymour iguanas on their second voyage a year later.

There is a supreme irony here. In committing what today would be considered ecological folly, Perkins and his associates actually saved a whole race of the Galapagos land iguanas from extinction. South Seymour, from which the iguanas were taken, is now known by its Ecuadorian name of Baltra, familiar to tourists as the place where they land when they fly to the islands.[16] During World War II Baltra was an American Air Base designed to protect the approaches to the Panama Canal. Having little to enliven a bleak existence on a volcanic rock covered with just enough sparse vegetation to support the limited animal life, the military personnel stationed there found relief from boredom by using their rifles to slaughter all living creatures on the island, starting no doubt with the largest, the land iguanas.[17] Today only sea birds are found on Baltra. The iguanas are no more, but thanks to Perkins and his associates their descendants continue to live on what is now Seymour Island.

However, the relocation of land iguanas was a side issue. Perkins was after live animals for the zoo. On the voyage down and back he bought or personally collected numerous tropical reptiles, birds, and mammals at various ports from Acapulco ("real clean, about 15,000 population") to Guayaquil. Since he had to care for every animal aboard (he was listed as a steward on the ship's roster—"sarcastically" one of the regular crew members told him), each

---

[16] Almost all the islands now go by the Spanish names favored by Ecuador, although a few still have the English names that once made the entire archipelago sound as though it were Admiral Lord Nelson's fleet—names like Albemarle, Beagle, Champion, Daphne, Duncan, Hood, Narborough, and Indefatigable.

[17] There were no tortoises on this island.

additional specimen added to his work. Moreover, little was known about the natural diets of many species taken aboard. Perkins' remedy for this deficiency was to use eggs, force-fed if necessary, whenever an animal refused other food. The great interest, of course, was in capturing Galapagos creatures which few zoos had, particularly the land iguanas, marine iguanas, and giant tortoises. The first two were easily collected. The colonies were sizable and like all of the Galapagos wildlife they had not been genetically programmed to flee from predatory man, since for most of their evolution the islands had been uninhabited by human beings. The tortoises were a different story. Once numerous on the islands, their numbers had been decimated during the era of sailing ships by naval vessels, whalers, and buccaneers whose crews found tortoise steaks and roasts an excellent source of fresh meat on long Pacific voyages because the tortoises would live eight or nine months aboard ship without being fed.[18]

By the early thirties the tortoises, sharply reduced in numbers, were found in the rugged interiors of the 10 islands that supported populations. Perkins was given time to make a two-day trek into the forbidding interior of Isabela (Albemarle), the largest island, where tortoises still live in the craters of extinct volcanos. Two days was not enough, and Perkins was forced to return to the ship scratched, aching, and tired—wishing, he noted in his diary, that he had a pitcherful of cocktails. He was perfectly willing to pay for tortoises if the price was not too high. Too high in his lexicon was $15 in one instance and $7 in another. Today a Galapagos tortoise, if it were obtainable, would bring up to $2,000.[19]

Nevertheless, on the second expedition, perhaps bolstered by the presence of Dr. Harry Wegeforth, founder of the Zoological Society of San Diego and the zoo, Perkins was able to obtain at Guayaquil and on some of the islands six of the tortoises, which

[18] One study of the logs from seventy-nine New Bedford, Nantucket, and Salem whalers, a small fraction of the ships that stopped by the islands to pick up tortoises, showed that in 151 visits they had taken off a total of 10,373 tortoises, unfortunately mostly females, which are somewhat smaller and more easily carried than the giant males.

[19] The animals cannot legally be taken from the islands, which are protected as a National Park by the Ecuadorian Government, so the only sources are poachers and the few zoos that have large herds.

were added to the 30 San Diego already had.[20] It was another sign of a more innocent era that the tortoises were not physically segregated according to the islands from which they had originally come. At the zoo the animals were put into one exhibit on the assumption that each individual came from the same species, even though there were two obviously different shell types, the domed and the saddleback. It took approximately forty more years to discover that many of the tortoise islands have seen the evolution of distinct species. In a monumental study of tortoise behavior and general body configuration Dr. Thomas H. Fritts shows significant differences in tortoises from island to island—differences so great that interbreeding between species is unlikely because of dissimilarities in physical makeup, behavior, and mating periods—all good reasons why propagation in mixed captive herds has been rare.[21]

Of the Galapagos animals that Perkins collected and brought back to the San Diego Zoo few, excepting the tortoises, lived for more than two years. It was typical of the times that zoos often acquired animals about whose dietary, sexual, and other biological requirements scientists had only the haziest knowledge. No deliberate cruelty was involved. Men like Perkins were eternally optimistic that they could learn enough about the newly captured animals to keep them alive, although they were bolstered in this optimism because they knew that many more animals remained in the wild to provide replacements for those that died. It is to Perkins' credit that when the marine iguanas succumbed within a short time, he made no further effort to keep the species because he conceded that too little was known about them. The marine iguanas are in fact marvelous examples of adaptation. They can go within a few moments from lava rock where the surface temperature may exceed 120 degrees into the cool depths of the ocean forty feet below the surface to seek the sea plants upon which they feed. They have also evolved the ability, necessary to their survival, to squirt

[20] Twenty of these came from a collecting and study trip led by Dr. Charles H. Townsend in the late twenties. Some are still alive. In addition ten more tortoises were brought in individually, several by tuna fishermen.
[21] Because of Fritts' study it was determined that the San Diego herd had one of three surviving males of the Hood Island tortoise. The Zoo promptly sent him by air to the Darwin Station in the Galapagos where, it is hoped, he can do his part in assuring the survival of the species.

in tiny white jets from the corner of their eyes the excess salt they imbibe with sea water.

For the land iguanas the change from the Galapagos to San Diego was not so extreme. These lived longer but they did not reproduce. The tortoises did best of all, and because Perkins and more particularly his successor, Charles E. Shaw, became interested in their captive propagation, they conducted some of the research required so that Shaw was able to hatch the first Galapagos tortoises to be born in captivity.

For thousands of years then, the movement of animals has been one way—from wilderness to captivity—and zoos have done little to repay their part of that debt. The taking of wild creatures from seemingly inexhaustible sources was done in innocence by men who simply assumed their vast superiority to the creatures they incarcerated. Future shock did not set in until the late 1960s and early seventies as zoo operators everywhere were hit with the realization that animals were getting scarce. Even with this revelation many zoo people continued to flounder, endeavoring to obtain their animals through the same channels that had been used for centuries. A few of the more farsighted zoos recognized the need to become self-sufficient by breeding their own animals. And of these still fewer appreciated the opportunity to begin repaying their long-standing debt to the wild by working to assure the survival of species that otherwise would go the way of the dodo.

The Orangutan
Escape Committee

I t is fascinating, though profitless, to speculate on the relative intelligence of advanced primates like gorillas, chimpanzees, orangutans, and humans, except to say that humans are probably smarter (although not all the evidence is in), and that intelligence has to be looked at more in terms of individuals than species. Some of the great apes, for example, can score up to 85 on modified intelligence tests, which makes them smarter than 10 percent of the people who make faces at them in the zoo.

Certainly the orangutans, who hail from Borneo and Sumatra,[1] and whose name in Indonesian means "man of the forest," are among the smartest creatures on earth. Orangs, especially the young ones, are great favorites of zoo visitors. They have a sad clown quality in their expression, an affectionate nature, a sly playfulness, and a curiosity which, when it is combined with their intelligence and incredible manipulative ability, makes the problem of containing them at a zoo a constant challenge. They have fingers so dexterous that they can neatly field-strip a camera accidentally dropped into their enclosure by an unwary visitor, yet so strong they can twist off large nuts that have been tightened with a torque wrench. They seem to enjoy taking things apart; consequently any structure in an orang exhibit has to be strong enough to resist the

[1] In prehistoric times orangutans inhabited much of Southeast Asia even up into Southern China, but constantly encroaching man has pushed them back into their last redoubts, where there may be 2,500 left in the wild. Another 600 live in zoos.

leverage of their long arms and be joined by welds, rivets, or bolts with nuts that have been countersunk. Orangs have originated their own version of Murphy's Law: Anything that can go wrong they will make go wrong.

In zoos orangs are normally kept in pairs or family groups. In the wild state they are loners, perhaps not because they want to be, but because the harsh requirements of searching for food day after day in the jungle forces them to spread out. Males go their solitary way while mothers and infants live in another part of the forest. Since there are infants, there exists a strong presumption that occasional meetings of a sexual nature do take place, and, in fact, field observations by people like Biruté Galdikas-Brindamour reveal that three-year-old orangs generally get their first lessons in sex by watching mother with father or sometimes with a strange male who has taken over the territory and mother by beating up father and sending him packing. The system results in a number of cut and bruised males, numerous half brothers and sisters, and a constant refreshing of the gene pool.

When the San Diego Zoo opened its new orangutan exhibit in 1975, five orangs were put in it together—three females, including a grandmotherly type named Doris, and two males, one of whom, Otis, became the father of twins just after he and his mate (on this occasion Robella) had attained maturity.[2]

Ranging in age and wisdom from bright young Clancy, just turned three, to wise old Doris, approaching 35, the five orangutans proved to be the right number to set up an escape committee. Their enclosure is a large one, covering about 4,000 square feet. Completely open, it has a turfed surface surrounded on four sides by unscalable gunnite walls 12 feet high. In the exhibit, slightly off center so that visitors can watch the orangs better, is a massive play and climbing structure, a kind of jungle gym made of logs the size of telephone poles held together by bolts with nuts that have been countersunk. At various places along this 14-foot-high edifice (not counting some single poles), there are metal handholds so the orangs can swing by their extraordinarily long arms or dangle head down while holding on with their feet—the kinds of exercise they would get in the wild.

---

[2] Seven sets of twins have been born to captive orangutans.

Adjoining the enclosure in the rear, completely away from the public's view, are heated bedrooms of cement block in which the orangs sleep at night, after being enticed in by the knowledge that there they will be fed their principal meal of the day. Each bedroom has a barred front facing a service corridor with barred safety doors at both ends. These doors are locked at night, but during the daytime when the orangs are in the enclosure they are often kept unlocked to make it easier for keepers passing in and out.

During the first few days after the orangs were put into the new enclosure, zoo staffers watched them carefully just in case there had been a mistake in design or construction that would allow them to climb the walls. The walls proved unscalable, but for a while it looked as though the orangs might be planning to tunnel their way out. At various points in the enclosure they dug deep holes in the turf, sometimes finding rocks in the soil, which the keepers carefully gathered each night lest one of the animals got the idea it might be fun to pitch them at visitors. The thought made zoo officials turn pale, especially after Otis used a fist-sized rock to crack the shatterproof glass in a viewer window built into the wall at the lower part of the exhibit. It appeared obvious, however, that the new home pleased the orangs, and they took advantage of all the play opportunities offered them. They wrestled, chased each other, gathered mouthfuls of water to spit at one another, and used every part of the exhibit from the turf to the highest point on the jungle gym. This, however, was most often occupied by Doris, who as senior officer in charge took it as her right, settling down each day in a kind of crow's nest from which she could scrutinize every part of the enclosure, the better perhaps to study escape possibilities.

Keys to the getaway, which came several months after the enclosure was opened, were two dissimilar objects that in the right combination provided a stairway to freedom. On the outside of the enclosure fairly close to the wall grew a magnificent stand of bamboo with tops some forty feet above the ground. For most of its height each bamboo stalk was largely bare, but about a third of the way down from the tip, shoots with leaves branched out. Inside the exhibit an additional play device had been installed for the orangs. A length of tough fishnet had been twisted into a simulated vine and firmly attached to the jungle gym so the orangs

could play Tarzan by swinging out over the turf.[3] The vine's length had been carefully determined. Even when a swinging orang extended an arm full length at the outer limit of the arc, it could not possibly reach the wall. Neither could it release the vine at the last possible instant like a trapeze performer, and use momentum to fly through the air to the top of the wall.

But the most closely figured calculations sometimes go wrong. This particular type of rope netting had a tendency to stretch, not much—the orangs could never reach the wall—but enough to make the swing the first indispensable step in the escape plan. It was an act of God that allowed the orangs to bring the swing into play. One evening a fairly stiff breeze caused a single fragile offshoot of one bamboo stalk to break so that it hung down from the main stalk. The shoot did not touch the wall but its tip, pointing downward, hung three or four feet inside the wall. So fragile was this shoot, so wispy and inconsequential, that nobody noticed it—nobody that is but one of the orangutans.

The shoot itself would not have supported an orangutan's weight, but it became the tool used by the smart orang—whoever that was—to pull in the flexible upper part of the main bamboo stalk. By swinging on the vine to the full extent possible, the orang could grasp the wispy shoot, pull it toward the inside of the enclosure and with it the main stalk of bamboo. The escape route was ready.

Whether or not the orangs made their discovery before the day of escape will never be known. The timing of the getaway, however, was exceedingly well chosen. It came just after the orangs had been released into their enclosure one morning but before any visitors were present to watch. As zoo staffers later reconstructed the break, one of the orangs, probably the genius who had seen the connection between the swing, wispy offshoot, bamboo stem, and wall, immediately went to the swing, swung out, reached for and got hold of the shoot and then the main bamboo stem. The stem was then pulled far enough to break it over the wall. Since green

---

[3] This swing resulted from an experiment sponsored by the zoo and conducted by Professor Chris Parker of San Diego State University. The object was to find diverse ways to provide a more interesting life for primates, who are often victims of boredom in captivity.

bamboo when bent splits but does not snap apart, the bamboo tip made a first-rate ladder to the top of the wall.

Two orangs (one of them probably the genius) made their break before the plot was discovered. Robella, a young female, went clear over the wall and lurched her way on long arms and knuckles along a path that led by some bird cages toward the main entrance of the zoo. There she was discovered by a surprised keeper who, in trying to turn her back, caused her to seek refuge on top of the cages. Dispatching one of the first visitors of the day as a messenger the keeper, who wanted to keep watch on Robella, got word of the break to both security men and veterinarians. For several moments while help was being rallied Robella merely sat on top of the bird cage either sunning herself or contemplating her next move. The security men who arrived at the scene carried real guns, a precaution designed to protect any zoo visitor whose life or limb might be threatened. The vets came with a dart gun loaded with the correct dosage to knock out a medium-sized orangutan. Within a few minutes Robella was shot with the dart. She soon fell asleep, was lifted from the cage and taken in a small truck to her bedroom. There she was given an antidote and left to sleep it off.

Meantime, back at the exhibit Otis, having taken the first step toward freedom, was apparently reluctant to venture further. He remained on top of the wall, shuffling back and forth, undecided whether to return or go on. Because darting is always risky the vet in charge suggested that Otis be lured into his night quarters, for he was on the wall just above the outside door to the bedrooms. Keepers put bananas at two points on the ground beneath the wall where Otis paced and in the service corridor for the bedrooms. The idea was to have Otis go after the first banana (for he dearly loved bananas) then, seeking the second banana, move through the open safety door into the corridor. At that juncture a keeper, hidden around the corner on the outside of the building, would slam and bolt the safety door. It would then be an easy matter to inveigle Otis into the familiar surroundings of his own bedroom.

The plan had one major flaw. No one fully appreciated Otis's powers of observation. The young orang climbed down from the wall, seized and ate the first banana, shuffled over to the safety door, peered in, saw the second banana, and moved on into the

corridor. Quickly the keeper slammed and bolted the safety door. So far the plan had worked to perfection. But Otis paid absolutely no attention to what was happening behind him. Almost without breaking stride he picked up the second banana and went on to the second safety door. Grasping the handle as though he had done it a thousand times before he opened the door and went on through. It was an astounding performance considering the fact that he had never opened that or any other door (as far as anyone knew); he had apparently learned by watching the keepers as they came and went.

Unfortunately for Otis the corridor he left merely led to another which was blocked at the end by a locked safety door. Soon he was lured back to his own bedroom and the great orangutan escape plan had been foiled.

In theory the orang enclosure is now absolutely escape proof. Nevertheless, whenever two or three of the orangs are seen with their heads together as though in whispered conversation, zoo staffers find themselves wondering. Is the escape committee planning another break? What if they learn to form an orang pyramid, or pile up turf in one corner of their yard? Maybe they are tunneling after all . . .

Through most of recorded history man has incarcerated animals in boxes, cages, or pens, which allow little or no vent for their natural yearnings. Hoofed animals have generally fared best, for they can be confined by fences like domestic sheep or cattle; although some of the antelope, even as large as the eland, can from a standing start clear heights that would make an Olympic high jumper envious. Carnivores and primates have fared worst; many have been driven to neurosis by the kind of close confinement which would be classified as cruel and unusual punishment if it were applied to human beings.

The ancient reasons for such treatment of animals—by no means entirely a thing of the past—are not hard to guess at. It is of course simply easier and less expensive to build a boxlike cage barely big enough to house a specific animal, and if all one wants to do is exhibit a curiosity, even as large as an elephant, the boxlike cage will do. More fundamentally, men have historically been insensitive to the needs of confined animals and have assumed the right, never granted, of subjugating them as beings vastly inferior to man. Perhaps the assumption of man's superiority came easily to people who hunted animals for food and proved one kind of superiority over and over again by outsmarting their prey, little noting that animal predators were also consistently outsmarting their prey.

From whatever first source the assumption of man's superiority came, it was given philosophical underpinnings by religion, particularly in the West. When a religion like Christianity granted man dominion over the beasts, then dominion could be interpreted not as trusteeship but as the right to kill or subjugate at will. In these circumstances the manner in which captive animals were treated became of little concern.

This inherent callousness was buttressed even more in western thought when in the seventeenth century, at the beginning of the "age of reason," the French philosopher René Descartes established to his own satisfaction a clear separation between man and animals with his famous dictum "Cogito, ergo sum." Since in Descartes' opinion animals did not cogitate, ergo they were not. However, the fact of animals, their undeniable presence on earth, had to be accounted for. Descartes' solution was simple. By his definition animals could not think and lacked souls. Therefore they had to be cleverly contrived machines, machines without the divine spark of man, driven, Descartes announced, by an internal system of gases and mechanical connections. Descartes' idea was not based on observation of the behavior of animals in their natural state, for as modern ethologists have demonstrated, any number of animal species are capable of thinking. But the Cartesian philosophy was widely accepted: Captive animals are little more than machines. Machines have no feelings. All they require is fuel to keep them going and perhaps some minimal repair from time to time. The manner of caging or confining them is of no consequence so long as it does the job. The Cartesian idea that animals are machines accounted for much vivisection as scientists and dilettantes alike subjected live creatures to the scalpel in order to determine the system of connections that made them run.

Yet there have been historical bright spots for captive animals. Roman aviculturists, as we have seen, often maintained well-furnished aviaries and even large flight cages, and deer parks for the more easily confined hoofed animals have been used since ancient

Egypt and China.[4] But most zoo animals, as old prints testify, were confined in cramped, barren quarters often without the solace of another of their kind. Alone, unable to exercise properly, given nothing to play with, the lot of the bear, tiger, or monkey was often one of endless empty hours relieved only by staring at visitors, picking at its own fur, rubbing against walls, licking up excrement, or masturbating. The people who came to zoos thought they were seeing the real wild animal—the real grizzly, chimpanzee, or Chinese leopard—but what they actually saw was a physical representation, alive, but far removed from the alert, mentally healthy wild creature. Zoos were in effect nothing more than museums in which the display animals were slightly mobile and stuffed with their own vital organs. One can still get the feel of what that kind of zoo was like by visiting the menagerie at the Jardin des Plantes in Paris. (Then, by way of startling contrast, visit the modern Paris Zoo at Vincennes.)

The pity of it all was that the conditions of captive animals can frequently be made better by small changes in their enclosures. Several years ago the San Diego Zoo built an exhibit for mandrills that was only a slightly enlarged version of the old-fashioned menagerie cage. It had a steel frame covered with wire mesh over a cement floor relieved only by large rocks to improve appearances for Zoo visitors. Barred bedrooms were built in the rear. In this exhibit were housed a large male and two female mandrills who at least had occasional sex to relieve the tedium.

Cooperating with nearby San Diego State University, the zoo several years ago agreed to have students study the daily lives of the mandrills. What their study turned up was the fact that the mandrills, rather pathetically, climbed the wire mesh sides of their cage each night and clung near the top until fatigued muscles could no longer support their body weight. Then they came down and slept on the cement floor. What the students were witnessing was characteristic of what the mandrills would be doing in the

---

[4] That deer parks were also found in Asia is evidenced by the fact that Père David's deer was kept alive for nearly 3,000 years in a large imperial reserve near Peking. The last Père David's deer in that walled reserve was killed for venison by foreign troops during the Boxer Rebellion. Fortunately the species survived thanks in large part to the Duke of Bedford who maintained a large herd on his estate in England.

West African forests where they had originated. Mandrills are forest animals. They spend their waking hours foraging for food on the jungle floor but at night, to protect themselves from predators, particularly their most constant enemy, the leopard, they climb trees and roost there high in leafy nests. In scrambling up the sides of their cage each evening the San Diego Zoo's mandrills were simply trying to do what came naturally but could not find the safe resting places they sought at the top.

Using the knowledge gained from the student observers, zoo officials built high platforms in each of the corners of two adjacent cages, the original mandrill cage and another which was connected by two tunnels of wire mesh. Two tunnels were required because the big male mandrill found it amusing and satisfying to his ego to block the single tunnel that was first constructed. He would sit at the tunnel's entrance and make fearful grimaces at any of his wives or numerous progeny who wanted to move from one enclosure to the other. As a final improvement simulated vines of nylon chain and woven fishnet were suspended from the top of each cage. The result of these inexpensive minor changes was to greatly enlarge the mandrills' living space without enlarging the cage. Now, from all appearances, there isn't a neurosis in the mandrill group. The male mandrill sleeps anywhere he wishes, but once he has chosen his spot, his wives and children find their own corner shelves high out of reach of the predators they are genetically programed to avoid. The changes also produced an added bonus for the zoo. The mandrills, once relatively morose and inactive, move about their cages much more; youngsters play games with one another and harass the adults by swinging down from the simulated vines. The almost constant movement during the daytime has changed the static, museumlike exhibit that used to be hurriedly bypassed by visitors into a crowd pleaser where people sometimes jostle one another to obtain front-row spots.

It has only been within the past quarter century that new zoo exhibits have been built with an eye to the underlying needs of the animals. In former times zoo exhibits, no matter how elaborate they might be, were generally constructed with the idea of pleasing visitors. The greatest innovation in zoo construction in several hundred years was the moated enclosure first developed by the

Hagenbecks at Hamburg shortly after the turn of the century.[5] But even these cages were freed of their bars so zoo visitors could get an unobstructed view of the animals. Moated enclosures give visitors a greater sense of openness and freedom, but removing bars does not necessarily improve conditions for the animals. Sterility is sterility whether it is behind a moat or behind steel bars.

The first theoretician to promulgate a concept that is becoming more widely accepted by zoo managers was Heini Hediger, a Swiss who was director first of the Basel Zoo and later of the zoo at Zurich before he retired in 1974. In several of the books Hediger wrote about zoo management, he contended that the most important consideration in moving an animal from a wild to a captive state is providing for the animal's psychological adaptation to its new surroundings. Often, Hediger was in essence saying, newly captured animals suffer from a kind of psychological bends when they are uprooted from one environment and thrown into another. Even if an animal is kept at the right temperature, properly fed, and allowed to rest, an unbridged move from wild to captive state can produce shock. What Hediger realized, as few before him had and many still don't, is that captive wild animals, depending on their relative intelligence and sensitivity, are like human beings in being influenced for good or ill by their ability to adapt to disruptive change. Caught, moved from familiar surroundings, possibly from an acknowledged and comfortable position in the hierarchy of a group, removed from the group itself and away from the system of sentries and known escape routes that help protect it from predators, often lacking in its new confinement sufficient flight space—the amount of territory normally needed to get away from enemies—undergoing, in short, a rapid series of shocks, the newly captive wild animal may suffer enough psychological damage to bring on physical weakness, disease, and, in some instances, death. Many if not most animals that come into captivity from the wild already carry viruses, bacteria, or parasites that cause various deadly diseases, but which are suppressed in a mentally healthy animal. But if the animal is psychologically weakened by the shift from the wild to captivity, the suppressed diseases may break out. In

[5] Credit should also be given to a Swiss designer, Urs Eggenschwyler, who was the architect of this innovation.

this respect postmortems are often misleading because they list the disease itself as the cause of death, not the psychological trauma that brought it on.

When animals first arrive at a large zoo they are most often quarantined for a month or so. This self-imposed quarantine has nothing to do with the required quarantines ordered by the United States Department of Agriculture (or their equivalent in Europe) in the interest of detecting and arresting exotic diseases like hoof and mouth in cattle or Newcastle in birds before they infect native and domestic animals. In their requirements, the USDA people may on occasion be overzealous and given to bureaucratic inflexibility, sometimes displaying a Procrustean approach that is unnecessarily harsh,[6] but the fact remains that the intent of the protective laws they administer is unquestionably sound.

When zoos impose their own quarantine they act to protect animals already in their collection. Just as a bad cold can spread rapidly in a schoolroom or crowded theater, so viral and bacterial diseases of animals can take devastating toll in a zoo if sensible precautions are not taken to stifle them before they can start. The zoo director's worst nightmare is of coming to work one morning and finding all his animals lying immobile in their cages and enclosures, victims of a fast-spreading plague. Nor is the fear unfounded. Not long ago the Los Angeles Zoo received a large shipment of antelope, including rarely seen gerenuk, lesser kudu, and bongo. The animals were in the zoo less than a month when within three days

[6] In 1977 United States Customs confiscated 10 Tahitian lorys, small beautiful members of the parrot family, which had been smuggled into Los Angeles by people who wanted to sell them in Europe, where private aviculturists would probably have paid up to 50 thousand dollars for the lot. So rare are the birds that stuffed specimens in Vienna's natural history museum carry the legend "Probably Extinct." Customs turned the birds over to the San Diego Wild Animal Park, where the staff wanted to start a captive breeding program. Officials of the United States Department of Agriculture claimed that under the law the birds would have to be killed because they had entered the United States without being quarantined. This claim was made in spite of the fact that Newcastle disease, the major concern, is not found in Tahiti. A compromise was finally reached after bird lovers throughout the United States had risen in arms whereby the lorys were sent to Great Britain then after a thirty-day quarantine returned to the San Diego Wild Animal Park. Had the USDA's application of sensible rules been less rigid the birds would not have been subjected to the additional strain.

six of the kudu, all females, and two gerenuk died of a mysterious virus.

A self-imposed quarantine also gives zoo veterinarians the opportunity to give incoming animals physical examinations to find any defects, cysts, malformed limbs, and the like that they might have. Sometimes, unfortunately, such examinations are so cursory that later events bring embarrassment to the vets. At Front Royal, Virginia, the 4,000-acre breeding farm of the National Zoo in Washington, D.C., a dozen or so female Bactrian camels were provided with a splendid looking male in order to get a breeding program started. When several months passed without any normal activity—heavy breathing, neck rubbings, and snorting chases—that precede breeding, let alone attempts to copulate, the splendid male was given a thorough physical examination. He was, it became clear, a eunuch. Sometime in the past he had been castrated, a not unusual way of reducing male yearnings in domesticated Bactrian camels and dromedaries among people who use them as work animals. The San Diego Zoo had a similar experience with a male bush dog, obtained on breeding loan from the Lincoln Park Zoo in Chicago. The animal had already been on loan to two other zoos before being sent to San Diego for pairing with a lone female. Left for several months in the exhibit with its putative mate, the dog developed a sore which required surgery. When it was on the operating table the veterinary surgeon discovered that it had long since been surgically rendered unsuitable for breeding.[7]

In the transition from wild to captive state young animals fare best, but all ages are better off if their human captors have established an environment in the animal's new world that allows it to retain as nearly as possible its natural patterns of behavior—with the obvious exception of allowing the hunting and killing of live prey by captive predators.[8] Parents of small children and humane

---

[7] Zoo people are often guilty of failing to make full disclosure about animals that they sell or trade to one another. It is of course possible that the first zoo that got this bush dog didn't know that it had been castrated, but somewhere along the line someone should have ascertained this rather vital fact. Slip-ups of this nature used to be compiled by the American Association of Zoological Parks and Aquariums for an annual "Zoo Goof" Award, now discontinued because it invariably caused some pain to recipients.

[8] A few zoos are now trying to simulate hunting behavior in predators.

society officials would very likely object to watching a lion kill a horse, even though that lion is probably living on a diet of horse meat or a prepared food made of horse meat.

In the effort to create an environment that stimulates natural behavior, zoo people are doing far more than helping animals adapt to change. They are also creating exhibits that attract more visitors because the animals are more fun to watch in this environment. Natural exhibits become popular attractions that gather crowds. People do not experience the boredom of walking past a line of live museum displays; instead they are frequently treated to live-action entertainment where animals vocalize, climb, run, fight, groom, and mate.

For captive breeders natural exhibits provide an additional benefit. If endangered animals are to be successfully bred, they must retain most of their wild characteristics. In the wild natural selection determines the characteristics that will be transmitted from generation to generation, but in a man-made environment natural selection is next to impossible. Knowing this, most serious captive breeders seek to approximate natural selection by using objective or random methods when they select the animals to be mated. Otherwise, as they know, the tendency of people to select for popular characteristics—long horns, wide chests, bizarre colors, smaller or larger sizes—will result in the original wild animals being lost. (Just as, over many generations, wolves were turned into poodles.)

One objective in the captive breeding of endangered animals is the return of species to the wild, but like the program to reestablish the Arabian oryx, this will most likely be done, when it is done, with relatively small numbers of animals. If the rehabilitated animals are not able to cope with a wild environment because captive breeders have overdomesticated them, groups will probably be too small to allow enough natural breeding for selection to once again fine-tune the animal for survival. It is axiomatic, for example, that where predators stalk, their game must be wary. The need for wariness has been thoroughly demonstrated at the San Diego Wild Animal Park. Because the Park is located in underdeveloped back country where native predators, coyotes, bobcats, and an occasional mountain lion are still to be found, Park officials diligently sought to remove all the coyotes and bobcats from the area fenced

in for the Park. The task proved hopeless. As soon as the large enclosures were built and stocked with virtually every known species of antelope, to say nothing of zebra, buffalo, wild cattle, deer, giraffe, and rhinoceroses, the natural population of ground squirrels and rabbits boomed as they waxed fat on the nutritious pellets used to feed the wild animals.[9] Then the coyotes began to move back, digging their way under the fences, setting up dens, even audaciously parading youngsters before startled visitors on summer nights when the Park runs trains with floodlights on its five-mile railway, the Wgasa Bush Line. Squirrels and rabbits were their principal prey, but coyotes are impartial, displaying a willingness to kill and eat any exotic animal small or weak enough to tackle. It soon was impossible for the Park to keep any birds smaller than an ostrich in the large enclosures. The Lilford's and other cranes, unable to fly because of pinioning, were easy pickings for the coyotes and Park officials had to move them into secure pens near Nairobi Village where visitors board the trains. Adults among the antelope species, including the smaller gazelles, were not threatened but their progeny were. Few were lost, however, because adults stood ready to defend them, and breeding results in the enclosures—the largest one is about 125 acres—were so good that the few losses could be sustained.

It can be argued that the coyotes are helping the Park officials to achieve their objective in preserving wild species. The herds of antelope and deer retain their natural defenses, their grazing and sleeping formations, their systems of sentries on the perimeter of the herd, their danger signals, their individual wariness.

In some animals natural wariness and instinctive defenses against predators may remain for several generations without the constant presence of predators to stimulate them. At the Marwell Zoo near the town of Winchester, England, the proprietor, John Knowles, has a fine herd of Przewalski's wild horses, the only true wild horses in the world. Lovely animals somewhat larger than ponies, they stand when mature about fourteen hands at the shoulder. Adapted to Mongolian plains and mountain foothills that run to extremes in temperature, they have shaggy coats light beige to golden tan in color with a black mane that stands straight and is

[9] No one knows for sure what percentage of the pellets are handouts to welfare rodents, but it may be as much as twenty percent.

cropped like the hair on the head of a Prussian general. The absence of a forelock, and a tail that changes from short to long hair a third of the way down, clearly distinguish them from domestic horses. All the Przewalski's horses now in captivity are descendants of wild stock brought into Europe around 1900, supplemented later by three additional wild caught animals. The 250 horses in several major zoos came through two main lines—the Halle-Prague Zoo and Askania Nova-Munich Zoo. There has been some worry among those who breed Przewalski's that through inbreeding the horses have begun to deviate from the original wild horses, now thought to be extinct, although sightings of a small herd was reported in Mongolia as late as 1966. Any deviations, however, have not totally removed their wildness, not if Knowles' herd is typical.

The Marwell Zoo is in green English countryside through which in the appropriate season fox hunters sometimes ride behind full packs of 25 to 100 baying hounds. Knowles forbids any hunting on the grounds of his large zoo, but he cannot control events in nearby fields. One soft English day several years ago his herd of Przewalski's, seven mares, two foals, and a stallion left their barn in the morning and trotted through a gate that led from a smaller paddock into a field of some five acres that Knowles provides for grazing and exercise. Beyond the outer fence of this field is open wooded country, roadless, but transversed by one trail normally used by hikers though sometimes by horsemen.

Knowles was having breakfast in Marwell Hall at the center of the zoo when he first heard the baying of foxhounds in the distance. Because it was hunting season he thought little of it. But as the baying grew louder and louder he began to take note. The sounds were coming from the direction of the Przewalski's enclosure. This disturbed Knowles who quite frankly acknowledges that he favors some animals more than others, and of all his animals none stand higher in his esteem than the Przewalski's horses. Any threat to them was like a threat to members of his family. So as the baying hounds came perceptibly closer, Knowles put down his unfinished tea, ran from the manor house, catapulted himself into his land rover and drove toward the Przewalski's enclosure. It was his intention to herd the Przewalski's into their barn before the baying foxhounds caused them to panic and stampede, for then some would surely injure themselves. The terrible thought crossed his mind that perhaps one would break a leg and have to be destroyed.

He need not have been so concerned. When he reached the Przewalski's field he found that the hunters had been pursuing either a lucky or extremely savvy fox. The animal had headed straight for the one place that promised safety, the forbidden grounds of the zoo. Unfortunately, the foxhounds were ignorant of the prohibition against their entering the zoo grounds. To a hound they had gone over, under, and through the fence of the field where the wild horses grazed.

For the Przewalski stallion the moment of truth had arrived. He had to rely on ancient instincts, programs for survival that had been developed in his ancestors during encounters with packs of hungry wolves. For the sexual favors rendered him by the mares, and for the instant and unquestioning obedience by all members of his herd, the Przewalski stallion is obliged only to provide leadership and defense against all enemies. Confronted by what to him was a large pack of wolves, Knowles' stallion pulled his wagons into a circle so to speak, shaping his herd into a laager with himself in front, then turning to face the enemy, snorting, prancing, head high, sharp front hooves ready for use.

It was a glorious moment. Far from panicking, the horses stood before the foxhounds as the 300 Spartans did before the Persian armies. For the foxhounds, intent upon their chase, it was a bewildering development. They, after all, were used to the obedient if sometimes spirited mounts of the fox hunters, but they had never been confronted by so fierce an animal as the Przewalski stallion, let alone the phalanx behind him. Their baying subsided somewhat as they milled uncertainly in front of the horses. At this moment the hunters reached the scene, took in the situation, and called off the hounds. For the moment the fox was forgotten and in the excitement made good his escape.

It became obvious over the next few months that the experience had greatly disturbed normal life in the herd. All the pregnant females aborted within a short time after the confrontation with the foxhounds, and in the brave stallion prudence replaced boldness. He decided that the large field presented too much risk, and even though its gate was left temptingly open, it remained unused. Any mare who ventured toward the gate was instantly nipped and directed back toward the barn, where in the stallion's mind all security lay. Day after day he kept the herd, himself included, in the barn leaving it only when the keepers drove him and the others out to clean. Then he kept the herd standing patiently a few feet off waiting until the task was done and they could return.

The natural reaction of the Przewalski's wild horses when they established their defensive cordon against invading "wolves" marks a third stage in the evolution of zoo exhibits. The first stage was that of barred boxes, barren cagelike prison cells, which showed no regard for the animal and very little for visitors, particularly after photography was developed and people wanted to take pictures of animals unobstructed by bars or wire mesh. The second stage saw the development of moated enclosures which gave viewers and animals an unobstructed view of one another, but which seldom took cognizance of the animal's behavioral requirements except by lucky accident.

Disregarding deer parks[10] and considering only those enclosures in traditional zoos, the first exhibits which allowed natural behavior by animals were probably the monkey and baboon islands; most of these in North America were built during the 1930s and 40s. The exhibiting principle was simple: Surround an island (either natural or constructed) with a moat, sometimes but not always filled with water, provide bedrooms to protect tropical animals against northern winters, and, then, except for feeding, occasional cleaning, and veterinary care of the sick, let the animals shift for themselves.

The first baboon island was established by the Cologne Zoo around the turn of the century. Operated continuously until World War II, it was partially destroyed by Allied bombs, but was rebuilt and restocked after the war with hamadryas baboons and has been a public favorite ever since. In 1928 the Munich Zoo constructed a one-acre island of hamadryas baboons on which all the animals now living are descendants of the original founding stock.[11] Families and troops form as they would in the wild. Domi-

---

[10] There is a tendency among Americans to think of deer as hoofed animals with branching antlers—a fairly recent definition which overlooks the fact that European languages in general and English in particular once used "deer" as a general term for all quadrupeds. Hence deer parks are not confined to animals of the family *Cervidae*.

[11] In the United States the old Milwaukee Zoo in Washington Park was the first to start a monkey island for rhesus monkeys. This island also has operated continuously with successive generations. In San Francisco an island for spider monkeys has existed for close to 40 years with new animals added only infrequently.

nant males take over as leaders only to be deposed in a few years by younger, more powerful males, while subordinate males and females work out their own hierarchies. All the elements are present that fascinate behaviorists, and for the public there is a continuous show, with squabbles among adults, mothers nursing cute babies, and numerous playful youngsters. The action on baboon island is so entrancing that the Cologne Zoo built an amphitheater around three sides of it, set off by a shallow, water-filled moat. Visitors sometimes sit by the hour watching the busy scene in front of them. Some bring picnic lunches, surreptitiously tossing tidbits across the moat to the baboons and throwing leftovers into trash cans provided. What these visitors may not realize is that no leftovers go to waste. Long ago a smart female baboon learned to wade through the moat each night, pick through the trash cans for food scraps, and return to the island by daybreak, even though she could escape if she wanted to. What zoo officials know is that the animals stay on the island because it offers them security, for patently, if one animal has learned to leave the island that knowledge has been imparted to others. As behaviorists have several times noted, whenever a particularly intelligent member of a primate group makes a discovery, the rest of the group soon learns from the pioneer. Perhaps the best-documented case is that of the wild female Japanese macaque who accidentally learned that food dipped in seawater is better for being salty and thereafter always dipped her food. Within days after her discovery all the members of her troop were also dipping their food.

Zoo designers are not as a rule animal behaviorists. The disaster that can be wrought when an otherwise outstanding architect attempts to design a zoo was well illustrated by what happened in Los Angeles where a zoo was built from the ground up for an opening in 1966. Exhibits designed for the public but not for the animals posed many problems. To name only one, the slippery, painted floor of the giraffe exhibit was the direct or indirect cause of the deaths of three giraffes (that were, incidentally, among the few Angolan giraffes in North America). Fortunately, the original mistakes in design are being rectified by the zoo's present director, Dr. Warren Thomas, a man firm in his conviction that zoo exhibits should be pleasing for the public, practical for the staff, and natural for the animals. And to those three criteria virtually every zoo director in the world would add in chorus "and economical to build."

To be natural for the animals an exhibit does not necessarily have to look like the habitat they occupied in the wild, even though such exhibits may be most pleasing to visitors. The objective these days is to build exhibits which allow their inhabitants to behave as they would in nature. In these exhibits birds can fly, monkeys swing, and zebras gallop. However, such obvious manifestations of behavior display only a small part of the enormously complicated repertoire of almost every living creature, particularly those higher on the evolutionary scale. One of the saddest commentaries on human beings is the vastness of their ignorance about the behavioral needs of creatures with whom they share the earth. The scientific study of animal behavior in the field is a recent vogue,[12] scarcely twenty years old, and behaviorists have tended to concentrate on popular animals, mostly primates. Yet despite the thousands of hours in the field spent by behaviorists like Jane Goodall, George Schaller, Dian Fossey, and others in their study of wild chimpanzees, gorillas, lions, and tigers, the behavioral profiles of these species are far from complete.

What zoo architects, advised by their scientific staffs, are finding is that certain elements must always be taken into account when they design an exhibit (as well as off-exhibit breeding enclosures) where animals are supposed to behave naturally. The allotment of space is a major concern. Not only must the use of space be related to the number of animals that will occupy an enclosure, it also has to be related to a species' known habits during food gathering, play, mating, establishing pairs or territories, or escaping from enemies—including from time to time the most well-intentioned members of the visiting public, let alone those who throw sticks, stones, and pop bottles to stir up some action.

Many animals, particularly among the monkeys and apes, are like people in wanting occasional privacy. Frequently, the desire

---

[12] Credit for the first extensive field study of primates has to go to a South African, Eugène N. Marais, who around 1900 lived with a troop of baboons for over three years in order to observe their activities and relationships. An English version of Marais's book *My Friends the Baboons* did not appear, however, until 1939, largely because Marais was such an Anglophobe that he insisted on writing in his native Afrikaans.

for escape or privacy can be satisfied by allowing animals unlimited access to their sleeping quarters from the on-view part of an exhibit. Sometimes refuges can be provided by windows or screens of wood, plastic, or plants that enable the animals to hide from the public and one another. These dividers actually give psychological enlargement to an enclosure by screening an animal when he doesn't care to be stared at. Zoo visitors who themselves would feel uneasy if another person stared at them for long moments will fix their eyes intently on a monkey or ape, not realizing that all primates feel threatened when they are under scrutiny. Gorillas are so sensitive about staring that they almost never stare at one another or at zoo visitors. Their own method of watching a visitor is that employed by a middle-aged American male when he ogles bikini-clad girls while his wife is present. The secret, gorillas know, is to pretend to be looking at something else while taking in the true object of investigation out of the corner of the eye. Gorillas would no doubt find sunglasses a great boon.

The proper allotment of space may not by itself be enough to prevent some captive wild animals from developing neuroses. The sight, sound, or smell of animals in nearby enclosures may produce tensions, disrupt normal eating habits, interfere with sexual activities, or simply drive an animal into a blue funk. At Gerald Durrell's Jersey Zoo, which among other accomplishments has an outstanding record for breeding marmosets, the first marmoset house did not originally include barriers to keep the marmosets from smelling their neighbors in adjoining cages. On some days, depending on wind conditions, the scent of many marmosets intermingled and were wafted from cage to cage. As a result tensions among all marmosets increased. These little primates habitually mark territorial boundaries by laying down their own specific perfume. Logically, each family in the Jersey marmoset house saw its own cage as a territory and marked the perimeter in various places, saying in effect, "Stay out—this is my territory." However, the strong invasion of smells from marmosets in adjoining cages caused acute distress to all the animals, perhaps because it was interpreted as the precursor to a physical invasion. Seeking to ward off the enemy, the poor little creatures drove themselves to the point of exhaustion and nervous breakdown by rushing around the perimeters of their cages trying to reinforce the scent markers. Tranquility was restored when plastic barriers were placed between cages so that the inhabitants could no longer smell their neighbors.

"Furniture" is a term zoo designers apply to objects—plants or structures—placed within an enclosure. Furniture may enlarge space, provide screens, or simply be good to look at, but its principal function is to stimulate action in the animals, action that· is natural. The furnishings meet a behavioral need that would cause distress to the animals if left unfulfilled. For example, wood shavings help satisfy elephant shrews. According to Dr. Devra Kleiman, a behaviorist at the National Zoo, a pile of wood shavings in the bottom of an otherwise plain cage kept the shrews busy and presumably happy in their own way by the hour. What the shrews do is spread the shavings and then build a maze of paths through them. It seems that in the wild male shrews and their mates control a large territory in a grassy habitat. Small,[13] defenseless elephant shrews rely on a complicated network of escape routes, trails they spend many hours building and rebuilding through the grass of their territory. Because they know their own maze of trails by heart they can readily escape predators or frustrate rival shrews that attempt invasion from adjacent territories. Left in a bare cage with no means of building trails, elephant shrews may suffer neuroses.

Zoo men tend to divide on the subject of natural versus artificial objects. Some insist on real trees, logs, and vines while others are perfectly willing to use metal, rope, and plastic structures, or for that matter, old rubber tires. In all probability the animals don't much care what is used. At the National Zoo designers have built erector-set jungles for monkeys out of the same multicolored plastic pipe that plumbers use. Each structure has plastic platforms at various levels where the inhabitants can display relative social standing by playing a form of king of the mountain, with the highest platform being the most desirable. From the monkeys' point of view the whole arrangement seems quite satisfactory. They swing through the maze of pipes as they would through a forest. Some visitors, however, may be offended by the "unnatural" use of a modern material.

Introduction into an enclosure designed to bring out natural be-

[13] The "elephant" refers not to size but to a trunklike snout.

havior can produce some startling changes even in animals habituated to old-fashioned enclosures—as the staff of the San Diego Zoo learned from a white rhinoceros named Mandhla, "the bold one." In 1972 virtually any zoo worthy of the name had at least a pair of white rhinoceroses, but none of these, second largest of land mammals, had ever bred outside of Africa. At the San Diego Zoo Mandhla, all 5,000 pounds of him, had lived with a female for eight years in a fairly large walled enclosure. While the two rhinos enjoyed each other's company, serious romance did not develop. The relationship, to employ an old-fashioned concept, was purely platonic.

The fairly common failure of paired wild animals to breed in captivity might seem strange to a farmer or owner of a stud farm used to placing bull with heifer or stallion with mare and getting quick results. But simple cause and effect in mating exists in few wild animals. The entire mating process may require a pattern of behavior as complicated as a computer program, which in fact the original genetic coding greatly resembles. Zoo researchers know that the way to successful matings always exists but may lie hidden in a complex of behaviors, which like the tumblers of a safe must first fall in place before the lock is opened.

The change that came over Mandhla is a case in point. In the spring of 1972 Mandhla was taken from his home at the San Diego Zoo and transported thirty miles north to the San Diego Wild Animal Park. The park is located in typical Southern California chaparral country, which in climate and appearance is much like the high veldt of Africa. Cactus, sage, and mountain sumac grow amid granite boulders on dry, grassy foothills that slope into the valley of San Pasqual, where was fought the principal battle between the United States Army and the lance-bearing Californians immediately before California was joined to the Union. Running through the foothills are rocky stream beds, waterless for most of the year, lined with sycamores and cottonwoods. When Mandhla first arrived at the park much of the vegetation still grew within the hundred-acre South African exhibit into which he was placed. Later the teeth and hooves of the many herbivores in the exhibit would devastate all but protected trees and shrubs.

Mandhla, a zoo animal for most of his life, was to join 20 wild, newly caught rhinos that had just completed a rough crossing from

Durban, South Africa. Five of these new arrivals were young, sexually immature males, but many of the 15 females were mature, the reason Mandhla was sent for.

Because Mandhla's history of continence indicated that he might have a sexual hang-up Dr. James Dolan, general curator at the Park, watched his behavior with keen interest. For the first two or three days in his spacious new enclosure, which even had a large water hole and mud wallow at one end, Mandhla didn't quite know what to do with himself. Used to only one companion in an enclosure one-three-hundredth the size of his new home, Mandhla found himself able to roam over a hundred acres that held, in addition to the other rhinos, numerous sable antelope, white-tailed gnu, gemsbok, eland, springbok, waterbuck, nyala, mountain zebra, ostrich, and a few other hoofed animals, not to mention the native coyotes, rabbits, and ground squirrels. Faced with new freedom in an unknown environment, Mandhla's disorientation showed in his continual brisk trot, vertically corkscrewed tail, and readiness to take on all comers, including the trucks used by Park keepers to distribute food and clean up.

It would be impossible to say at what point in those first few days Mandhla discovered he was king of the mountain. No other animal in the enclosure was as large as he; all were willing to stand aside when he approached except for one possible mental case, a tiny springbok male not much larger than a good-sized jackrabbit, that continued to challenge Mandhla's supremacy by periodically charging him—a slingless David trying to overwhelm Goliath.

Mandhla discovered also that there were females. Before a month had passed he secured himself a harem, seven rhino cows who stayed with him in a selected part of the enclosure. This was Mandhla's territory, designated by trotted boundaries and corner markers of dung (which were, frustrating to Mandhla, cleaned up each day by the keepers), forbidden ground to all rhinos save Mandhla and his wives.

Whether Mandhla selected the females or they him, the results were the same. His relationships were platonic no more. Whenever a female indicated that she was in heat, he stood ready to oblige. Soon, allowing for an 18-month gestation period, his offspring began to arrive one by one.

Speculating about the reasons for Mandhla's change from pla-

tonic companion at the zoo to successful lover at the Park, Dr. Dolan pointed to three possibilities. The male white rhino apparently needed room enough to establish his own territory, the stimulus provided by rival males, and enough females on hand to assure that if choice by females was a factor some would choose him.

Mandhla's was a short happy life, although he survives today an outcast male in the place where he once was king. The end of his reign provided an illustration of that complete indifference nature has to the individual in the evolutionary process, which helps to assure that the fittest genes will be transmitted to future generations.

By the spring of 1976, after Mandhla had sired eighteen youngsters, Paghati, one of the juvenile males, was no longer juvenile. Large, strong, and filled with the lust for dominance, he challenged Mandhla. The battle, on a darkling plain, was not seen by any of the Park's staff, but its outcome was obvious. When keepers arrived for their morning count of the animals, they found an exhausted and battered Mandhla lying on muddy ground near the water hole far from his territory—or what had been his territory—and his seven wives. He was a king deposed. For a while at least, a new king would reign. It would have happened that way in the wild.

Beware an Affectionate Elephant

If zoos were armies, the front-line troops would be keepers. Directors and curators make the decisions about what animals to exhibit. Veterinarians take care of sick and injured animals and help the curators select diets, and together all these (and sometimes others like architects and committeemen) determine how an exhibit will be designed and built. But at every phase save perhaps the original selection of animals, smart directors, curators, veterinarians, and designers consult with the keepers. For finally it is the quality of its animal husbandry that will make or break a zoo, and the chief husbandry people are the keepers who each day feed the animals, clean their enclosures, watch for significant changes in their behavior that might indicate pregnancy or illness, and sometimes care for them when they are ill. To be better than mediocre a zoo must have a force of well-trained, highly motivated keepers. Conversely, if zoo managers view their keepers as mere carriers of fodder and shovelers of dung, their zoo will not prosper.

It would be easy to exaggerate the dangers that zoo keepers face in their work. In all probability the hazards are about the same as those faced by people who work around moving machinery in factories. But zoos present one element not found in factories. Machinery is predictable, not eccentric or mindless. When accidents occur they are almost always the result of poor maintenance or operator error. Animals on the other hand are unpredictable, often eccentric, and each has a mind of its own, however infinitesimal it may be. Peanut-brained storks or cranes may inexplicably turn and poke a sharp bill at their keeper's eyes.

80

So while the keepers are infrequently attacked by the animals they serve, they are exposed to daily risks, and during a career keeper's occupational lifetime he is likely to have one or more brushes with death.

Sometimes the dangers are obvious. Most zoos with reptile houses take elaborate precautions to protect keepers from venomous snakes—rattlesnakes, vipers of various sorts, cobras, kraits, mambas, and such deadly Australian creatures as the taipan, tiger snake, and death adder. To avoid mischance at least one zoo, Zurich, exhibits no venomous snakes while others avoid swift-moving poisoners like the taipan and green and black mambas, particularly the latter, which can attain a length of 14 feet and may be the fastest snake on earth.[1]

Yet knowing that the public is fascinated by the deadly snakes, especially those like mambas or cobras that are surrounded by fanciful legend, most zoos want some on exhibit and seek to minimize danger to the keepers. The doors of cages are plainly marked with skull and crossbones, red dots, or other signs indicating the dangerous nature of the inhabitants. As a further precaution these cages are kept padlocked except when they have to be cleaned or the snakes fed. Most are provided with a peephole or mirror so that the keeper can pinpoint the location of each snake inside before opening the door, and if the snakes have to be moved they are handled at arm's length with hooks or snake sticks with loops that can be closed around the snake's neck or body. In spite of all precautions, accidents or near accidents will occur. Normally, these come from momentary lapses. A keeper climbs in to wash the inside of the window on an exhibit of Australian death adders which, though they seldom grow more than two feet in length, are among the world's deadliest snakes. New to the job the keeper assumes that all snakes have been removed from the exhibit. He spends some fifteen minutes on his knees in the rather confined space when he sees reflected in the glass he is polishing two death adders in the rear corner of the exhibit, coiled about 18 inches from

[1] Legend has it that a black mamba, an African snake, can outdistance a man on a galloping horse. Actually, legend has outdistanced fact. The black mamba can go about seven miles per hour on level ground and hit maybe fifteen going down a slope, fast enough if one happens to be coming toward you.

the partially exposed calf on one of his legs. The speed of his escape through the small exhibit door is still a topic of conversation in the zoo where he works.

Another keeper has been asked to transfer a harmless African egg-eating snake from a storage cage to a display window in the reptile house. A knowledgeable herpetologist, he apparently has something else on his mind as he picks up in his bare hands what he thinks is the right snake. A second keeper standing nearby turns pale, but has sense enough to tell him sotto voce, "Hold still. Now do as I say. Real easy-like drop that snake back in the cage." Sensibly the first keeper does as he is told. Only then does he discover that he has been holding a saw-scaled viper, a small, very deadly, short-tempered snake from the dry areas of northern Africa and Asia whose form and color pattern are almost perfectly imitated by the African egg-eating snake.[2]

A third keeper is assigned to open a box labeled "Turtles" which has just come in from an animal dealer in Africa. Inside the box he finds a bag, opens that, and thrusts his arm in to pull out one of the turtles. To his horror he finds that he is up to his wrist in snakes. Examination proves that the bag contains a half dozen horned puff adders, an African desert snake with extremely toxic venom. Two days later a letter arrives from the dealer cautioning the curator of reptiles that one box in transit has been mislabeled Turtles, but actually contains poisonous snakes.

If one is struck by a taipan, mamba, or king cobra, all large snakes with virulent venoms that attack the central nervous system, one can die swiftly—sometimes even before readily available medical treatment can be administered. Virtually all zoos that exhibit venomous snakes keep antivenins under refrigeration for every species in their reptile houses. There is no universal antivenin to cure snakebite; a few will counteract the poisons of several closely related species like the rattlesnakes, but a number have been developed that are good for only one species. Recognizing that panic

---

[2] Mimicry is not uncommon among some species of deadly, mildly venomous, and harmless snakes within the same geographical area and for much the same reason that bees, wasps, hornets, and some perfectly harmless flies all have black and yellow bands on their bodies. Stung once or twice, a predator thereafter tends to avoid all creatures that look like the ones that stung him. Thus mortality is reduced for every species in the mimetic complex.

brought on by the fear of death often seizes a snakebitten person, zoos seek to hasten the administering of antivenins by placing numbered or color-coded cards on the doors of cages that house venomous snakes. These are keyed to specific containers of anti-venin in the refrigerator so that no time need be wasted finding the correct medicine. In addition panic buttons are often installed so that bitten keepers can summon aid from another source, a security office for example, where people are on call twenty-four hours every day. Finally, most zoos have on call at least one expert in treating snakebite who can be summoned to advise in a particular case.

There are other obviously dangerous animals. The big cats can never be trifled with. All are capable of swift and sometimes inex-plicable attacks on unwary keepers. Leopards have probably caused more deaths to zoo keepers than any other cat. Alert, resourceful animals, they may not at first appear as dangerous as a full-grown Siberian tiger or male African lion. For one thing they are smaller and less conspicuous. But among the big cats leopards' agility and tree-climbing skill combined with their fierce, untamable natures and alertness makes them the most difficult cats to contain. Moated enclosures will seldom hold them; they are most often exhibited in cages with four sides, a top, and an antechamber or safety cage that enables keepers to close an outer door before opening the door leading into the main cage. Even so leopards will sometimes position themselves slyly so that any lapse on the keeper's part may be fatal. One black leopard[3] at the San Diego Zoo had concealed itself when the regular keeper entered its cage with a broom. For some unaccountable reason the man must have believed the leopard to be safely locked in its bedroom. When he became aware that it was behind him, between him and the door, he made the worst possible mistake. Instead of using the broom as a lion tamer uses a chair to ward off an attack, while he backed out of the cage, the keeper turned and ran. Swiftly, the cat attacked, leaping onto the keeper's back as it would have leaped on an antelope and biting through the neck to bring instant death. Then it dashed into the antechamber only to find the road to escape barred by the closed outside door.

[3] Not a separate species but a color phase of the common leopard (*Panthera pardus*).

Oversights by keepers in leaving cage doors open have created some hair-raising moments in every zoo. At the San Diego Zoo one bright morning in the 1930s a mature Bengal tiger walked through a cage door carelessly left open by a preoccupied keeper and calmly strolled up a macadam roadway that would soon be frequented by zoo visitors. The enormous cat was quite amiable about the whole affair. It seemed more to be out for a stroll than to be making a break for freedom. But it was a tiger, capable of killing the strongest man with one slashing swipe of a paw or bite through the head. Informed of the escape by a keeper who saw the tiger and quickly telephoned, Dr. Charles R. Schroeder, then the zoo's veterinarian, immediately directed that the zoo's gates be closed and any visitors already on the premises be directed to leave. Then he put out a call for all available keepers to meet him near the fence on the side of the zoo toward which the tiger was leisurely walking. No one had a rifle (as would now be the case) so any effort to contain the tiger would have to be undertaken without the comfort of knowing that if all else failed, the animal could be shot. The stark truth was that the tiger had to be captured—*had to be*. Ticklish is not a strong enough word to describe the dangerous situation.

When his force was assembled Dr. Schroeder found he had nine keepers, scarcely a formidable army. Then as now a short, somewhat stocky, energetic man, Dr. Schroeder displayed tension about the outcome of any matter by repeatedly flexing his left shoulder to his chin the way a boxer might. As he spoke to the keepers the shoulder flexed. The only course open to them, he explained, was to drive the tiger back to its cage, the outer door of which remained open. They must not corner the animal, for then, fearful, it would very likely turn savage and charge. They were to form a line, spacing themselves about ten yards apart, and then with any object handy, their clapping hands if necessary, make as much noise as possible as they advanced, slowly, very slowly toward the tiger. He dispatched one keeper to flank the tiger, but stay high on the hill above it, telling him to report any dangerous developments.

By this time the strolling tiger, pausing every now and then to sniff the air or peer at other animals through the wire of their cages, had reached a point about halfway between its cage and the six-foot-high fence topped with barbed wire which then enclosed

the zoo, a fence over which any full-grown tiger could easily leap.

What happened next could have come right out of an old movie about a tiger hunt by the Maharajah and his guests in the days of British India. The line of keepers, Dr. Schroeder in the middle, moved slowly forward. Some beat sticks together, one had found two short lengths of pipe, another used a tweeter which he habitually carried to summon emergency help; others simply clapped their hands and shouted or whistled. Whatever personal trepidation Dr. Schroeder and his force felt, and they unquestionably felt some, theirs was a brave advance. There was no doubt also that they extracted the most noise possible from whatever beater's tools they carried. The tweeter was blown more shrilly than usual, sticks clacked together with a vigor that knocked chips off, and the pipes clanged together like hammer striking anvil.

As the thin line moved forward, ragtag skirmishers with makeshift fifes and drums, the tiger paused. Clearly, now the noise began to penetrate its consciousness although the beaters were not yet in sight. For the big cat the sounds represented an unknown, disturbing element, not familiar and possibly dangerous. Tigers are no braver than most animals. When they attack they attack out of desperation, not because they lust for battle, and no one was going to push this tiger to the point of desperation, not if he could help it. In the game of chicken that was being played, Dr. Schroeder, the keepers, and the tiger had one thing in common. Nobody wanted an eyeball to eyeball confrontation.

It became apparent thereafter that the tiger's thoughts had turned to the idea of finding safety. The keeper-spotter on the hill above reported later that the animal showed signs of agitation and indecision. As the sounds from the beater's line became louder, the tiger made up its mind. It was no exception to a general rule about zoo animals. For any captive animal the place of greatest security is the exhibit to which it has grown accustomed, the place where it eats, sleeps, and lives out its life.

So the tiger turned and increasing its leisurely pace to a brisk lope started back down the macadam road. Uppermost in its mind, one must suspect, was an overpowering desire to get back within the four walls of its bedroom, the den where it slept at night, the place of greatest security. Never once did this tiger deviate from its chosen course. Continuing at a lope it moved down the road, turned, and without pausing went on through the open door of the tiger exhibit. Once inside, it stopped, then fell all at once in a striped heap on the ground. When keepers reached the cage door to slam it shut, they found the tiger with paws hugging the earth, panting rapidly as though it has just escaped the rifles and elephants of the Maharajah's hunters instead of ten men with two pipes, some sticks, and a tweeter. The keeper who had left the door open in the first place never showed up at the zoo again, not even to collect his pay.

Elephants, female elephants that is, are seen by most zoo visitors as simple, lovable creatures, given to making loud trumpeting noises, tossing dirt onto their backs, addicted to joyous, splashing baths, and cadging peanuts or other goodies by reaching out with their trunks. That picture, as far as it goes, is reasonably accurate. But elephants are not simpletons. Field studies have shown them to be highly intelligent creatures that ordinarily live in well-organized matriarchies, sometimes leisurely browsing, sometimes pacing across a savannah in a deceptively fast and soundless gait as though, in a memorable line from Isak Dinesen, they had "an appointment at the end of the world."

In captivity elephants best display their great intelligence in shows of various types, rapidly learning complex acts where it seems the trainer is constantly at risk and never harmed, or in the heavy, often difficult tasks they perform in India, Bangladesh, Sri Lanka, and Thailand. But elephants have a devilish side. One of the oldest bits of conventional wisdom about them is that they have long memories, and while many of the stories about elephants killing men who as small boys put a hot chestnut or peppercorns in their trunks are exaggerated, some elephants do hold grudges against people who have hurt them, or whom for some reason they dislike.

Captive elephants frequently develop great affection for a particular trainer or keeper, but experienced elephant men, who may feel reciprocal affection for their animals, nonetheless know that they must be on their toes around even an affectionate elephant. For elephants play various games to test their keepers. An elephant may use its trunk, that marvelously intricate instrument with one or two fingers at the end, either as a lasso or straight-arm to pull a

careless keeper down or punch him to the ground, methods which overwhelmingly demonstrate the elephant's dominance. Another popular game, which might be best described as "squash," though it bears no resemblance to the human sport of that name, can be played by one elephant with a keeper and a wall or in the doubles version by two elephants and a keeper. In the first version the elephant's objective is to sidle around in an innocent and sly way until it traps the keeper between it and the wall. The elephant wins if it can lean against the wall with the keeper in between. In the more difficult doubles version two elephants maneuver until they can trap a keeper between them. Then they lean together and *voilà*, the keeper becomes meat in a sandwich. Smart elephant keepers who know that these games will be played carry a shortened elephant hook, marlin spike, or hunting knife whenever they are around the elephants. If the game starts and the keeper is outmaneuvered he can still win by poking his opponent sharply in the side. Knowing also that the real contest is to determine who is boss the best elephant keepers establish a dominance over their animals that a matador would envy. The test of this dominance can be seen whenever keeper and elephant are walking toward one another on a narrow road or path. The dominant keeper never deviates. Without batting an eye he continues forward until the elephant steps aside.

Elephants may also, if they get the opportunity, play little games with unwary visitors. One kindhearted lady who was trying to feed an elephant at the San Diego Zoo made the mistake of holding her purse and the peanut in the hand she stretched out across the moat while she clung to a no feeding sign with the other. Instead of taking the peanut the elephant grabbed the purse, which in the process fell open. The elephant then turned the purse upside down and emptied its contents on the ground. For the next several moments, while the formerly kindhearted lady watched helplessly, the elephant picked up all the objects one by one—lipstick, car keys, comb, compact, hair curlers, coin holder, wallet, and ballpoint pen —that were in the purse. Eventually the purse and its contents were rescued, but not quite in the shape they had been before the elephant got them.

While female elephants, even those that play games, are generally friendly and affable and in the Asian species fairly easy to handle and train,[4] male elephants are a different story. Among both circus and zoo people legend holds that for every captive bull elephant a keeper has been killed. The truth is that several keepers have been gored or trampled to death by bulls during the animals' "musth," when for periods of up to five months the males become unpredictable, unmanageable, and possessed of superelephant strength. A human male in this condition would be called mad. Little understood, but probably related to sex drive, musth may give a bull elephant the determination, ability, and don't-give-a-damn attitude to drive off rival males and break through the largely female herds in order to mate. The condition is more pronounced in Asian elephants, but in either species it spells trouble for keepers.

One elephant keeper, an apocryphal story goes, had been made so nervous by the tales of male elephants killing their keepers that he played the leading part in a modern version of the legend about the appointment in Samarra. That legend told of a man who heard that Death was coming to fetch him. Living at the time in Damascus, he sought to avoid his fate by moving to Samarra. On his first day there he encountered Death, who smiled and said, "Ah, my friend, I see you have come to keep your appointment with me in Samarra." The apocryphal keeper, when he heard that the zoo where he worked was acquiring a bull elephant, quit his job and took one like it at another zoo which had only female elephants. One of the females became agitated, pushed him to the ground and trampled him to death.

Some of the stories about keepers and bull elephants are more amusing than tragic. Lothar Dittrich, director of the zoo in Hanover, Germany, tells a story about his elephant keeper and a large African bull elephant named Tembo. As is often the case with bull elephants, Tembo had developed an affection bordering on love for his keeper, a type Dittrich calls an "alpha keeper" because he easily dominated the animals in his care. He became one with them, but at the same time their seldom-challenged leader.

It was the closeness of the relationship between this keeper and Tembo that created a serious problem for the zoo. The keeper,

[4] Although the African elephant can be trained. Hannibal probably used a North African subspecies on his famous march across the Alps. Some have been trained in Zaire, and the legendary Jumbo was African.

who tended other animals besides the elephants, was working one day in a pen of Masai cattle, large, tough, half-wild creatures that are the principal basis of wealth among the fierce Masai tribesmen of Kenya and Tanzania. Intent on his work the keeper failed to notice a challenger, a cow who got into position to butt him hard against the wall. The keeper managed to escape, but with a cracked, dislocated vertebra that necessitated his being placed in traction on a hospital bed.

On the first night the alpha keeper was in the hospital, a substitute keeper was assigned the task of putting Tembo and his two female companions into the elephant barn that abuts the rear side of Hanover's small African elephant exhibit. This exhibit, adjacent to one holding Asian elephants, is bounded on three sides by a narrow, shallow moat, which had given the zoo a good deal of trouble. Several times elephants had either fallen or been pushed into the moat, and some had been injured. Consequently, whether the weather required it or not, the elephants were always chained in the barn at night to prevent them from falling into the moat.

When the substitute keeper attempted to order Tembo into the barn the big bull would have none of it. For him, it appeared, the substitute was a beta keeper, practically a nonperson, unfit to command his respect and obedience. He flatly refused to enter the barn, trumpeting his displeasure and waving his huge head, ears laid back, massive tusks raised ominously. Moreover, he wouldn't allow the females to enter the barn either. Clearly, he was laying down a statement of his newly assumed authority. "If I stay out, everybody stays out. And I'm staying out!"

The keeper was a reasonably brave but not foolish man. Instead of pressing the matter further he reported the rebellion to his superior. That first night the African elephants did not go in the barn.

On the following day Tembo found he was up against a stubborn and resourceful man in Director Dittrich. The heart of the problem, Dittrich well knew, was the close relationship between Tembo and the alpha keeper. It appeared that no one else could command the big elephant's respect. Very well, Dittrich thought, we'll let Tembo hear the alpha keeper—on a tape recorder. So he drove the twelve miles to the hospital, explained the situation to the alpha keeper, who was lying flat on a hard bed with weights attached to his feet, and had the man record a message to Tembo ordering him to enter the barn.

That evening Dittrich, the substitute keeper, and several other zoo officials stood by the rail of the elephant enclosure while Dittrich played the tape, turning the volume up so loud the alpha keeper's words cracked out loud and clear, like a German noncom's. But Tembo was not to be fooled. The voice was not the man. He listened, showed signs of interest and recognition, but he would not go in the barn.

Now Dittrich saw the full extent of the challenge and determined that no elephant in his zoo was going to defy him. A handsome man in his forties, Dittrich is a dedicated zoo man who fled with his family from East Germany just a few days before the Berlin Wall was built. In the manner of most German zoo directors he made rounds of the zoo each day, getting to know his animals by name and personality. Now he realized that Tembo was not going to be satisfied with anything less than the real thing—the alpha keeper in person.

And the real thing was what Tembo got. Dittrich made arrangements with the keeper, his doctor, and the hospital to have the keeper taken out of traction, strapped to a stretcher, and brought by ambulance to the zoo. Attendants then carried the keeper over to the guardrail around the elephant enclosure and held him up so that Tembo could see him. Otherwise immobile, the keeper was allowed the use of one arm and was able to raise his head a few inches above the bed of his stretcher.

What followed no doubt seemed strange to the few visitors left in the Hanover Zoo that evening. A man lying flat on a stretcher between two ambulance attendants raised his head a few inches and fixed stern eyes on a large elephant that was looking fondly down at him. Pointing with one arm toward the barn at the rear of the elephant exhibit, the man commanded in a firm voice, "Tembo, go in! Tembo! Go in!" For an instant the tableau held. The man continued to point while he looked the elephant in the eye; the elephant looked down on him. Then obediently, the elephant turned. He had gotten the word from the highest authority he cared to acknowledge. The rebellion was over, the old order reestablished. Placid now, Tembo allowed the substitute

keeper to shepherd him into the barn, the two females falling in behind. From that moment until the alpha keeper returned Tembo seemed to understand that the command was permanent. Each night he let the substitute keeper drive him and the females into the barn.

There is a sad epilogue. After the alpha keeper returned, and after Tembo had sired one male calf, the elephant broke a tusk, causing himself great pain and requiring dental work to cap the tusk. Shot with a dose of M-99 to put him under for the operation, he fell in such a way that one leg, twisted beneath him, was severely broken. Because of their great bulk and the danger of being suffocated by their own internal organs, full-grown elephants cannot be treated for broken legs. Tembo had to undergo euthanasia.

The formation of bonds between good keepers and the animals they serve is common, although not always desirable where captive breeding is an objective. In zoos without special nurseries it is keepers (and often their wives and children) who take over the function of raising orphans or trying to save sickly newborn infants. Not infrequently, this becomes a twenty-four-hour task; keepers take baby animals home and raise them like children until they are old enough and strong enough to be put back with their own kind. Imprinted by human beings from birth, such hand-raised animals develop ties with their keepers which, because they and the keepers often remain in close proximity means that the effects of imprinting do not wear off. In many instances imprinted animals, particularly primates, become sexually confused and do not make good breeders. Most zoo directors agree, however, that in the trade-off between saving the newborn and running the risk of imprinting them, they prefer to save the animals and deal with the sexual problems as they arise.

Even without taking animals home to be hand-raised, keepers will imprint some of their charges. It is proverbial, more in European zoos than American, that keepers stand by expectant mothers, remaining all night if need be to see that a delivery goes smoothly and to help out if it doesn't. Because the knowledge of how imprinting can affect some species is recent, starting really with Konrad Lorenz and his goslings, and the tradition of conscientious husbandry by keepers is a long one, it would be almost impossible for a zoo director to instill the kind of objective husbandry, which keepers would probably call indifferent, that would be necessary to avoid imprinting by keepers altogether.

Keepers are well aware that many of their charges will sicken, some will suffer and all eventually will die,[5] so they try to avoid becoming emotionally attached to their animals. If each time an animal died, a keeper were to grieve, his job would be too difficult to bear. Nevertheless, situations do arise that would cause grief to any person not made of stone. One such situation occurred to William B. Crytser, now one of two Animal Care Managers for the San Diego Wild Animal Park, when he was a keeper with the ape string at the San Diego Zoo in the 1960s.

The zoo then housed its gorillas, orangutans, chimpanzees, and gibbons in adjacent cages of chain link wire mesh with cement floors, various climbing apparatus and items of furniture including in the gorilla cage a dangling rubber tire and a children's slide. The resident chimpanzees at that time, all full grown, were Esther, Molly, Katie, and her son George. Although George was fully mature he and his mother were inseparable. There were occasions, for example, when all four chimps would walk arm over shoulder around the cage but at no time did Crytser ever see Katie and George when they weren't beside each other. Their relationship, he added, was one of familial affection, nothing overtly Freudian. If George were sexually inclined he looked to Esther and Molly, not his mother.

The heartbreaking event took place on a particularly beautiful San Diego day under a faultless blue sky when the air has that softness that comes with just the right mixture of cooling breezes from the Pacific Ocean and balmy winds from the California desert. For several hours Katie and George had sat close together, with Katie fondly grooming George. At last George took it into his mind to get some exercise by swinging in a leisurely manner on the various steel bars, smooth from much use, that crisscrossed the cage all the way to the top. He had reached the highest bar and was just starting to walk along it, balancing himself with his arms and grasping

---

[5] Because most animals are shorter lived than human beings a keeper of more than five years' tenure will see many of his charges die, unless they are parrots or elephants. The oldest living animal in the San Diego Zoo, a cockatoo named King Tut, has been in the zoo since 1926.

the bar with his toes, when he clapped one hand to his breast, opened his mouth in a grimace, and fell head first some fifteen feet to the cement floor. There he lay inert, the only movement coming when the breeze stirred a few black hairs on his back. Katie, who had been watching him, immediately ran over and picked him up in her arms, large as he was. It was obvious to Crytser, looking on the scene from outside the cage, that George was dead. The tableau is still deeply etched on Crytser's mind. Katie held George in both arms, his head against her shoulder, as she gazed intently into the dead face with its staring eyes and slack lips. To this day Crytser swears that Katie started to weep. Genuine tears moistened her eyes and wet the hair on her cheeks. For almost a day she was inconsolable, refusing to leave the body of her son even to eat, and in those days before capture guns nobody dared enter to remove the corpse. On the second afternoon Katie left George when she heard Crytser bringing the evening ration of fruit and vegetables to Esther and Molly, already in the bedrooms behind the cage. The instant she entered the bedroom area Crytser shut the door. Then, unhampered, he dragged the body out. A postmortem revealed that George had suffered a fatal heart attack. Crytser has never forgotten the terrible occasion. He still awakens sometimes with the image of the weeping Katie and her dead son uppermost in his mind.

Although they may try to avoid emotional attachment, keepers are often so dedicated to their animals they may risk their own lives to help one. When researchers started a project to breed cheetahs at the San Diego Wild Animal Park, they fenced in ten acres of rocky, cactus-covered hillside completely away from public view and installed ten cheetahs, five of them males, brought directly from southwest Africa. The keeper hired for this project, a young man named Robert Herdman, was also a trained scientific observer who, when he wasn't carrying feed or otherwise caring for the animals, spent many hours watching them through field glasses from a high seat specially raised near the nine-foot chain link fence on one side of the enclosure.[6] Herdman had just climbed the ladder to his seat one morning and focused the glasses on a

---

[6] Unlike the leopard, the cheetah is not a climber. Born with sheathed claws, cheetahs soon lose the sheaths and grow up with relatively small feet more like those of dogs.

group of cheetahs some 100 yards away when he realized that one of the females had borne cubs during the night. This was evident because one of the infants, its eyes tightly closed like those of a newborn kitten but apparently alive, lay on the rocky ground near a clump of cactus about three yards from four or five adult cheetahs. As Herdman continued his sweep with the glasses he saw the remains of two more cubs. It was certain that something horrible had happened to them, the first cheetahs born in the new project. Herdman's first thought was to save the remaining cub before it met the same fate as the others. Standing on the high seat he jumped over the fence into the enclosure, landing so heavily that he nearly lost his balance. Shouting and waving his arms to scare off the adult cheetahs, he sprinted to the cub, scooped it up, and without pausing ran back to the fence. Because he had to hold the cub he had trouble climbing the chain link, but motivated no doubt by the fact that one adult cheetah, sex unknown, but possibly the mother, was starting toward him, he managed to scramble up to a point where he could reach the high seat and pull himself over the fence. Herdman made his dash knowing that cheetahs are not as dangerous as lions, tigers, or leopards. But being large enough at 125 pounds to knock a man down and rip his throat, their method of killing prey, these wild caught animals couldn't be considered tame either,[7] particularly since the mother might object to someone's carrying off her cub.

This cub, named Juba, was one of the first zoo-born cheetahs to live more than one year,[8] a record that has since been exceeded several times at different zoos. After the incident of Herdman's dash, he and his mentor, Dr. Lynn A. Griner, who was responsible for the cheetah breeding project, reviewed possible causes for the

[7] Cheetahs were once tamed to hunt. Literally thousands of the Asian and North African subspecies were captured when young and trained as hunting leopards, at first by Summerian nobles and Egyptian Pharaohs around 3,000 B.C.; later by many Middle Eastern and Asian nobles. Hunting cheetahs were even used in southern Russia, and Emperor Leopold I of Austria kept a stable of them to hunt deer in the Vienna woods. Because these tame cheetahs never bred, the continued drain on wild stock to provide new hunters was one of the reasons for the near extinction of the Asian subspecies and the extinction or near extinction of those in North Africa.

[8] Two cheetahs born at the Zoological Society of London's Whipsnade Zoo, born in 1967 and 1968, still survive.

infanticides and concluded that one of the males had been the cannibal, for little remained of the murdered cubs but some pitiful patches of skin. The two men then decided that females and males should be separated except during actual mating. Each female was assigned her own special pen, which was connected by gate to a corridor leading to the male's bachelor pen. Now, whenever a female comes into heat, the gate to her pen is left open so the males can respond to her calls. During the two or three days of her desire, she can choose whichever males she wants to mate with. When the brief season is over, the gate is once again closed on the males and the female left in solitude to bear and care for her young. As a result no more cubs have been killed and out of litters of up to eight very few have died. The best sign of the success of this program, originally funded in part by the Donner Foundation of Washington, D.C., is the fact that cheetahs born at the Wild Animal Park have since bred in other zoos.

From time to time keepers in any zoo also have to risk their lives to save visitors who through bravado or ignorance place themselves in mortal danger of being clawed, gored, bitten, trampled, or crushed by one or another zoo animal. More frequently than not the animal is one that doesn't appear very dangerous, a Bambi-like gazelle or small antelope, a wolf that looks like someone's German shepherd, or a somnolent crocodile. The crocodilians (crocodiles and alligators) mostly lie in their exhibits like so many fallen totem poles, mouths sometimes open, but more often tightly shut, and to all intents barely alive. Lying there they give the impression that a person on crutches could evade them easily should they ever be inclined to move.

What the unwary don't realize, or don't stop to think about, is that wild crocodilians have to catch their dinners, either by outswimming them if they are aquatic or moving swiftly enough to seize them the way the crocodile seized the elephant in Kipling's fable about how the elephant got its trunk. A big crocodile or alligator, ten or twelve feet long, say, has the agility and immense strength needed to seize an animal up to the size of a horse, pull it into the river and tear it into bite-sized pieces. The crocodilians can lunge swiftly, forward or to the side, with massive tooth-studded jaws, or they can strike hard against ankles with their tails.

It bothers some zoo visitors and tempts others when crocodilians don't move much. In an open enclosure these are probably the most persistently harassed of all zoo animals. Visitors throw stones, bottles, sticks, and other hard objects in an effort to make them move, with the predictable result that many crocodilians are blinded or otherwise injured. If there doesn't seem to be a zoo employee in the vicinity, visitors, inevitably male, may be tempted to jump into an enclosure with a crocodilian in an attempt to stir up some action. Not all these unwise men are young, either. At the San Diego Zoo several years ago a well-dressed man in his eighties climbed with great difficulty over a waist-high wall that fronted an alligator exhibit. The wall was, of course, clearly designed to keep visitors out and alligators in, but for this old man it was merely an irritating obstacle between him and the immense 12-foot alligator that he wanted to photograph. The alligator was lying by itself on the sand near a small pond in the center of the exhibit about 25 feet from the wall.

Because the man was old, and because, fortunately, visitors don't climb into exhibits every day, other zoo goers became curious and rushed toward the scene. This sudden movement attracted the attention of head reptile keeper Tom Schultz, for any sudden movement of people into a crowd is a tip-off to zoo employees that something may be amiss. By the time Schultz had hurried to the exhibit and broken through the crowd to the wall, the old man had unlimbered his camera and was about to take a close-up of the alligator's head. Schultz couldn't believe his eyes. The old gentleman was barely able to shuffle along, was obviously rheumatic, yet so intent on getting this special close-up that when he put the camera to his eye his elbows were not two feet from the alligator's nose. The loud shutter noise when the picture was snapped caused the alligator to open one eye. Before the man could snap another, Schultz vaulted the wall and unceremoniously jerked him back several feet from the alligator's nose. Protesting that he meant no harm to the alligator—"I just wanted a close-up of that head to show my son"—the old man was led back to the wall. But his exertions from climbing over the wall in the first place proved too much; he couldn't climb back out. Schultz had to shout for another keeper to help him literally lift the old man over the wall. Flus-

tered, a little embarrassed perhaps, because of the crowd the man shuffled off without another word.

Schultz, a well-built man about five feet seven with one or two tattoos that bespeak his former career in the Merchant Marine, understood from personal experience how dangerous crocodilians can be. A few years before, he and another keeper were assigned the task of uncrating a crocodile that had just arrived from a dealer. What they didn't know was the vital fact that the dealer's men had not crated the five-foot reptile properly. There was no inner restraining bar or buffer to keep it from coming out of the crate before they put a noose around its neck so they could thrust it into the exhibit at the end of a pole.

The two men had set the crate down on a sandy spot near the back of the crocodile exhibit. The other keeper took up the pry bar to remove the nails and other fasteners that secured the front of the crate while Schultz watched from the other side. When the last fastener popped the front of the crate fell to the ground. Almost before it hit, the crocodile was out. Mouth agape, the testy animal charged the first living thing it saw, the keeper with the pry bar.

When Schultz saw the crocodile come out as though propelled by a spring, his only thought was to keep it from getting the other man. Leaping to the top of the crate and over in one move, Schultz threw himself on the crocodile's back, grasping the animal's jaws in both hands the way alligator wrestlers do in the movies. He was confident that he could hold on until the other man came to his aid so that between them they could wrestle the beast into the exhibit. Unfortunately for this plan the other man vanished. Schultz was left by himself on top of an agile and angered crocodile. Now, like the man riding the tiger, his main difficulty would be in finding a way to dismount. Crocodiles he also learned firsthand are loaded with muscles and this one was using every one in its frantic effort to free itself. Straining to hold on, Schultz realized he was beginning to tire. He decided that his best bet lay in jumping rapidly back and to one side before the crocodile could get him. Like Captain Hook, he had no doubt that the crocodile was out to get him. Doing a mental countdown, he shouted "now," and using his remaining strength to push the crocodile's snout into the sand, threw himself back and to the side and scrambled to his feet. At this juncture the second keeper reappeared with a third and the three of them were able to get the still-struggling animal into the enclosure. After the crocodile was secured Schultz noticed for the first time that he was bleeding. Taken to a clinic, he was given a thorough examination. It turned out there were two deep cuts, one in his hand that required nine stitches and a longer one in his leg that took sixteen. It is a measure of the crocodile's speed that to this day Schultz isn't sure exactly when the animal got him.

Zoo people sometimes become morose about the fact that certain visitors, fortunately a small proportion, disregard obvious and often formidable barriers that are placed between them and the animals and apparently can't read warning signs. One man threatened to sue the San Diego Zoo because he had stuck his finger into a cage full of squirrel monkeys and promptly had it bitten to the bone. Being a reasonable man, he relented when the keeper to whom he complained pointed out that he had pushed his finger through wire mesh about two inches under a sign that stated in bold letters: "Warning. Squirrel Monkeys Bite Fingers!"

Hoofed animals, deer, antelope, gazelle, and others are among the most dangerous in zoos, particularly if they have been hand-raised, for then, in an enclosure, unafraid of people, they don't maintain the respectful flight distance of wild-caught or mother-raised animals and may suddenly kick out with knife-edged hooves or gore with sharp horns and antlers. For a public familiar with a Walt Disney world of soft-eyed, gentle deer it is inconceivable that small, delicately stepping antelope or gazelle would hurt anyone. This conception is correct as far as it goes, but since it leaves out an essential element it is misleading. Even normally docile creatures that have been preyed upon for millennia have developed responses to what they perceive as threats. These responses range from flight, which is preferred, to attack as a last desperate measure. And an attack by even a small antelope or gazelle can be both dangerous and embarrassing.

At the San Diego Zoo some Persian gazelles, small desert-brown and white animals that came originally from Asia Minor, lived in an enclosure behind a shallow moat, which on the visitor's side was edged with both a hedge and a guardrail. These animals, graceful as all gazelles, stand no more than three feet at the shoul-

der. Only the males have horns some six to eight inches long that extend almost straight above the head, diverging so that their exceedingly sharp points are about four inches apart. A male with its head lowered in attack position would stab a six-foot man at a point no higher than his belly button, and possibly, to his consternation, a little bit lower.

It was precisely in this manner that a young man visiting the zoo was attacked one day. The man, in his early twenties, later claimed that he had climbed into the gazelle enclosure to retrieve a cap thrown in by a prank-playing friend. He couldn't believe, he explained, that such inoffensive animals would hurt him. This belief was rudely shattered when the male gazelle, who in a confined place felt threatened, hurled himself at the intruder. The astounded young man could do no more than grab a threatening horn in each hand and allow himself to be shoved back against a wall at the rear of the enclosure, while, no doubt, his prankster friend laughed as he watched a slender, fragile-appearing animal that couldn't have weighed more than 50 or 60 pounds successfully attacking a full-grown man.

When a keeper arrived on the scene the young man had been forced completely back into a corner formed by the back of the exhibit and one wall. At this point it was impossible to say whether the gazelle wanted to break off the attack or not, for the young man didn't dare release the continually jabbing horns to find out. It was a perfect impasse. To break it the keeper had to enter the enclosure and assume the task of holding the gazelle's horns, taking them from the young man one at a time. When the grateful man was safely out of the enclosure, the keeper allowed the animal to push him to a point near the moat. There he thrust the gazelle's head away from him long enough to take two or three undignified bounds across the moat and to jump the hedge and guardrail, unscathed except for a few scratches.

Keepers agree that adventures like that with the Persian gazelles are what make their occupation one of the most interesting in the world. The pay scale is not high and shows great disparity among zoos, for the head keeper in a major zoo will probably draw more pay than the director of a small one, but the job is never monotonous despite the daily round of cage cleaning and food toting.

Both animals and visitors, separately and interacting, produce a mix that brings the keeper constant change and frequent challenge.

In earlier times when there were more farm and circus folk, most zoo keepers had at best a high school education and were frequently old farm or circus hands who had gotten used to working with animals before they ever saw a zoo. Within the past ten to fifteen years, however, the complexion of keeper forces has changed somewhat and not always, some critics feel, for the better. As a rule European keepers, particularly those in German and Swiss zoos, are better trained for their occupation. Zoo-keeping is seen as a career. In West Germany and Switzerland keepers learn their trade through a three-year apprenticeship program, during which they are imbued with the traditions of animal care which bring European zoo keepers as a group closer to their animals than their American counterparts. During their apprenticeship, the keepers-to-be, who can start at age 16, are given both written and oral examinations. For the written exams they are required to learn basic zoology, mathematics, and political science. The oral examinations are intensely practical, emphasizing techniques of cage cleaning, diet preparation, and the shipping of animals. For this test an apprentice may be required to describe how he would build crates for such diverse species as a peacock, an antelope, and a tiger.

The zoos in eastern Europe, which in most matters are greatly influenced by the Tierpark in East Berlin and its prominent director Dr. Heinrich Dathe, who chairs a committee of socialist zoo directors, follow the same basic apprenticeship program as the one in West Germany but shorten it to two years. Most apprentices train in the large (325 acres) Tierpark, but take their exams at the Leipzig Zoo.

In European zoos it is a common practice to send keepers on educational trips to other zoos. The Basel Zoo extends this process even further. All proceeds from pony rides, elephant rides, and the like go into a special fund to provide money to send eligible keepers, one at a time, to East Africa where they can see in the wild some of the reptiles, birds, and mammals they care for. American zoos have no comparable program. One keeper at the San Diego Zoo who wanted very much to see East Africa actually took a month's leave of absence to travel there at his own expense.

Because this was before the jet age and regularly scheduled airline flights to Africa, he hopped a boat in New York, went through the Suez Canal to Mombasa, Kenya, and from there by train to Nairobi where he hired a car and driver to visit the nearby game parks. He returned to Mombasa, caught the boat back and barely made it to San Diego before his month was up. For all his pains he had exactly three days in Africa.

American zoos do not as a rule have true apprenticeship programs for keepers. They use instead on-the-job training, with all the wasted time, inadequate instruction, and transmission of error that is inherent in that method. American zoo keepers, however, benefit from programs not found in Europe. A group of keepers in San Diego started a professional organization, the American Association of Zoo Keepers, now headquartered in Washington, D.C., to provide for a national exchange of ideas and techniques at annual conferences; and those keepers who are promoted to supervisory posts may be selected to take a course in zoo operation and management offered once a year by the American Association of Zoological Parks and Aquariums.

The people who become keepers in American zoos are generally selected from applicants or employees who have gained familiarity with animals, sometimes by starting in such a menial zoo job as sanitician, whose function it is to collect and dispose of animal feces in sizes ranging from droppings the size of BB shot to the considerable deposits of elephants who consume up to 800 pounds of fodder a day.[9]

Within the past five years, two developments have brought some changes in the keeper forces of most American zoos. As in other occupations, more women have been hired and a greater number of college graduates have entered the occupation. Both these changes can be at least partially credited (or blamed, depending on the point of view) on the impact of scientists like Jane Goodall, Dian Fossey, George Schaller, and Biruté Galdikas-Brindamour, whose work in field research on animals has been glamorized through articles, books, and television. However, there are two

[9] Most manure generated in zoos goes to waste, being either buried or burned. One or two enterprising zoo directors have bagged and marketed manure from exotic animals. The Portland, Oregon, Zoo does a nice business with brightly bagged elephant manure.

other factors. Veterinary schools, more difficult to enter in many states than medical college, look favorably on applicants who have worked in zoos, and higher unemployment has made fewer jobs available to college graduates in general.

This new breed of keeper, most often a college graduate in biology, zoology, or anthropology, doesn't as a rule view the keeper's job as a career, but as a stepping-stone to field research or better paying, more challenging positions in zoo management. Inevitably, the new style keepers are resented by old-timers, mostly men whose education ended with high school or before, who see the keeper's job as an end in itself and are likely to feel inferior around the college graduates.

The new breed of keepers argue with some justification that the old-timers don't know about recent scientific discoveries about genetics, wild animal behavior, and conservation needs. The old-timers claim with equal justification that the college kids, both men and women, either become childishly sentimental about the animals or go to the other extreme and see them as textbook abstractions instead of living, breathing creatures with distinctive personalities of their own. Moreover, the old-timers charge, too many of the college kids are anxious to put their book-learned theories to work rather than rely on long-established and tested procedures of animal care. The view may have some merit. There have been a rash of recent accidents involving young keepers, usually female, often with elephants.

A college education, the old-timers contend, is no substitute for learning about captive animals the hard way, by dirtying one's hands in their service and getting to know them by name, disposition, and eccentricity. The argument is compelling to the extent that many zoo mammals, some birds, and even a few reptiles develop unique characteristics and behavior that in sum create a stand-out personality. Animals such as these must become known as individuals if they are going to be properly kept.

Whenever they reminisce about their jobs, old-time keepers recall best the animals that were unique, for example, a spectacled bear that became one keeper's favorite at the San Diego Zoo. Spectacled bears are so named because their otherwise largely black fur is relieved by great white circles around the eyes, giving them the appearance of a clown with painted-on glasses. Full-

grown spectacled bears, native to jungles on Andean slopes, are about the size of the familiar American black bear. The particular animal in the keeper's story was described as a Houdini of bears because it tended to turn up where it wasn't expected, apparently in constantly foiled efforts to escape from its open, moated grotto. Thwarted in its efforts everywhere else, the animal turned its attention to a manhole cover inside the exhibit. How he knew that the manhole cover might offer a road to freedom, no one could say. But he seemed to know, for one day he succeeded in working the cover out of its recess in the floor—a considerable achievement because there was barely room for a thin knife to be inserted between the rim of the flush cover and the surrounding cement.

What the bear found was a pipe that led to a covered storm drain three feet in diameter, installed to take run-off from all the moated exhibits built side by side for nearly half a mile along the bottom of a canyon. The bear could not know, of course, that in its early days the zoo had once been flooded by heavy rains that swept some startled sea lions all the way through a storm drain until they were flushed out onto the streets of downtown San Diego. There, equally startled citizens had to spend several hours rounding them up. As a consequence, the zoo had installed wire mesh at the lower end of storm drains. So the Houdini of spectacled bears, it was later conjectured, found himself once again thwarted. Undaunted, he turned and made his way back up the storm drain. Then, whether confused or still hoping to escape, he took the wrong tunnel from the drain. Finding another manhole cover, he pushed on it from below and popped up into the tiger's grotto.

In retelling this story the keeper had to stop for a moment because he got to laughing before he reached the denouement. One of the zoo's bus drivers who had just pulled to a stop in front of the exhibit with a load of visitors was the first to see the bear in the tiger's grotto. Down front in this enclosure was a shallow pool and in the exact center of the pool the spectacled bear sat upright on its haunches, constantly shifting its position so it could face the single tiger circling it on the outside of the pool. Tigers are not afraid of water; indeed they seem to like it, but this tiger wanted to discover the nature of its opponent before it plunged in. So it contented itself with pacing just out of reach of the bear's cocked paws, meantime taking an occasional swipe with one of its own front paws, which like an inept boxer's left jab never quite reached the mark.

Few zoo visitors have or ever will witness such a drama. But some of the passengers on the bus apparently thought the bear-tiger boxing match was being staged for their benefit. One of the passengers, a middle-aged man, couldn't get over it. Turning to his wife, he exclaimed, "See dear, what did I tell you? Best damned zoo I've ever seen. Look at that action!"

The bus driver, who recognized potential disaster when he saw it, didn't stop to explain that matching spectacled bears and tigers was not a daily event in the zoo. He climbed down and raced off to find a keeper. Fortunately, the tiger's keeper was coming down the service road behind the grotto. Alerted to the situation, he didn't wait until more help came. He began to call the tiger in a low, persuasive voice through the window of a bedroom that opened into the exhibit. Either the tiger took the opportunity to escape from what might have become a painful escalation of the shadow boxing, or he thought the keeper was about to offer him a chunk of raw meat. In any event, he stopped circling and bounded into the bedroom, which the keeper, using an outside lever, promptly shut off from the main exhibit. The spectacled bear was safe. His keeper later cajoled him into another bedroom, worked him into a crate, and returned him to the proper grotto—after, of course, the manhole cover had been secured by bolts. From that day until his death several years later the Houdini of bears made no more attempts to escape—as far as anyone knows, that is.

A Stitch in
an Aardvark's Tongue

T he story of Krinkles is of a tongue that went too far. Krinkles was an aardvark (the word in Afrikaans means "earth pig") who lived for a time in the San Diego Zoo. Like all aardvarks he looked like the result of an illicit union between an anteater and a domestic pig. His body was shaped like that of an anteater, his front feet strongly clawed, and his snout long. Nevertheless this snout greatly resembled a pig's, being flat and rounded at the end as though someone had dulled the point by pushing it in. The crinkled flesh that gave this aardvark his name was also porcine in its pale fleshy tones.

One day Krinkles became a hospital case. There was no immediately ascertainable reason, but the keeper reported he was not eating his special diet of ground meat, eggs, and broth, laced with a dash of formic acid to give it the flavor of ants. Fearing that he had some mysterious aardvarkian malaise, the veterinarians put him in the zoo hospital for observation and treatment. There he was assigned to the only available cage, which happened to be next to one occupied by a female gelada, sometimes called gelada baboon, who was recovering from a minor operation. Between the two animals a solid wall of concrete block made it impossible for either animal to see the other. On the front, however, both cages were covered by wire mesh with openings that left plenty of room for an aardvark's tongue.

That tongue is a fascinating instrument. In their native Africa aardvarks live almost exclusively on termites, which build earthen nests that rise in pinnacles as high as a man above the savannah.

For a 90-pound animal to make its living by eating termites it is helpful to have a long, sticky tongue that can be poked into the entrances of termite mounds, lashed about a bit and then withdrawn with dozens of termites mired on the surface like flies on flypaper.

To preface what follows it is necessary now to consider the nature of geladas. These primates are foragers that spend most of their waking hours moving across rocky African foothills looking for edible roots, eggs, and fat grubs. Some of these grow quite large and juicy and their color resembles that of an aardvark's tongue. Geladas are also social animals likely to become morose and bored if confined alone in a cage with no furniture or playthings.

The scene is now set. Both the gelada and Krinkles, after medication, are recovering their health. On a particular day, nearly his old aardvarkian self again and rather hungry after his illness, Krinkles apparently decided to explore his cage for termite holes. He sniffed his way across the concrete floor, poking the tongue from side to side, finding nothing. At last he reached the front of his cage on the side nearest his unseen neighbor, the gelada. There he stuck his tongue through the first real opening he had found, one of the squares in the wire mesh. He first thrust the tongue forward but drew in nothing but empty air and cold concrete. Then, quite innocently, hoping still to find some termites, Krinkles turned the tongue sideways, found another opening, and reeled the tongue out as far as it would go. At this point it entered the gelada's cage.

The point of view now shifts to the gelada. You (the gelada) are getting well. In the hospital they feed you well enough, it is true, but for long hours your only occupation is picking hair from your body and staring at three walls and an empty corridor beyond the wire mesh. Sitting there morosely on your haunches you are pleasantly surprised to see what looks like a rather substantial grub inching its way into your cage. Your old foraging spirit is aroused. What do you do? Right. You pounce on the grub with both hands.

Only it isn't a grub. It's a tongue, and at the other end is a startled, hurt, and powerful animal who clearly resents having his tongue grabbed by what he must feel is the world's largest termite.

A tug of war ensues, with the gelada holding fiercely onto her grub and the desperate aardvark trying to reel in its tongue. At last the aardvark, motivated by pain and the urge for survival, wins the pulling match but at the expense of a severely lacerated tongue. The gelada, having had at least momentary surcease from monotony, goes back to glum hair-picking until she can rejoin the gang back at the exhibit.

The lacerated tongue of an aardvark, root canal dental work on an orangutan, cataracts on a tiger's eyes, Caesarean on a gorilla, broken leg on a Komodo dragon—these are but a few of the many unusual problems that make the life of a zoo veterinarian considerably more challenging than that of a private practitioner who takes care of pets or farm and range stock, even though the latter can earn a good deal more. Not all zoos can afford their own veterinarians, being content to use the services of a local private practitioner, augumented on occasion by medical doctors, especially pediatricians when young apes are sick, for their ailments often resemble those of human children. What the vet always and the pediatrician frequently doctors is a patient who cannot say where it hurts. Diagnoses must sometimes be made and even operations performed where symptoms in the sick animal or child are infinitesimal deviations from healthy norms. Nor can the vet always summon up help from a large body of medical literature on such topics as repairing an aardvark's tongue. He has to use years of experience with exotic animals, a lot of extrapolation from other cases, some solid common sense, and then plunge ahead. The repairs on Krinkles' tongue, for example, required both stitches and the tying off of a damaged blood vessel. The operation was a success. Within a short time Krinkles had recovered enough to resume active duty back at his exhibit, a wiser aardvark no doubt, who in the future would be a lot more careful about where he stuck his tongue.

There is an afternote to the story of Krinkles. The aardvark was traded by the San Diego Zoo to the Melbourne, Australia, Zoo. For a while during the long ocean voyage (required then because no exotic animal could legally enter Australia except by ship),[1] it

---

[1] A provision designed to protect the sheep and cows on Australian ranches. Restrictions on importing animals are still the most stringent in the world, although some exotics can now be brought in by air. Most hoofed animals,

appeared that Krinkles would not survive. Two or three days after his departure from San Francisco Dr. Phillip T. Robinson, San Diego's chief veterinarian, received an urgent ship-to-shore telephone call from the Aussie who was shepherding Krinkles and some other animals. The Australian was a keeper, not a veterinarian, and he had become alarmed because the aardvark looked poorly and wouldn't eat. Dr. Robinson, whose boyish looks belie his skill as a diagnostician, asked several questions about Krinkles' behavior, and then came to the only reasonable conclusion the described symptoms would allow. Krinkles was seasick. The prescription was dramamine. Two days later he got another call from the now far-distant ship. Krinkles had his sea legs and was eating well.

Stitching an aardvark's tongue would actually be classified as routine by most zoo veterinarians. Far from being routine was an operation done at the San Diego Zoo on a Komodo dragon. Some people at the zoo called this the case of the broken dragon, for this largest of lizards, which can grow over ten feet long and weigh 300 pounds, is appropriately called dragon. A voracious flesh eater that will wolf down its own young,[2] the dragon has a long, scaly, muscular body with a thick-based tapering tail that can be used as an offensive weapon. These creatures, like so many island species, are endangered because it doesn't take too many of them to overpopulate Komodo and the two or three other Indonesian islands where, unthreatened for several millennia, the species evolved. There are few dragons in captivity and of these the San Diego Zoo has three, a powerful nine-foot, one-eyed male and two seven-foot females, the only Komodo dragons in the western hemisphere.

One of the San Diego females broke her right front leg. No one knows how, but keepers speculated that she slipped or was pushed from a fake boulder which used to be in the enclosure and landed with her full weight on the leg. The break was so severe that the

---

however, cannot be imported at all. This has caused a shortage of antelope, deer, wild cattle, and hogs in Australian zoos, which must breed their own or not exhibit them.

[2] For this reason evolution has provided that the young dragons spend most of their time in trees while their parents—who don't know their own children—are hunting on the ground.

bones snapped asunder, which meant that the animal was virtually immobilized, a serious impairment for a Komodo dragon. These reptiles use their legs both to walk, sometimes quite rapidly and with a head-down intentness and inexorability that can be awesome, and to lift up their bodies as one means of regulating their otherwise unregulated body temperature. Like all reptiles the dragons have no internal regulator like the one that keeps the temperature of people at a constant 98.6 degrees. When the sun grows hot and air temperatures rise, a Komodo dragon can cool itself either by moving into shade or rising up on all four legs to expose more body surface to whatever cooling breezes may be present. In the wild the blood of a dragon that could neither move nor rise would most likely grow too hot and the animal would die.

As a first step in repairing the dragon, Dr. Robinson and his team bound the reptile's leg tightly to prevent further damage. A major decision, they knew, was selecting the right anesthetic to use in the operation that had to be performed. No one fools around with Komodo dragons. They don't breathe fire or turn people into stone with a baleful stare, but their sharp teeth, made for cutting and ripping, can make hamburger out of a hand, and they are so muscular that several men would be required to hold the injured creature down if a local anesthetic were used.

Robinson and his cohorts felt that the search for the right anesthetic merited some tests. The operation they contemplated to fix the shattered bone properly would involve a relatively new technique of bone plating that had been developed for human beings. The delicate engineering required would necessitate an extraordinarily long operation, a critical reason for choosing the right anesthetic from among those available.

What the vets realized was the somewhat disquieting fact that they were venturing into unmapped territory. No one had ever fixed a broken dragon before. There was no standard text nor article in a veterinary magazine to tell them how to proceed. They knew also that in dealing with a valuable endangered animal they would be kibitzed both by the zoo administration in general and the Curator of Reptiles, Dr. James Bacon, Jr., in particular. Moreover in the close, critical world of zoos, word about botched jobs on precious animals soon gets around.

The vets decided that a few days could be spared for some experiments, not on the injured dragon but on a close relative that didn't enjoy endangered status. The best bet, they decided, would be an anesthetic called Halothane, an inhalant that has worked in operations on other reptiles. They persuaded Dr. Bacon to loan them a large monitor lizard that came from the same genus, *Varanus*, as the Komodo dragon. Calculating all the variables from age to weight that enter when a general anesthetic is used, they administered Halothane to the stand-in monitor, while Dr. Bacon, who favors the big lizards, looked the other way.

Although it couldn't count backward, the monitor went smoothly to sleep and stayed out the length of time Dr. Robinson and his team calculated the operation would require. While the animal was under, the vets, without harming it, studied the ways to cut through the tough outer layer of scales, using as their maps x-rays of both the injured Komodo and its stand-in. Finally they settled on a method of securing the leg so the animal would be unable to reinjure it while the bones were setting.[3]

The four-and-a-half-hour operation was almost anticlimactic. Halothane worked as well on the dragon as it had on the monitor and the preoperative planning showed its value when the scalpels started cutting. Within a few weeks the dragon could move around once again on all fours, although somewhat stiffly. Now she is fully mobile. A slight limp has not in the least diminished and possibly even enhanced her in the eyes of the one-eyed male who, when the season is right and she is within range of his good eye, often pursues her with obvious lust. The situation is rather sad really because the lusted-after female remains standoffish, whereas the other female tends, figuratively, to blink her eyes and swish her hips whenever the male comes near. Apparently, however, she hasn't found the right perfume, for the one-eyed male ignores her hints and continues his pursuit of the disinterested one. This confused *ménage à trois* troubles Dr. Bacon, who very much wants to propagate Komodo dragons.[4]

---

[3] Reinjuries often occur to animals with broken bones, particularly flighty ones like antelope. For this reason at the San Diego Zoo's new hospital surgical wing, some recovery rooms have floors and walls padded in foam rubber.

[4] Herpetologists who have studied these animals believe they may form permanent male-female relationships (pair bonds), an unusual, but not unheard-of custom among reptiles.

Dr. Bacon, a tall, thin, handsome young man with a good deal of compassion for the reptiles and amphibians in his charge, figured in another unique story of zoo medicine. One of the zoo's Indian pythons grew a large and terribly disfiguring tumor in its mouth. Wishing to save the animal if he could, Dr. Bacon called on the zoo's vets to help. A section of the tumor was removed and tested in the cancer laboratory at the nearby University of California Hospital in San Diego. Back came a strange diagnosis. Dr. Bacon's python was suffering from a malignancy called Burkitt's lymphoma, an oral cancer ordinarily found only in humans. Although marvelously equipped, the San Diego Zoo's hospital is not set up to give intensive radiation treatment for cancer. Consequently, for a period of several months personnel in the radiation treatment rooms of the University Hospital were treated to the unusual sight of Dr. Bacon and one of his helpers carrying in an eight-foot python taped to a two-by-four so it could be given deep radiation for cancer of the mouth. Before and after photographs of the stricken snake show that the outward manifestation of the cancer was greatly reduced. When it started the treatment, the python could neither close its mouth nor eat; at the end it could do both. Unfortunately, the treatment had come too late; the cancer had already spread. After five months of treatment, the python died.

The presence of full-time veterinarians on zoo staffs is a relatively recent development. The first zoo vet, a man named Charles Spooner, was hired as "medical attendant" for a collection of animals in Regent's Park that was later to become the London Zoo. This was in 1829. For three-quarters of a century thereafter most zoos continued to get by without vets or by calling in vets as any animal owner might—only when they were urgently needed. Around the turn of the century the Bronx Zoo in New York put Dr. H. Amling, Jr. on staff, having hired him from Bostock's circus where he had gained valuable experience with exotic animals.

Vets are not yet common in zoos. In the United States there are only 40 to 45 practicing zoo vets in the 60 or so zoos that can be classified as major because they possess 1,000 or more animals. And when one considers that two of these major zoos, the San Diego Zoo and Wild Animal Park, have five vets between them, not counting pathologists and interns, it becomes clear that many zoos have none. These zoos must depend on local practitioners or graduate students and faculty members from nearby veterinary colleges if the zoo is fortunate enough to have one nearby.

Zoo veterinarians are not, it should be noted, universally acclaimed as white knights. Some zoo officials and curators, particularly old-timers, echo the sentiments of Carl Hagenbeck who preferred to rely on his own "old-established and well-known remedies," which could be anything from herbal salves to powdered bone in the sick animal's diet. Sometimes a good deal of ingenuity went into Hagenbeck's cures. He tells of one instance when seven of his elephants simultaneously came down with what he diagnosed as "colic." His prescription was a liberal dose of rum in each elephant's water. In a few hours six of the elephants were either cured of their affliction or tipsy enough to forget it. The seventh, unfortunately, was an unruly drunk who when everyone else wanted to sleep kept trying to pick a fight with its neighbors. Hagenbeck rose to this emergency by giving the irascible animal another large shot of rum. This did the trick. The elephant fell into a drunken sleep, no doubt with loud snores and occasional hiccups.

There are still zoo people who see any vet as "Dr. Stickneedle," to employ an old term of contempt, overanxious to give medicine or wield a scalpel and likely to kill more animals than he cures. As Dr. Charles R. Schroeder, director emeritus of the San Diego Zoo and himself a veterinarian of considerable stature,[5] has observed, "Too frequently the veterinarian was called too late for successful treatment and too early for a postmortem."

One of the reasons for the contempt expressed by old-fashioned zoo keepers and curators is seen in a story that Dr. Theodore H. Reed, director of the Washington Zoo, tells on himself. As a recently graduated D.V.M. on his first job in Oregon Dr. Reed responded to a call from a nearby zoo. While passing in front of a row of cages his eyes were drawn to a female baboon who, to put it delicately, had the enormously swollen, tumescent, dark pink buttocks that signaled her readiness to acquiese if any male baboon cared to respond. In brief, the animal was in heat. But for Dr. Reed, who had never before seen this phenomenon, her condition was one of "gross contusion requiring immediate surgical intervention."

[5] Among his many contributions Dr. Schroeder developed the skin test for tuberculosis that most zoos now use on their primates.

Koala , San Diego Zoo.

North Chinese leopard, San Diego Zoo.

Southern white rhinos, San Diego Wild Animal Park. Since the arrival of the herd of 20 southern white rhinos from the Umfolozi Game Reserve in South Africa in 1971, a total of 31 calves have been born and raised at the Park.

Impala, San Diego Wild Animal Park.

Mandrill, San Diego Zoo.

White-fronted lemur, San Diego Zoo.

Hamadryas baboon, San Diego Wild Animal Park.

He was set straight by the keepers and departed with his first valuable lesson in exotic animals.

The old arguments against vets have now for the most part died out. For many years, the joke goes, the zoo veterinarian's standard prescription for most animal ills was "fresh water, good food, and cage rest." Not only were underlying diseases that afflict exotic animals unknown or hazily understood (as many still are), but administering treatment was extremely difficult and sometimes hazardous to both the animal and the men trying to help it. The detection of incipient illness in animals has always been enormously difficult. Animals cannot announce that they have a headache, upset stomach, or pain in the chest. Moreover, like people, they are individuals in their reaction to oncoming disease. Some display sickness sooner, some later, and some not until they are at death's door. Many species, particularly those that are prey to carnivores in the wild, have been coded by their genes to avoid showing illness or weakness, for in the wild it is not the healthy animals the predators pursue, it is the laggard—the old, the infirm, and the sick. Delayed diagnosis of illness in an animal means that the disease, when it is discovered, may already be well developed and require immediate medication. In the old days giving medicine to most animals was both difficult and dangerous; the animal had to be caught and restrained before it could be doctored. If it were of a nervous or high-strung species, a gazelle or antelope for example, the application of Leake's rule became critically important. Promulgated by Charles D. Leake, a pharmacologist at the University of California at Davis, this rule states that "the therapeutic hazard should not exceed the disease hazard." An English translation is "the cure shouldn't be a greater threat than the disease." The hazard to the animal of being chased, roped, or netted, and tightly restrained in a squeeze cage (which can be closed like a vise) often exceeded the danger from its disease. To avoid restraining nervous animals vets often concealed medicine in their food the way human mothers used to hide castor oil in orange juice, but because one of the characteristics of a sick animal is often loss of appetite, vets could not be assured that the medicine went where it was supposed to.

What changed the world of veterinary medicine in zoos was a simple invention, the capture gun. Either rifle or pistol, the capture gun allows a charge of compressed gas to fire a dart, essentially a strong hypodermic needle, accurately up to 20 yards. With this tool and adaptations of two more primitive weapons, the blowgun and the crossbow, veterinarians can stand outside a cage or enclosure and shoot a previously selected drug into a sick animal. Sometimes the object is to knock the animal out so that the vet can administer to it. At other times capsules in the dart carry antibiotics or any other medicine the vet wants to inject. Beyond a brief pain when the dart strikes, the animal scarcely notices it. When knockout drugs are used, there is some risk that the animal will receive an overdose and die, but constant refinement of the technique (at the cost of some lives) has eliminated much of the risk. For example, rhinos and elephants shot with the drug M-99, originally developed for a massive capture and relocation of white rhinos in southern Africa,[6] have been safe in ninety-nine cases out of a hundred. On many other species, however, vets use knockout drugs only as a last resort, for the mortality rates are higher. Knockout drugs are seldom used if some other approach will accomplish the task.

Armed with their new techniques vets in most leading zoos are now emphasizing preventive medicine designed to keep diseases from starting or arresting them during their earliest stages. In preventive programs zoos cannot achieve the exacting standard set by the Lemsip Primate Center of New York University. At this center hundreds of macaques, baboons, and chimpanzees are kept and bred for use in medical research. None ever leave the center. Healthy animals are required for several reasons. Animals must possess the stamina to undergo numerous experiments, some of them requiring surgery under anesthesia. The presence of disease in an animal might skew the results of an experiment. Finally, and most important, any disease in one animal would quickly spread to others in rooms very much like hospital wards closely packed with individual cages. To prevent disease the center uses Draconian measures. Vets inspect each animal visually (an eyeball physical) every day, looking for any deviation from the animal's norm—

[6] This famous conservation program, developed because two South African reserves were being overcrowded, saw the shipment of many white rhinos to other parts of Africa and to a few zoos in Europe and the United States. The story is excellently told in Ian Player's *The White Rhino Saga* (New York: Stein and Day, 1973).

change in eye expression, loss of luster in hair, weight loss, strange patterns of behavior. Every three months each animal receives a complete physical on an operating table after it has been immobilized with a dart gun. Cages are periodically steam cleaned. Each building in the compound is maintained as a separate sanitary zone. Personnel and visitors cannot enter without donning all the regalia of an operating room—surgical gown, mask, nurse's cap, gloves, and shoe covers. There are undoubtedly many hospitals less rigorous in enforcing sanitary procedures.

No zoo could, or would, want to go to such extremes. The diversity of animal forms and size of exhibits, to say nothing of the costs involved, would prohibit complete physicals. And extreme sanitary precautions are impossible where many people visit. Zoo vets have to content themselves with visual inspections, reports from keepers, other employees who see the animals daily, and sometimes visitors, particularly those regulars found in any zoo. Physicals can be given whenever an animal has to be immobilized for another reason. Moreover, preventive medicine can be used. Most zoos require that all cats and dogs, including tigers or wolves, get distemper shots. Primates, particularly the anthropoid apes, are vaccinated (orally) against polio, and the common childhood diseases of humans, and are skin tested for tuberculosis. At the San Diego Zoo on one occasion three baby apes, an orangutan, a chimpanzee, and a gorilla came down with chicken pox, quite obviously passed along by either a keeper or visitor in the children's zoo, where they played together. Anyone who has gone through the process of caring for human children with chicken pox can readily imagine what it's like placating a hair-covered baby that has broken out all over.

Because newly born zoo animals frequently have to be taken from mothers that can't or won't care for them, and thus deprive them of the agents in mother's milk that help build immunities to many diseases, some zoos have achieved the ultimate in preventive medicine by installing equipment to produce gamma globulin, that multipurpose fortifier against disease.

Parasites are common in zoo animals, particularly those recently arrived from the wild. To find and eradicate these multifarious creatures, which come not singly but in hordes, zoo vets rely on close examination of animal feces. In zoos without adequate laboratories daily visual inspections, generally done by keepers, may catch the big parasites like a 24-inch worm that afflicts zebras but overlook microscopic creatures like malaria bugs (which more frequently infect birds than mammals). Only a lab technician or pathologist with a microscope can detect these tiny creatures, which may be under two microns in size.

The life of a zoo veterinarian is not without its risks. People have been known to shoot themselves accidentally with capture guns, sometimes taking, as one South African game ranger did, a dose designed to knock out a 5,000-pound white rhino within twenty minutes, which doesn't leave much time before sleep and probably death for a two-hundred-pound man. The ranger was saved, only because he acted fast to inject an antidote and send out a radio call for help before he passed out.

Animals being ministered to do not understand that needles and syringes or clippers are being wielded for their own good and are inclined to kick, bite, and scratch their nearest tormentor, often the veterinarian. For the same reason many animals—once stung, twice shy—become vet haters. Normally placid and lovable gorillas, for example, have been known to bear grudges against a vet who months or years before gave them a painful shot. The vet can bear not being loved, but he knows that intelligent creatures with grudges may, if they get the opportunity, play "gotcha," with him as the gotchee. In such cases constant vigilance may be the price of keeping one's limbs.

Possibly the greatest danger faced by most zoo vets comes immediately after they have knocked an animal down with a capture gun. At this point somebody must enter the cage or enclosure to see if the animal is in fact unconscious and beyond suddenly flailing, biting, or cutting with sharp claws or hooves. Because vets would consider themselves somewhat less than heroic if, after drugging an animal, they turned to a keeper and said "after you," it has become the code of zoo veterinarians to go first into an enclosure to inspect a presumably unconscious patient. On rare occasions the presumption is wrong. Unconscious animals have suddenly come alive to score some hits, many near misses, and near tragedies that in retrospect could be laughed at, with perhaps some insincerity by actual participants. One time when Dr. Charles Sedgwick, he of the blue bear, was a veterinarian at the Los An-

geles Zoo, he used a capture gun to shoot a knockout drug called sernylan into a full-grown Bengal tiger named Hilda so he could examine her badly swollen jaw.[7] Allowing a margin for error, he counted down the number of minutes that theoretically would be required for the sernylan to do its job. When he felt certain that Hilda was completely out, he went into the cage and stood for a moment looking down at the sleeping animal. Because heavy animals like tigers can quickly collapse a lung when they lie unconscious on their sides Dr. Sedgwick, with considerable effort, heaved Hilda over onto her chest. Then he took her head in both hands to begin a close inspection of the swollen jaw. At that instant he noticed something disturbing. The eyes he was looking into were looking back at him. They were dazed, but in them was a glint of fear, which in any animal may be the prelude to escape, or in close quarters, savage attack. For a moment Dr. Sedgwick knew panic. Yet even as his legs pleaded with him to run from the cage, he strove to keep his cool. One does not run from any of the big cats. Their most frequent point of attack is from the rear, for it allows them to knock prey down as they bite quickly and decisively through neck and spinal cord. Don't run, Dr. Sedgwick instructed himself. Stand up slowly and back out of the cage. But as he stood, so did Hilda. Rearing up on her hind legs she loomed over him so that his head was barely level with her front paws. Before he could make a move Hilda placed both paws against his chest and in a single swipe raked him from breast to knee, stripping him of his khaki shirt, cutting through his leather belt, pulling his trousers halfway off. As he stood there with blood beginning to well from the deep scratches across his now bare abdomen Dr. Sedgwick realized that Hilda was now lying blissfully unconscious at his feet. The sernylan had at last taken full effect. Holding up his trousers, Dr. Sedgwick walked calmly to the door of the cage. But when he had slammed and bolted it behind him, he became conscious of perspiration streaming down his face and knees that were urgently signaling him to sit down.

[7] Dental problems are common in zoo animals and often contribute to other disabling diseases. One study, made many years ago at the Bronx Zoo, showed that virtually every animal had some dental ills that needed attention and many were serious. Unfortunately, veterinary dentistry does not get anywhere near the attention that it should in zoos.

Some zoos, though by no means all, assign primary responsibility for nutrition to their veterinary staffs. Selecting the proper diets for animals creates one of the toughest problems in zoo husbandry. Not only are there many species of amphibians, reptiles, birds, and mammals (and sometimes insects and fish), each with its own requirements, but food for the newly hatched or born often differs greatly from that eaten by their mothers and fathers. Then, too, there are individual preferences. Not all animals want the same food that their cage companions eat. Some must be pampered.

Up until the 1940s zoos had to warehouse many different kinds of fruits, grains, and meats. Horse meat was the universal food for carnivores, although it wasn't always good for them in pure form without internal organs like the heart and liver, and unsupplemented by grasses or some other vegetable food that the animal might deliberately eat in nature. Ungulates were fed hay of various types; sea mammals got fish; and birds, depending on their nature, ate various fruits, grains, or meats. Snakes were often the easiest to feed as long as there was a supply of fish, frogs, mice, rats, or rabbits, depending on whether the snake was aquatic or terrestrial and large or small. The problem of warehousing and distributing the proper food for each animal was sizable.

The great leap forward in zoo diets came with the invention of scientifically mixed foods that could be packaged or distributed as pellets. The greatest innovator was Dr. Herbert Ratcliffe, then director of the Penrose Research Laboratory of the Philadelphia Zoo. He was the first to apply a scientific approach to the development of diets for exotic animals, giving his concoctions the name Zoo Cake. His genius lay in determining not only precise amounts of animal fats, carbohydrates, and proteins, but also in putting into the diets rare earths, amino acids, and vegetable oils as needed. This approach was refined and carried forward by Mark Morris, both a Ph.D. and D.V.M., who developed balanced meat diets for cats, specialized diets for monkeys, and many others that are now sold under the brand name ZuPreem by the Hills Division of Riviana Foods. Even before Dr. Morris the old-line professor of feeds for domestic animals, Ralston-Purina Corporation, had begun the manufacture of foods for exotic animals with Monkey Chow, and now distributes several other types of pellet foods.

Dr. Morris's son, Mark Morris, Jr., carries on his father's work

at a research center near Topeka, Kansas, that covers several acres with pens full of various animals. Morris and his staff have even developed a pellet for snakes to be used by those zoos that find it difficult to obtain or raise mice and rats, which is seen by conservationists as a great deal better than feeding the reptiles strips of whale meat, as the Japanese, who raise snakes for food, have done.

While nearly all major zoos have now turned to the use of pellet or packaged meat diets, there remains a good deal of controversy over their use. Those who favor pellets argue that they assure a scientifically balanced diet for zoo animals and greatly reduce the amount of warehouse space required. While few professionals oppose the use of prepackaged diets, there are many who point to possible shortcomings. When little is known about what natural foods a species of animal eats in the wild, it is possible that pellets will lack some essentials that the animal must have to stay healthy and very possibly achieve the sexual arousal that is, needless to say, necessary to all successful captive breeding programs. Furthermore, pellets do not sit well in the stomachs of some animals unless they are combined with other food. Leaf-eating monkeys like the langurs or colobuses, for example, have evolved stomachs very much like those of ruminants in that food passes through several compartments during digestion. It is a process both subtle and incremental, and pellets may lodge in the leaf eater's stomach the way logs do at a narrow part of the river.

Some critics of pellets note also that they don't satisfy an animal's behavioral requirements. Wild animals spend most of their waking hours in a ceaseless hunt for food, with sex and other social activities a poor second in time consumption except perhaps for play among the very young. Food gathering, in other words, is habit forming and in captivity the pellet-fed animal finds it hard to kick old habits. Even though its nutritional requirements may be satisfied, the animal feels deprived. In the large enclosures of the San Diego Wild Animal Park the herbivores, largely pellet fed, soon reduced the native grasses and shrubs to the bare ground so that for a while each enclosure was as bleak and barren as the surface of the moon. When Park officials installed sprinkling systems and seeded the enclosures with grasses, the herbivores, it was observed, appeared more content. They still got their nutrition from pellets, but as repeated waterings keep the grass sprouting, they spent hours nibbling it down again, passing their time as they would in the wild.

A continuous source of friction in zoos is the running battle between those who set diets and kindhearted visitors who want to share their food with the animals. That most visitors are well motivated when they toss peanuts and popcorn to animals is undisputed, as is the fact that animals enjoy being fed. The more intelligent ones like bears and monkeys soon learn to beg for handouts, developing in the process their own acts that become part of the zoo show, and often growing morose when feeding by the public is stopped. What troubles the zoo professionals is the knowledge that feeding by the public creates many ills. Human diseases are transmitted on the food. Animals fight one another over scraps, causing bruises or wounds that may require medical attention and disrupting otherwise harmonious social groups. Animals overeat to the point of obesity, as dangerous to them as it is to humans. Worst of all, not all zoo visitors are well motivated. There are always psychos, poor sick souls of the type who put razor blades in apples for Halloween trick-or-treaters, or pseudo-scientists who toss a lighted cigarette into a cage to see if a monkey will blow smoke rings.

Postmortems have turned up an incredible number of different objects in the stomachs of zoo animals. Coins are commonplace. At the San Diego Zoo the former pathologist Dr. Lynn A. Griner had in his desk a can containing $2.57 (not counting several pesos) in pennies, nickels, and dimes that were taken from the stomach of one harbor seal. Harbor seals go around the bottoms of their zoo pools like vacuum cleaners, scarfing up virtually any object they can swallow. This particular fellow had the misfortune to be in a pool that had temporarily achieved the status of a wishing well, probably after the first coin tosser had thrown in a nickel that other visitors could see glittering on the bottom until, that is, the seal swallowed it. The fact that most of the coins in this seal's stomach were pennies speaks of the desire of most Americans to get their wishes cheaply.

Coins, of course, are not highly digestible. Neither are some of the other items Dr. Griner has found, ranging from a child's woolen socks (both of them) to a condom. The socks, fortunately, were in the stomach of an aoudad, or Barbary sheep. Had they been in the stomach of a crocodile, zoo officials would have been

much more concerned, especially if some parent had reported a missing child. The socks were well preserved, but old enough to have become mineralized through an accretion of salts. The condom had also been swallowed by a Barbary sheep. There was some speculation in the pathologist's office as to whether it had been used before the sheep swallowed it, but Dr. Griner declined the further investigation that would have been required to prove or disprove this point on the grounds that he was concerned with what caused death or illness in zoo animals, not with the possibly outlandish sex habits of zoo visitors.

In the United States only three zoos, Washington, Philadelphia, and San Diego, employ a full-time pathologist, although most of the major zoos have arrangements with nearby universities or research centers to have postmortems performed on selected animals, or leave the task to the staff veterinarians. At San Diego nearly every animal that dies is posted, a task which often exhausts the pathologist, since the collection of both the zoo and Wild Animal Park numbers around 7,000 amphibians, reptiles, birds, and mammals. In these circumstances, with an annual mortality running around 15 percent, the pathologist may have to post 10 to 15 animals on a peak day, in sizes ranging from tiny tropical tree frogs to elephants. (Although on a day when an elephant is posted little else can be done.) Complicating the pathologist's task is the fact that particularly good or rare specimens are desired by museums and so must be posted cosmetically, with due attention to preserving the skin.[8] Dr. Griner once literally crawled inside a three-ton white rhinoceros in order to extract the lungs without creating unsightly cuts in the hide.

The first pathological lab in the United States was appropriately established at the Philadelphia Zoo, the nation's oldest.[9] Called the Penrose Laboratory, it was the pathologist's task there to dig out the causes of animal deaths with a view to correcting as soon as possible any condition that might cause more deaths in the collec-

[8] Seldom thought about by conservationists who accuse zoos of being a drain on the wild is the fact that zoos provide many skins for museums which were once also a severe drain on the wild.

[9] If one does not count the original Central Park Zoo, which opened in 1853. The present Central Park Zoo was built by the WPA during the 1930s. Philadelphia was the first zoo to be operated by a zoological society, opening in 1874.

tion. At San Diego the pathologist sends presumptive findings on each animal to the curators and vets within twenty-four hours after its death. The findings, which most often speak for themselves without any recommendation from the pathologist, are generally routine. All animals must die and for most zoo animals, which live longer as a rule than they would in the wild, death comes from the deterioration of teeth and tissue that can be characterized as old age, frequently culminating, as in humans, in the old folks' friend, pneumonia.

Sometimes though, a single finding, or more likely a series of similar findings, point to serious trouble in the collection. After San Diego had opened its tropical rain forest flight cage, a structure nearly the size of a blimp hangar, with a stream which starts from a waterfall at the top and rushes downward through a luxuriant forest of tropical plants, Dr. Griner began to turn up numerous cases of malnutrition in birds from the rain forest. When he called this to the attention of Kenton C. Lint, then curator of birds, an investigation turned up an interesting behavioral problem that was causing some birds to die. The hang-up was in distribution of the food. Like tough street gangsters, some of the territorial birds had established their own turfs around the principal feeding stations, and then using the bird equivalent of bicycle chains and shivs, they beat up on any birds who didn't belong to their gang. With plenty of food temptingly close, the less aggressive and less territorial birds simply starved to death, a fact which doesn't, one hopes, carry a message for human beings. To solve the problem Dr. Griner and Lint worked out a system of putting out more feeders set at various levels in the forest. This allowed the territorial birds to hold their turf, which appeared to satisfy them, but assured that there would be some feeders open to all.

The case of the starving birds was fairly easy to solve. The case of the Cretan goats was much more difficult. Several years ago Dr. Griner began to find lungworms in the Cretan goats, an endangered form with a few survivors on the island of Crete[10] and in two small herds at the San Diego Zoo and Wild Animal Park. The parasitic lungworms do not bring death swiftly but debilitate,

[10] Where they run the risk of being genetically swamped, one way to extinction, by interbreeding with common goats of various nondescript types and thus losing themselves in other forms.

opening the way for other, faster diseases. (Parasites seldom want to kill their hosts, not out of any sense of gratitude for the provender, but simply because they would themselves die in the process.) After several postmortems it became clear to Dr. Griner that the Cretan goat herd was infected throughout. Only the newborn were without lungworms, and before many days had passed they too carried the parasites.

But lungworms are not easy to eradicate. Dr. Griner decided that the first attack should be directed at the common garden snails, intermediate hosts for the parasites, and the reason for their spreading because goats swallowed snails when they grazed. Poisoning the snails was considered too risky, for the pesticides might harm the goats. Brought in for consultation, the zoo's chief horticulturist, Ernest Chew, provided an ingenious way of taking the battle to the snails. He was familiar with a new pesticide for leaf-eating insects that used as its killing agent that chemical which in bubble gum provides the impermeability, stretch, and stickiness.

When this pesticide, Polytrap, is sprayed on the plants that snails eat, the mollusks soon find their chewing mechanism hopelessly clogged. Since they apparently don't know how to blow bubbles to thin out the gum, they are unable to eat and soon starve to death. Sprayed on the vegetation in the Cretan goat enclosure, Polytrap worked, but only for a short time. While thousands of snails gummed up their mandibles and died, their advancing armies proved overwhelming. The decimated ranks in the enclosure were soon reinforced by outside regiments that pushed into the Cretan goat enclosure. In the end it came down to the fact that there wasn't enough Polytrap in the world to deal with every snail in the zoo. Dr. Griner decided that the lungworms had to be attacked directly.

Working with two colleagues over the course of one summer he experimented with various types of commercial worm medicines. After three months the three scientists developed a cure by dipping the goats' regular food pellets in a commercially available worming medicine. The impregnated pellets were given to the goats every day for two weeks. Now all the Cretan goats are free of worms, and the garden snails that live in their enclosure chew contentedly on, no longer plagued by sticky jaws.

A pathologist at work may create anxieties in both veterinarians and zoo managers. In a commentary about the first zoo pathologist, James Murie, who was hired by the London Zoo in the 1860s, zoo historian P. Chalmers Mitchell notes with admiration that during his tenure Murie autopsied over 4,000 animals. From these autopsies, Mitchell adds, "He drew inferences . . . which appeared to me to be sound, but were presented in such a way that they were a direct criticism of the management of the Gardens . . . That he was correct there can be little doubt; that he was offensive, whether deliberately so or not, no doubt whatever."

Criticism is inevitable if pathologists are independent, as they must to be effective. In performing postmortems the pathologist exposes—whether deliberately or not—those mistakes which physicians, the old joke goes, bury with their patients. When zoo veterinarians and managers are motivated by purely human emotions they are likely to resent findings which reveal mistakes in husbandry, diagnosis, prescriptions, or surgery. In their professional souls, however, both vets and managers know that feedback from a pathologist can both correct and redirect them in ways which may in the future save many animals from untimely death.

There are times when a zoo veterinarian has to be more than a medical practitioner. When Jane E. Meier studied veterinary medicine at Purdue University with a view to becoming a specialist on horses, she hoped she might one day work for a zoo, but never dreamed she would become the surrogate mother of an infant koala or save the life of an elephant through a feat that was more engineering than medicine. Now Jane E. Meier, D.V.M., she works at the San Diego Zoo. A short, intense, freckle-faced girl with somewhat unruly dark hair, she is fiercely devoted to her job. She was the obvious choice, therefore, when Zoo Director Charles L. Bieler decided that Gumdrop, a four-month-old koala, needed a mother 24 hours a day. Gumdrop's real mother, one of six koalas that came to the zoo as a bicentennial gift from the government of Australia,[11] had died while Gumdrop was still in the pouch, but fortunately at the stage when he could start taking some solid food. At the zoo hospital Dr. Meier put Gumdrop into an incubator

[11] Australian law forbids the export of platypuses, lyre birds, and koalas. San Diego's koalas are the only ones outside that country.

with a large teddy bear to the back of which he could cling as he would have to his real mother.[12]

Every night for several weeks Jane took Gumdrop back to the home she shared with another girl who worked at the zoo. There Gumdrop spent his time in a crib with a second teddy bear, Jane's own childhood bed companion, which had come with her from the Indiana farm where she grew up. At every opportunity Jane and the other girls picked the tenderest of leaves from those of the zoo's eucalyptus trees that koalas like best to eat. Given constant, tender loving care Gumdrop grew to independent koalahood without missing his real mother. He lives now, contented and somewhat spoiled, in the zoo's new koala exhibit.

Smallest in stature of the zoo's three regular vets, Dr. Meier once had to confront one of the biggest problems a zoo can produce—an elephant in distress. Around five o'clock one evening when the day shift people had gone home and no one was left in the construction and maintenance yards, Sumithi, a Ceylonese elephant, was deliberately pushed by a larger companion into the dry moat that surrounds the elephant exhibit, itself about the size of a football field. Such incidents had occurred before but in every case the victimized elephant had landed on its side so it had no trouble getting to its feet. But when Sumithi went into the moat she was flipped completely over onto her back. As Dr. Meier later reported it, Sumithi's back fitted the bottom of the moat the way an egg fits into its carton. Like some enormous gray-brown beetle she could do little more than wave her legs helplessly in the air.

Called to the scene within moments, Dr. Meier found that she was the highest ranking zoo official on duty. Strictly speaking, Sumithi had not yet become a veterinary case as the fall had not visibly bruised or cut her, and she had been a perfectly healthy elephant. From her studies, though, Dr. Meier knew that she faced what mystery writers call the ticking bomb plot.

In this case the bomb was in Sumithi herself. An upside down elephant has little more than an hour to live unless it can right itself, or be righted. Its internal organs are designed by evolution

[12] An irony, in a way, for teddy bears were patterned after koalas, which frequently and incorrectly are called koala bears.

to hang down, not up, and their considerable weight pressing against the elephant's diaphragm will slowly bring normal functions to a halt. The compressed lungs will not take in enough oxygen to sustain life. Death is certain.

Within the next few minutes, no more than 60 at the outside, Dr. Meier realized that she had to come up with a way of getting a four-ton elephant to her feet before she died. There were few people around to help, one or two keepers, some salespersons from a nearby refreshment stand that had just closed, and two security guards. Biting her lip pensively, Dr. Meier tried to concentrate on possible alternatives. A derrick might do it. They could run a telephone pole lengthwise between Sumithi's legs, chain the legs to the pole, then lift Sumithi with a derrick the way African porters lift a dead game animal on a pole carried between them. Instantly, Dr. Meier dismissed that idea. For several reasons it wouldn't work, but most of all because no derrick large enough to lift an elephant could be obtained within the short time she had. The bomb, she knew, continued to tick. Might not all the people available, the six or seven of them including her, get into the moat and shove Sumithi from behind? Hardly. They would like be ants trying to push an egg out of its carton.

Then she noticed a coiled rope that one of the keepers had brought. It was a stout rope, nearly an inch in diameter, tough enough to stand considerable strain. Doubled it would be nearly strong enough to support an elephant. They could tie it around Sumithi's neck, not with a hangman's knot, but as a sailor might, with a bowline to keep it from throttling Sumithi. Then they could use one of the other elephants as a living tractor (if only she had a tractor!) to pull Sumithi up to a sitting position. Once on her hindquarters Sumithi might be able to find purchase for her legs.

They tried. One keeper jumped into the moat to fasten the rope to Sumithi and the other made the other end into a harness for one of the larger elephants in the enclosure. The direct haul was too much. The second elephant tugged as directed, but Sumithi didn't budge. The bomb was continuing to tick. Dr. Meier knew they were on the right track. Their only hope was to get Sumithi up to where she could somehow get to her feet. And the rope had held. The failure had been a failure of strength, not of will, in the second elephant.

The mammal department truck! One of the keepers had come in it. It was a regular pickup used to haul everything from bales of hay to crated animals—not a large truck, not a tractor, but maybe it would work. Because the truck was on the outside of the enclosure, they could bring it in closer to Sumithi than the second elephant had been. The truck didn't weigh as much as Sumithi, but in low gear it just might work.

For a brief time after the rope had been secured to a trailer hitch on the back of the truck, Dr. Meier thought they were going to fail again. When the keeper-driver started to let out the clutch, taking care not to jerk Sumithi's neck, the wheels spun on the asphalt road. Sumithi's head was raised a little, but not nearly enough. At no time during the entire operation did Dr. Meier's thoughts even turn to eventual failure and a dead elephant. It was not until later that she realized what failure might have meant to her. In what had largely been a man's world, that of zoo veterinary medicine, she and one or two other women were beginning to win acceptance. And even though anyone would have conceded that she used every resource available to her, the stark fact that an elephant had died when it might have been saved would have rankled some zoo employees. Inevitably, there would have been those who would think—if not say—that a man in charge might have done better where engineering and mechanics, instead of medicine, were needed to save the day.

Confident, though, that they would succeed, Dr. Meier was de-lighted when the truck's wheels began to catch. Then, straining like the little engine that could, the truck began to inch ahead, and slowly, very slowly, Sumithi came to a sitting position. As Dr. Meier had hoped, Sumithi now began to take part in her own rescue. Flailing out with her legs, she managed to get enough purchase to right herself. Then, shakily, she rose to a standing position. Amid cheers from the assembled employees, Dr. Meier included, a keeper led the elephant, her pachydermic dignity fully restored, down the moat to a ramp up which she could climb into the enclosure. When Dr. Meier looked at her watch, she saw that just under fifty minutes had elapsed.

As zoos get more involved in the problems they face when they seriously set out to breed their own animals and provide a final reserve for endangered species, the role of veterinarians will take on an even greater urgency than it does now. Fortunately, the old antagonisms against zoo vets have largely disappeared. They were all too often based on emotional responses to the loss of favored or extremely valuable animals. In smarting over deaths that were conveniently blamed on vets, because they were the last to minister to the animal, no one bothered to make a scientific study, using controls, to compare mortalities in the zoos with vets on call and those without. Beyond question veterinarians, using techniques that have been rapidly advanced, prolong the lives of most zoo animals just as physicians and modern medicine prolong the lives of people. Animal doctors like people doctors may sometimes dispense pills that aren't needed and do surgery that isn't required, but the fact remains that a modern zoo without the availability of vets is a city without doctors; only the animals don't realize the terrible consequences to them of living in such a place.

The Two Resurrections of Lazarus Lemur

The entire question of keeping animals alive and healthy has never received more attention in zoos than it does now. It is not that zoo people failed in the past to take a humane attitude toward the health and physical well-being of their charges (with some rare exceptions), but that concentration on the ways to keep animals alive increased as replacements became expensive, scarce, or impossible to get. These days zoo officials are looking sharply at all causes of mortality in their collections, and especially at the causes where the death rate is highest, among the neonates or newborn animals. In all zoos it is during the hours immediately before, at, and shortly after birth that death takes its greatest toll—one out of three or more of the baby animals.

Because reproductive strategies run to extremes in animals, the loss of newly born animals is not so serious when it occurs in some species at it is for others. Some animals have high rates of reproduction and some low. Among mammals one extreme is represented by the brown rat. Female rats, who reach maturity in a little over three months, regularly average eight young to a litter and produce seven litters a year. Mother is soon burned out, but by the time she dies she has left behind an astounding number of progeny, many of whom are alive, well, and dropping their own litters—to the point where the original mother's lineal descendants may number in the thousands after little more than a year. Thus, if these ubiquitous rodents didn't have numerous enemies like snakes, hawks, owls, cats, dogs, and exterminators, the land surface of this world would soon be knee deep in rats.

Rats did not, of course, decide upon their reproductive strategy

—natural selection did—but if they had selected the approach one can imagine the concluding statement at their convention: "Very well, it is agreed then that we'll offer our enemies more rats than they can possibly eat. That way there will always be some of us left to carry on the species."

Another extreme in reproductive strategy is represented by the elephant. Young elephants arrive singly after their mother has carried them for 22 months (as opposed to the same number of days for the brown rat), and mother, helped by several aunts who act as baby-sitters, has to invest several years in feeding and caring for baby, with the result that she can generally produce no more than seven young (about the size of one rat litter) during her long lifetime. In brief, while a mother rat produces 100 to 150 babies, the female elephant produces one. But elephants, once they have grown beyond infancy, have few natural enemies except bacteria, viruses, some fungal diseases, and man. However, because life offers no free lunches, the elephant's penalty for being large and safe from predators (except man) is that it requires a lot of food. If too many elephants try to eat the available grasses, leaves, and bark in one area, many soon starve—as has been sadly demonstrated in some African game reserves like Tsavo in Kenya. Consequently, a high reproduction rate in elephants would be counterproductive in the struggle for survival.

Animals that have a slow birthrate and devote a long period to raising their young, cause the chief problems of neonatal mortality in zoos. Virtually all of the most popular animals fall in this category, as do, logically enough, many endangered species. It is the big, slow-to-produce creatures of the world, especially those man fancies as dangerous or too competitive, or which exist precariously in a limited area (like an island) that approach extinction first in the uneven contest between man and animals as to who will live on the land. In zoos when a newly born Indian rhino dies, or an orangutan, or okapi, the officials know that many months will pass before the mother can bear another, assuming, that is, that necessary ingredients for propagation remain constant, from the availability of an interested male to the ability of the mother to produce more young.

Obvious to zoo managers is a cold mathematical fact. If neonatal mortality can be reduced by half, the number of survivors

in a captive breeding group will be doubled. The economic implications of this fact boggle the mind when one remembers that an Indian rhino can be sold for around $45,000. Whether or not zoo managers hope to preserve animal species as a conservation measure, they know that every newly born animal kept alive represents potential income to the zoo, and eventually, if increased reproduction of any rare species drives the market down, a lowering of costs for all zoos. Once Mandhla, the southern white rhinoceros, and his counterparts at Whipsnade in England and Dvur Kralove in Czechoslovakia busied themselves siring babies the asking price for southern white rhinos sharply dropped.

It should be no cause for wonder then that the leading zoos are putting much thought, effort, and research into saving animal babies. Many have established procedures similar to those in a general hospital with, for example, alert boards for keepers that indicate the approaching term of pregnant females and tell the keeper what to look for and what problems may arise when birth commences. Many zoos have established special care centers devoted primarily to infant animals that have to be taken from their mothers. Frequently, young women act as nurses in these centers, which may keep round-the-clock watches. Some of these centers, or nurseries, are as elaborately equipped as nurseries for human babies, with much of the same paraphernalia, including incubators and respirators to keep premature or sickly babies alive. If the nursery has a viewing window for the public, the zoo visitor will often be treated to a kaleidoscopic show of young animals. In one section of the nursery lies a premature aardvark whose hairless, wrinkled skin is a light blue color, indicating an oxygen deficiency. He will gradually turn pink in the oxygen-enriched atmosphere of a special incubator. Seated in a chair, an attendant holds a spider monkey as though it were her own baby while she feeds it a formula that she concocted after consulting with the zoo librarian, curator of mammals, and veterinarian. On the floor of the nursery an infant pygmy chimpanzee with typically unruly hair that gives it the appearance of an unkempt black gnome sits with his arm around a teddy bear as he watches television.[1]

[1] At the San Diego Zoo the infant pygmy chimpanzees prefer game shows and cartoons. Males tolerated sports, but one female pointedly turned her back on football games.

Zoos have discovered, of course, that nurseries make good viewing. Nothing so charms visitors as baby animals, particularly cute and cuddly ones. In deference to the public some zoos have installed two-way loudspeaker systems that enable visitors on the outside of germproof partitions to ask questions of the nursery attendants. Most questions are innocuous and predictable: "What's its name? What's it eating? When was it born? Why does it wear diapers?" (To this the answer is: for the same reason human babies do, to localize the messes. Otherwise baby apes in particular engage in what is delicately called "finger-painting" on walls, floors, and furniture.)

Many times visitors use the communication system to offer advice or call attention to what they think are inhumanities being done to the young animals. One elderly lady, a regular visitor at the nursery in the San Diego Zoo, took it into her head one day that John Muth, the burly ex-Marine superintendent of the Children's Zoo, was a cruel and vicious man. Pointing to him, she said in a shrill voice that caught the attention of visitors within a fifty-foot radius, "See that terrible man! He beats and maims little animals." On the first occasion Muth strove to maintain his dignity and go on with what he was doing. But every time thereafter that the lady visited the zoo, which was about once a week, the same scene was repeated. After a while it began to tell on Muth. He found himself looking guiltily at the visitors as though in fact he did beat and maim innocent young animals. By the lady's fourth visit, Muth started taking refuge in a men's room whenever he was fortunate enough to see his gray nemesis before she saw him. Relief did not come until the woman stopped visiting to the zoo several months later. How she developed her fixed idea Muth never determined. One possible source, he concluded, was that the lady had seen him playing with a young baboon that had only two fingers on one hand, a congenital defect. During their play, which the baboon greatly enjoyed, Muth sometimes cuffed the animal's head the way human fathers do while playing with their sons.

A second woman visitor threatened to summon the humane society because the nursery attendants on duty wouldn't stop the play between two Siberian tiger cubs and a young pygmy chim-

panzee who, in the manner of young animals, were happily rolling on the nursery floor, pouncing on one another and ferociously but harmlessly biting. The woman apparently believed she was witnessing a struggle to the death of the sort that were put on in Roman arenas. At last, when the tiger cubs pinned the chimp beneath them, she could stand it no longer. "Stop them," she screamed. "Can't you see they're killing him?"

As the result of an overdeveloped sense of humor in another girl attendant, this one in the petting paddock of the Children's Zoo where the San Diego nurseries are located, one woman actually did call the humane society. She had stopped to allow her young daughter to pet some goats when she noticed that three of the animals had nothing but unsightly holes on that part of their heads where ears should have protruded. "Good heavens!" she exclaimed, "what happened to their ears?" Whatever devil possessed the paddock attendant was never identified, but he caused the girl to lean over and in a confiding tone reply, "Don't tell anybody, but they were frozen off last night." Without another word the woman took her child by the hand and left to call the humane society. Only later when Muth called to apologize did she learn that the earless goats were La Manchas, who are born that way.

Zoo directors endeavor to keep employees from giving flip answers to the countless questions, however stupid they may seem, that visitors ask. Verbal pranksters do more than create poor public relations and misdirected calls to the humane society; they can provide the springboard for misinformation about animals that is later repeated as gospel. Attendants at the San Diego nursery are still wondering how far one falsehood has spread. It got its start when a keeper was delivering to the nursery a very young wallaby whose mother had died. The little marsupial, a close relative of the kangaroo, would, when full grown, be about the size of a jackrabbit. At this stage in its life it was no bigger than the keeper's little finger. Inevitably several visitors gathered to see what the keeper had brought into the nursery. In response to their obvious curiosity, he held up the animal, which was lying on a wad of cotton in a small cardboard box. Inevitably also, one visitor asked, "What kind of animal is that?" With the air of a man who found it hard to believe that such ignorance existed, the keeper replied, "Why it's a baby elephant, of course." (A newborn elephant actually weighs around 200 pounds and stands nearly three feet tall.) As no visitor seemed surprised by this statement, or moved to contradict it, the nursery attendant, who went along with the gag, later concluded that at least one person from this particular group of visitors might be traumatically disillusioned when at some future cocktail party he or she bets that newborn elephants are no bigger than a finger.

Offers of help are often proferred to nursery attendants, most coming from teenaged girls who find the young animals adorable and want to mother them. Many offers, however, come from adults who believe they can help to solve what they see as problems. One pediatrician visiting the San Diego nursery was convinced that the wrinkled skin on the blue baby aardvark indicated a severe case of dehydration. His solution, generously given to the attendants through the two-way communication system, was to wrap the aardvark completely in plastic wrap "to hold in the moisture."

Zoo managers appreciate displays of concern for their animals, for respect for other forms of life is one of the objectives in their educational programs, one of their stated reasons for being. Too often, however, concern is based on the erroneous anthropomorphic belief that every animal has the same desires and needs as human beings. Feeling this way, visitors sometimes see mistreatment of animals where none exists. San Diego's nursery attendants received many protests when that same blue baby aardvark, now pink and healthy, left his incubator and was demoted, as some visitors saw it, to living and sleeping in a decrepit plastic garbage container. Surely, these visitors thought, the wealthy San Diego Zoo could afford a better place to keep a young aardvark. Nursery attendants were not always convincing when they explained that the aardvark slept in the garbage can out of choice, not because he was forced to. Some visitors were outraged by seeing a jungle cat asleep in a box of kitty litter, feeling no doubt that the attendants were doing the equivalent of keeping a human infant in an outhouse. Actually, the cat didn't use the box for its intended purpose; for some reason peculiar to him he preferred to sleep in kitty litter and was allowed to.

Love for animals, and ignorance about them, can sometimes lead zoo visitors into dangerous actions. An attendant in the San Diego Zoo was horrified one day when she saw a young couple lift their

four-year-old boy across a small moat into the enclosure that housed a young elephant. Small, but grown beyond the baby stage, it was capable of stepping rather heavily on a young boy. When the attendant shouted at the couple to take the child out, they hastened to reassure her. "He's a good boy," the young mother explained. "He would never hurt the elephant."

Because nurseries full of baby animals do make attractive viewing for visitors, they pose a dilemma for zoo decision makers. Zoo directors, especially those beset by boards concerned for the dollars generated by public attendance, are often tempted, and many succumb to the temptation, to keep baby animals in their nurseries even if they have to take the infants from mothers who are properly caring for them. Increasingly, zoo directors are being caught in a tug-of-war between the zoo's traditional role as a place of entertainment and education and its new role as an animal preserve concerned with captive breeding. A conflict arises between showmanship and scientific conservation. Twenty-five years ago, possibly even ten years ago, some zoo directors would have decided invariably in favor of showmanship, arguing that the public who pays the bills has to be kept amused. Today the new breed of zoo director (and some of the old breed who had foresight to see the problem coming) knows that his zoo's future, and therefore its status as a place of entertainment and education, lies in assuring a supply of the exotic animals, and only through effective and sustained captive breeding programs will this be done.

The dilemma posed each time the director is tempted to take a baby animal from its mother and hand-raise it in a nursery goes deeper than depriving either the mother or baby of the other's love and companionship. In many species, most of all the monkeys and apes that become the star attractions among nursery babies, hand-raised youngsters develop abnormalities that cause them to be ineffectual breeders.

Increasingly, therefore, zoo directors are not inclined to have neonates taken from their mothers unless they are what the girls in the San Diego nursery refer to as "ice cubes," babies that have been rejected or for some other reason are barely clinging to life—infants worth saving, but only through arduous nursing and constant monitoring. These are the runts, the untended, the sick. Some have to be destroyed, for in the wild they would not survive more than a few hours before falling prey to the elements or predators. In zoos with nurseries most will be constantly attended and periodically visited by the vets. In zoos without a nursery, a keeper or curator, even the zoo director may take them home. In spite of these efforts only half of the ice cubes will live.

A baby giraffe requires surgery shortly after birth for a dislocated hip, possibly because a newborn giraffe drops six feet to the ground when its mother expels it. When this one is taken to the nursery, it is weak and soon develops jaundice. The girls alternate in coddling it, trying to get it to eat, making certain that it is warm under a sunlamp in the straw-covered stall where it is kept. Yet after a few hours it dies, choked by its own vomit after regurgitating medicine that it had previously kept down. But when a Tasmanian Devil that comes to the nursery "shriveled like a prune" gets the same unceasing care, it lives to become such an unregenerate, fierce little fellow that the girls call it Doberman because it displays a mouthful of needle-sharp teeth whenever anyone comes near.

Then comes a black lemur,[2] found some hours after its birth lying still in its mother's nesting box, its eyes tightly closed, shrunken, obviously near death. Rushed to the nursery, it is placed in an incubator where every few movements that first night the attendants look to see if it is reviving so they can offer it some nourishment. As the hours pass and one shift of attendants relieves another, the situation remains unchanged. The tiny animal, smaller than a newborn kitten, continues to lie inert. No movement betrays life, not even an occasional expansion and contraction of the chest to indicate breathing. On a routine visit to the nursery, where he has several patients, the duty veterinarian examines the lemur thoroughly and pronounces it dead. But as one of the attendants lifts the little body to place it in a plastic bag for delivery to the pathologist, she feels, or fancies that she feels, a slight stirring. Unconvinced, but knowing the girls' concern for animals they spend so much time trying to save, the vet agrees to leave the infant in the incubator until his next round. Several minutes later the lemur perceptibly moves, striving, it seems, to pull itself forward on the

[2] Only the male black lemurs are actually black. The females are a rufous color. For this reason they were seen as two separate species by the first scientists to classify them.

soft bed of the incubator as though looking for its mother's teats. Using the kind of nursing bottle that little girls get for their dolls, the attendant who first felt it move cajoles the lemur into taking a few swallows of formula. That is the beginning. Within a few days the little prosimian is eating regularly and growing. When the girls know that it will live, they don't have to spend much time deciding on a name. Only one is appropriate. This black lemur is called Lazarus.

When Lazarus grew to young adulthood, he was the size of a small cat, covered with fluffy black fur, and strong enough to live with other lemurs in a special colony near the zoo's hospital. There several species of lemurs are being bred in a program designed to help preserve them, for on Madagascar and some of its adjoining islands, the natural home of lemurs, ancient forests are fast disappearing under the woodman's axe to provide lumber for houses and fuel.

For a year or so Lazarus lived content with others of his kind. Then late one night when the moon was a sliver and darkness enveloped the zoo, a person or persons unknown, but patently a lover of lemurs, climbed the zoo's outer fence, cut through the wire of a large perimeter cage, broke a lock off the cage where Lazarus lived, and kidnapped him. During the next two days the theft of Lazarus caused a stir in the San Diego newspapers and on television. Pictures of the black lemur were shown and Charles Bieler, the zoo director, promised that no questions would be asked if Lazarus were returned unharmed. Privately, though, Bieler and his staff held little hope that their appeals would get results. People who steal animals take them either in hope of gain or more often because they fancy the idea of having exotic pets. Not three years before the disappearance of Lazarus a cheetah cub, one of three in the Animal Care Center of the Wild Animal Park, had been stolen during the night and never heard from, and cheetahs when they grow up are the size of leopards.

Lazarus, however, lived up to his name. His second resurrection took place twenty miles from the zoo in a trash container on an elevator at the headquarters of United States Customs by the multi-gated border crossing between San Diego and Tijuana, Mexico, the busiest border crossing in the world where thousands of people pass through in automobiles or on foot. A custodian entered the elevator and noticed what appeared to be a discarded bag of trash. As he reached for it he heard stirrings and scratchings and saw movements not normally made in inert trash. Hesitant, not knowing what he was getting into, he gingerly opened the bag and looked in. Staring back at him from the depths of his tomb were the intent, unblinking yellow-green eyes of Lazarus lemur.

The aftermath proved the value of publicizing such thefts from zoos.[3] When the custodian took Lazarus, trash bag and all, to the office, one customs official remembered the newspaper and television stories and called the zoo. Lazarus, of course, couldn't tell how he happened to wind up in a trash bag at the border, nor how long he had been there, nor for that matter what had happened to him in the intervening days. He lives now with his companions in the lemur breeding colony. Those who believe in predestination would probably say that he is destined to achieve greatness. If so, it won't be as a father of future black lemurs, except by involuntary contributions in a program of artificial insemination. The sad fact is that Lazarus was so spoiled by all the attention the nursery attendants gave him that he now lacks the grit and determination that a male lemur must have if he is to be successful with females, who tend to be dominant, henpecking types.

The girls who staff zoo nurseries are generally selected because they have had previous experience taking care of animals, at the very least their own horse. Consequently, they have become accustomed to the seamy side of animal husbandry, grooming their charges, coaxing them to eat or take their medicine, cleaning up their messes. If at the start they aren't used to animals dying they soon will be, or they won't last in the job. Yet they never become wholly detached, for those of their charges that survive the first few days of life develop distinctive personalities that often make them immensely engaging and attractive, contributing to a greater sense of loss if they die. If they live, and most wouldn't but for the ministerings of the girls, many of the infant animals become surrogate babies who, when they are grown and on exhibit in the

[3] A survey taken after the Lazarus affair revealed that all United States zoos lose some animals to thieves. Mostly they are cuddly animals or much sought after birds like cockatoos and falcons. All too often such thefts are not reported to the media.

zoo, the girls regularly visit and sometimes worry about, wondering if their new keeper really understands them.

As they acquire personalities the young animals also develop demands and eccentricities that challenge the attendants' patience or ingenuity. Kalind, a young male pygmy chimpanzee, becomes a night animal in the nursery. He prefers to sleep during the day and play or watch television at night, creating the impression in visitors who always see him during the day lying still in his crib, that he is a weak and sickly creature. The girls on the night watch, who are hard put to keep up with his demands for attention, know the truth. Lock and Lisa are day-old twin orangutans. In the nursery Lisa is perfectly content to drink a formula that has worked in the past, but Lock refuses to take his bottle. For several days the worried attendants and the veterinarian think he may have an obstruction in his throat. Finally, after repeated experiments with various new formulas the attendants find one that Lock drinks with such noisy gusto that he seems to be saying, "It's about time. This is what I've been waiting for."

In the drive to reduce the number of neonatal deaths zoo researchers have tried first to identify the principal causes. Prominent among them, curiously enough, is the fact that many baby animals arrive as a complete surprise to all except their mothers, who have managed to conceal their condition. Many female animals do not show their pregnancy because they are covered with hair like a bear or are already fat like a hippopotamus, and they have no way of asking their keepers to go out in the middle of the night and get them pickles and ice cream, or the equivalent in their diets. Quite inconsiderately, they also frequently drop their babies when nobody is around to observe them. Thus, the newly born are sometimes strangled by umbilical cords, crushed by inexperienced mothers, weakened and made susceptible to pneumonia by exposure at birth to cold or rainy weather, or in the case of some carnivores eaten by father or mother. Possibly mother becomes confused as to where the normally eaten afterbirth leaves off and baby begins. More likely though, in the wild father would not be present at birth and mother, secure in some den, has no distractions that cause her to have bad nervous habits.[4]

[4] At the Cologne Zoo, which has had success in breeding polar bears—animals that are often guilty of killing their newborn cubs in a zoo—a

Within large enclosures that have different species of hoofed animals mixed together, there may be an additional danger. Neonates of one species are often deliberately cut down immediately after birth by the sharp hooves of another. When the San Diego Wild Animal Park first exhibited Grevy zebras, they were mixed with other animals, mostly various species of antelope, in the 125-acre East African exhibit. Zoo officials soon found, however, that the Grevy zebra males viciously attacked and killed newly born antelopes. The Grevy zebra herd had to be moved into a separate exhibit.

To detect pregnancies before baby animals are dropped, most zoos have to rely on keepers, who are generally the only people who see their animals several times a day, and are most likely to notice deviations in behavior that indicate either pregnancy or illness. A female becomes secretive and spends more time away from others of her kind, or begins eating more, or develops some idiosyncrasy the keeper has never seen before. Even the best of keepers, however, may overlook or simply not see changes that are significant. Much more promising in the early detection of pregnancies, and consequently in reducing neonatal deaths, is the application of urinalysis in endocrinology labs. So far, though, only one organization, the research department serving both the San Diego Zoo and Wild Animal Park, has such a lab (see page 153).

The most common cause of neonatal deaths in zoos is the exposure of young animals who have not developed natural immunities, to the high concentration of bacteria and viruses present in any zoo, no matter how large or clean. Many of these disease "vectors" have come in with other animals, but several species, particularly among the primates, are susceptible to the full range of human diseases. These are obviously spread in a zoo by visitors and keepers through such normal means as sneezing and coughing and frequently because visitors persist in tossing germ-laden tidbits to the animals.

---

pregnant female is put into a large wooden box in the rear of the enclosure and left there undisturbed. Keepers know when the cubs are born because they hear them, but the crate is not approached until the mother wants to bring her cubs outside for the first time. Everyone walks on tiptoe around that box and speaks in hushed tones.

In trying to protect infant orangutans, chimpanzees, and gorillas, all of whom are particularly susceptible to human diseases like polio, measles, and tuberculosis, those in charge of zoo medicine are divided. Some favor isolation of the infant animals and programs of vaccination, including in some instances the use of gamma globulin; others use vaccination, but prefer to expose the infant apes at an early stage so that like human infants they can build their own immunities. Children visiting the Jersey Zoo are often delighted to discover that they can play with young gorillas, some of them barely able to crawl, on the lawn in front of Gerald Durrell's Les Augrès Manor. Both apes and children are watched carefully by a curator or his wife to make certain that nobody of either species gets too rough with the other, but play often takes the youngsters to all parts of the rather sizable lawn and its surrounding hedges. Allowing the young gorillas to mix so freely with their human counterparts is a deliberate strategy on the part of Durrell and his associates, motivated by the near loss of a young gorilla who had been brought up in isolation and came down with a severe intestinal disorder caused by that omnipresent human intestinal bacteria, *E. coli*, ordinarily harmless, but sometimes a killer.

In addition to keeping their pregnancy a secret and sometimes killing and eating their own babies, zoo mothers, particularly new ones, cannot always be relied upon to handle the responsibilities of motherhood. Among some species the relationship between mother and infant is based almost entirely upon instinct in both. Some of the lower animals, in fact, have no mother-infant relationship. A mother reptile's investment in the future of her children normally ceases when they are hatched or born. From that moment on the young must rely on built-in genetic programs to guide their initial actions, tell them which way the ocean is if they are sea turtles hatched on a beach, or what kind of food to hunt for if they are little snakes. No doubt to some people the process has a lot to commend it.

Higher on the evolutionary scale, hoofed animals raise their young after birth, but once a baby deer or antelope has risen on wobbly legs, it is directed by instinct to mother's teats, and she by instinct knows how to nurse it. Consequently, the problems that zoos may have in keeping young reptiles or hoofed animals alive are infrequently caused by ineffectual mothers.

But somewhere in the evolution of higher mammals the ability to raise young through reliance on instinct was lost and the necessity for learning how to be a parent began. Evolution had created a market for Dr. Spock.

Among captive apes motherhood, beyond the imperative of giving birth, requires an education the females do not always get. Female gorillas, for example, are not instinctively good mothers. They can conceive the infant with the help of a cooperative male and bear it stoically during pregnancy, but after the baby is born, they seem unable to take up the real tasks of motherhood, feeding, fondling, protecting, disciplining. In a troop of wild gorillas these motherly responsibilities are apparently learned by the adolescent females through observation and imitation of experienced mothers and by occasionally baby-sitting their infants. The process is not unlike the child care that human children learn by playing with dolls.

In captivity, however, the inexperienced gorilla mother may bear her infant and then for long hours sit dumbly staring at it as its life ebbs away. Perhaps realizing that she ought to be doing something, she is immobilized by not knowing what. This inability to cope characterized Dolly, a female gorilla at the San Diego Wild Animal Park, after she gave birth to Jim, largest at birth of any gorilla ever born in captivity. The birth occurred in Dolly's bedroom, one of several heavily barred rooms behind the half-acre enclosure in which the gorillas are exhibited at the Park. In keeping with the most frequent timing used by many primates, including man, the birth took place between dusk and dawn, a strategy that in the wild reduces exposure to predators by assuring the cloak of darkness and the presence of protectors. Jim's delivery was uneventful, but afterward Dolly's only further concession to motherhood was to bite through the umbilical cord and eat the afterbirth. That done she displayed no further interest in the infant as he lay several feet away from her on the warm cement floor, helpless, eyes tightly closed, unable to do more than squirm and make small noises.

At moments like this in most large zoos one of the professionals, a curator or veterinarian, has the power to make the critical choice.

He must decide, and be able to back up his decision, whether or not the infant shall be taken from its mother and raised by hand, unless as a matter of policy his zoo always hand-rears baby apes. It is not an easy decision, nor can it be made in haste unless it is clear that the newborn has some defect which requires immediate attention. Moved perhaps by some atavistic compulsion even inexperienced mothers have been known to start nursing their infant after several hours have elapsed. The tension at this time is heightened because the decision maker knows that the loss of an infant gorilla, sad in itself, will probably mean a long wait for another, and an economic loss to the zoo of from $20,000. to $25,000.

At the Wild Animal Park that night Dr. Lester Nelson, a grayheaded, normally calm veterinarian, felt the tension grow as first minutes and then hours passed while Dolly did nothing but sit, exhausted, motionless, looking first at the people and then at the wizened creature lying before her. Finally, with obvious reluctance, Dr. Nelson made his choice.

"We'll raise it by hand."

This simple declaration would begin a long, complicated, and relatively expensive process. Jim would be taken from his birthplace to the Park's Animal Care Center. There for the next year and a half he would become the center of delighted attention from the girl attendants—a kind of locum tenens for the love and affection that they lavished or would like to lavish on their own children. Jim would be cooed over, hugged, petted, and tickled (because he laughed so obviously and happily). Day and night the girls would feed him his formula, burp him, change his diapers, and if he wasn't sleepy, play games with him that would become increasingly rough as he developed both strength and teeth that far surpassed those of a human counterpart at the same age.

It would appear that Jim, pampered and loved, his every physical want cared for, even blessed for a while with an infant orangutan as playmate, was growing up in the best of all possible worlds. Not so, Park officials knew, for sooner or later he would have to go back with the other gorillas, and because of his growing strength, sooner would be better. At the moment of reunion Jim would have to face a stark reality, one that might produce psychological trauma. It boiled down to one question: Could he understand he was a gorilla?

When she was reunited with the gorilla troop, Dolly once more inflamed the passions of Trib, Jim's father, the dominant or silverback male. Within two months his frequent attentions, which she by no means rejected, had her pregnant. This time, Park officials decided, she would have to be given a short course in motherhood. In this decision more was involved than the desirability of having baby animals reared by their own kind to avoid the kind of psychological problems that faced Jim. Dolly's own well-being was at stake, for the gorilla mother that cares for her own infant will normally go three years between pregnancies, a natural, life-prolonging interval, but a female who is "bred back" as Dolly was, may be weakened for lack of recuperation between births to the point of illness and a shorter life than the thirty-five to forty years accorded healthy gorillas.

Selected to be Dolly's mentor in the motherhood course was Steve Joines, a graduate student in animal behavior at San Diego State University. To the unenlightened observer Steve might have appeared a curious choice. A blond male in his early twenties, the size of a football lineman, he was little experienced in animal husbandry and would obviously have to approach the teaching of motherhood as a theorist, not a practitioner.

He began with the air of one who knew precisely how to proceed. After he had searched the literature, both about wild gorillas and techniques of animal training, he sought to ingratiate himself with Dolly by spending many hours with her when she was in the bedroom. Separated by the formidable bars between bedroom and service corridor, he and Dolly at last reached the point of delicate (on both their parts) hand holding. This phase of the training could not take as long as Steve might have wished, for time, Dolly's increasing girth told him, was not on his side.

The first attempt at actual teaching was a failure. There had been reports in the literature that primates showed some evidence of "monkey see, monkey do" learning when they watched motion pictures or television of sexual acts, for example. Steve borrowed a film that depicted in exhaustive repetition the daily routine of a gorilla mother caring for her infant at the San Francisco Zoo. However, attention span, that old bugaboo in all education, proved an obstacle. When the pictures were projected in bright detail against the pale yellow sides of Dolly's bedroom, she watched

them for a few moments with mild curiosity—it was, after all, a new experience—but then she turned away in apparent boredom. Perhaps, Steve felt, she did not accept as real the flickering shadows on the wall of her cave.

Because haste was required, Steve discarded further experimentation with audiovisual aids and reverted to techniques of an earlier time, reward for tasks well done and punishment for those that are muffed. He decided, in short, that Dolly would have to learn motherhood by the numbers, with him as the drill sergeant. Keepers told him that Dolly's favorite delicacies were Natal plums (which grow in the Park) and soy beans, neither included in her regular diet, but occasionally given as tidbits. These became his rewards for obedience. Since one does not spank or otherwise physically punish a two-hundred-pound gorilla, Steve concluded on the basis of their hand-holding relationship that his reprimands would have to be expressions of extreme disappointment—Dolly, how could you—and, of course, he would withhold the rewards whenever she failed to obey.

As a simulated baby Steve chose a pillow, soft, easily grasped, and with a tough cover that was relatively indestructible. Dolly seemed perfectly content to take it from him, and it was not long before he could place it on the floor of her bedroom, order her to "pick up the baby," and if she obeyed, give her a Natal plum or soy bean. Seldom did he have to speak sharply or withhold rewards. The next command, however, was more difficult. "Show me the baby" was designed to help the veterinarians inspect the new baby, determine its sex, and detect possible defects or ailments that might require immediate attention. Obedience to the command meant Dolly would hold the baby out at arm's length toward the bars of her bedroom. It was a difficult command for her to learn, since it was less natural than holding a baby to the breast. In the end, though, Dolly got the hang of it, apparently seeing the gesture as part of a game that she and Steve were playing.

The third command, "be nice to the baby," meant that Dolly had to perform two simultaneous actions, hold the pillow to her breast and pat it gently. By now Dolly was catching on to the system well enough to realize that faster response brought more frequent plums and soy beans. Soon she knew how to be nice to the baby.

Satisfied that Dolly had mastered the fundamentals, Steve carefully reviewed his approach for possible flaws. It seemed as though nothing had been left to chance . . . He paused. Projected on his mind's eye was the shocking specter of failure. In vivid detail he saw a well-intentioned Dolly holding the infant gorilla to her breast just as he had commanded, but with its little head dangling, and its naked bottom up. His training aid, the pillow, held no key to the difference between head and tail. He resolved, therefore, that he would have to teach Dolly a fourth command, no longer with the pillow, but employing a simulated gorilla that had a clearly distinguishable head and tail. The first stand-in was a stuffed gorilla from the Park's gift shop. This, for some reason, Dolly rejected utterly and unmistakably by hurling it to the floor, a gesture with implications that caused Steve to shudder inwardly. Determined, he made his own doll, an awkward, primitive toy that an untutored but loving pioneer farmer might have fashioned for his daughter. Although it bore no resemblance to a gorilla, or to any other living creature, it did have arms, legs, and a head. Best of all, Dolly liked it, although true to Steve's vision she sometimes picked it up the wrong way. For this reason he was glad to teach her the fourth command, "turn the baby," which told Dolly to reverse head and tail at her breast. When she had mastered this move, after an appropriate number of Natal plums and soy beans, Steve believed his student was ready, and with precious little time to spare.

On the night Dolly's labor began, Steve was there by her side, speaking soothingly to her, trying to comfort her, but not holding her hand, since during labor pains she might accidentally squeeze his a bit too hard. In the way of second babies, this one came faster than the first. Once more Dolly bit through the umbilical cord, ate the afterbirth, and left the infant on the floor. It was time now for the test of three months' dedication. As though he were talking about the doll, Steve gave the command, "Pick up the baby." There was a flicker of hesitation, but Dolly had been well taught. She grasped the infant in one big hand, took it up from the floor, and clutched it to her breast right side up. Taking a breath, Steve gave the next command. "Show me the baby." Obediently Dolly held it out toward Steve and the nearby Dr.

Nelson. It was a girl, a well-formed gorilla female apparently in perfect health.

Named Binti, the new arrival was thereafter cared for by Dolly, who needed no more commands, but who from time to time in the days immediately after the birth practiced a little extortion on Steve and her keeper. They swore that her eyes glinted maliciously as she made a show of being nice, excessively nice, to the baby. Holding Binti to her breast as she had been taught, she would start patting the infant, gradually increasing the tempo and sharpness of the pats until she was rewarded with Natal plum or soy bean. As time passed her motherly affection triumphed over racketeering and Binti has grown under an umbrella of proper gorilla love.

Major attention now went to Jim, spoiled, lovable, increasingly strong Jim. The time had come to deal with what Park staffers sometimes called the reentry problem, the problem of accustoming Jim to his own kind. He had to face the possibly startling fact that he was a gorilla. Up to this point he had no inkling. Raised by humans and with an orangutan as playmate, how could he know? There wasn't even a mirror for him to note the difference between him and those around himself if, in his happiness, he would have noted it.

The problem Jim faced is a serious one in the husbandry of wildlife. Deprived of their natural mothers, young animals develop fixations on human "parents." The process, demonstrated quite dramatically by Konrad Lorenz and the goslings that followed him because he was the first object they saw after hatching, is called imprinting. In a surprising number of species young wild animals become imprinted by a particular person, frequently their keeper, if that person acts as a stand-in mother. With all the problems posed by imprinted animals, however, most zoo professionals believe that animals raised in an atmosphere of tender, loving care are much better off than those left in isolation if their own mother can't or won't raise them. The more serious difficulties arise when the hand-raised animal approaches sexual maturity after he has been placed once again with its own kind. Very few of the higher animals are immune to sexual hang-ups that spring from their fixation on a particular human being as a love object, if one can use that expression. There are some zoo men who believe that the failure of zoos to breed the fascinating shoebill in captivity may arise partly from the fact that these large stork-like birds with a head like a size twelve man's wooden shoe are generally acquired singly and tend to become rapidly attached to their keepers, often ignoring members of their own species that are introduced later as companions or mates.

Yet if the effective captive breeding of wild animals by zoos is to be called successful, all available resources will have to be used, including animals made abnormal by imprinting on humans. Increasingly, situations arise where the only obtainable male or female for a breeding program may be an imprinted animal. For this reason the peculiar problems of sexual neurosis in hand-raised animals will have to be solved, perhaps in some instances through carefully tailored programs in behavior modification.

Possibly, because of their similarities to people, young primates like Jim have a greater tendency to be imprinted by human foster mothers than other animals, and may find it extremely difficult to adjust, or win acceptance, when they once again must go among their own kind. The problem seems to be more pronounced in females, who don't receive the education from their foster parents they would get from being raised with well-adjusted members of their own species. Among gorillas particularly, well brought up young ladies learn the obedience and acquiescence to the will of their master that turns male gorillas on. Feminists can make of this what they will, but according to many knowledgeable observers, hand-raised female gorillas usually develop an independent nature which, when they are out with their own kind, leads them to believe they can willfully reject an amorous male. In a gorilla troop there is no room for disdainful females. Among human beings pursuit may be half the fun of eventual seduction and the hard-to-get female all the more desirable, but for male gorillas the ideal mate is apparently a gal who can't say no and doesn't try. For the record, however, it should be stated that hand-raised males may develop their own hang-ups—a morose nature, ineptitude in sex, or a difference in behavior that causes them to be rejected by others of their kind.

When Park officials decided that Jim, aged one and a half, would have to rejoin the gorilla troop, their greatest worry was

that he would run afoul of his mighty father, Trib. From many years of living with and observing wild gorillas, primatologist Dian Fossey has concluded that the key to normal development in a young male is the fathering he gets from the troop's dominant male or silverback after the youngster is a year or so old. But the father-son relationship is not always one of pats on the head and fishing trips together. It appears that some, if not all, silverbacks may be the equivalent of human fathers who beat their children. On apparently infrequent occasions a particular silverback may inexplicably run amok. Then woe betide any of his troop that gets in the way. Miss Fossey found to her horror that on these occasions young males may be killed by the silverback. She made the discovery by running across the skeleton of a very young male in the gorilla's jungle habitat. Death had come to this youngster from a tooth, a fang really, imbedded in its skull. Miss Fossey's first thought was leopard, since leopards are about the only local predator that might kill a small gorilla, but when she compared the fang with others in her collection she found it had come from a large male gorilla.

Even if Trib didn't deliberately attack Jim, a single cuff delivered with too much force could injure the youngster for life. Possessed of two or three times the strength of a Russian weight lifter and a good deal more agility, Trib stood over six feet tall and weighed close to 400 pounds. Jim, on the other hand, was about the size and weight of a three- or four-year-old child.

It should be noted that some zoos regularly, as a matter of policy, take infant apes from their mothers, hand-raise them, and routinely reintroduce them to others on exhibit. Most youngsters quickly adjust, but the risk is always there. Because Jim would grow to be a valuable animal and, Park staffers hoped, carry on as a breeding male when Trib had passed his prime, it was thought best to minimize all risks.

As a first step in reintroducing Jim, his nurses at the Animal Care Center began carrying him in their arms over to the bedrooms behind the gorilla exhibit. The idea was to let him see his kin and they him. Focal point in this visual acclimatization was Vila, a female who could best be described as Jim's aunt. Normally he would have been reintroduced through his mother, but

Dolly was busy caring for Binti, another relationship in which the possibility of trouble for Jim existed. Suppose, for example, that Dolly saw the rough-and-tumble Jim as a threat to Binti? She knew for certain that Binti was her daughter, but would she know that Jim was her son?

After a few days of repeated trips from nursery to bedrooms, Jim had apparently begun to accept the fact that other gorillas were nice creatures, not so different really, save in their manner of dress, from the creatures that had raised him. One day he reached an exploring hand through the bars to touch Vila. When she didn't draw back or show any signs of rejection, zoo staffers knew that the time had come for stage two. Jim was moved permanently from the Animal Care Center into a bedroom with his aunt. Kept away from the other gorillas for several days, the two soon became friends. Vila looked on fondly while Jim frolicked, and indulged him from time to time by joining his games.

The next step, which involved some breath holding by zoo staffers, was to put Jim and Vila with Dolly and Binti in a large sun room adjoining the bedrooms behind the gorilla exhibit. For all Dolly knew Jim could have been Vila's son. She showed no concern or worry about Binti, and soon brother and sister were playing together.

The introduction of Jim to his father turned out to be the easiest part. Jim was simply loosed into the main part of the gorilla enclosure along with Vila, Dolly, Binti, and from his separate bedroom, Trib. This enclosure is about two thirds the size of a football field, affording numerous opportunities for a chased gorilla to escape its pursuer. At one end is a log structure designed to allow the gorillas both play and shade from the hot summer sun. Various log pillars and screens give the animals plenty of opportunity for artful dodging. Nevertheless, Park veterinarians were ready with a dart gun if Trib made any move to threaten Jim. There was no threat. Possibly Trib, secure in his leadership, didn't even bother to review his troop every morning, so the addition of a juvenile meant nothing. Who, he might have asked, is counting? Nor did Jim in any way show fear of his father. He had been raised with affection by the girls at the animal care center, his aunt and mother were, if not affectionate, certainly kind

and indulgent. He did not expect to be harmed, and he wasn't. The troop had accepted him and he the troop.[5]

Jim did have a comeuppance of sorts sometime later, but the cause was not another gorilla. One day two geese flew into the gorilla enclosure, landed, and proceeded to pick at the grass that covers it. The birds fascinated both young gorillas, and Jim, the bolder, who expected no harm, went over to investigate closer. When he was a few feet away, the gander, not to be run off, lunged at Jim the way geese sometimes take after children in a park, hissing and fluttering their wings while they charge. If gorillas can turn pale, Jim did at that instant. He may have been more astounded than frightened, for never in his life had a living creature threatened him. Tumbling backward he got tangled with his own feet, finally righted himself and scooted off on all fours to the comforting arms of his aunt. Shortly after, the geese departed and the incident was forgotten.

No accountant kept track of the costs involved in hand-raising Jim, to say nothing of the labor that went into teaching him he was a gorilla. Quite obviously these costs were far greater than they would have been had Jim been raised by his own mother, for the hundreds of hours spent by staffers at the Park's Animal Care Center would not have been required, nor for that matter would the vast quantities of milk for his formula. It is ironic that Jim's sister, Binti, who would fetch far more in the open market, incurred perhaps a tenth of the costs.

Zoos, of course, use standard accounting practices. They know that day-to-day costs of administration, labor, and food, and can tell the average costs of feeding any given species. One gorilla, a vegetarian, eats about $500 in food a year, far less than a lion or tiger at $1,800 because meat is more expensive. However, the only project accounting done by zoos is on the construction of individual exhibits and buildings, not on hand-raising a particular young animal. The fact is, such costs don't normally enter a zoo director's mind. If asked, a director would probably state that

---

[5] He later developed the annoying habit of pulling hairs from his head one by one until he grew quite bald. This behavior did not seem to spring from boredom, for he and Binti played together constantly.

zoos have a moral obligation to give the best possible care to the creatures they keep, and if mothers won't care for their own babies then somebody has to.

The increased need for research into ways to prevent neonatal deaths, in developing intensive care units for nurseries (or nurseries themselves), and using behavioral engineering techniques to train both inexperienced mothers and hand-raised children in the habits of their own species—all of these will continue to impose a greater burden of cost on the modern major zoos. But the cost, most zoo directors agree, will have to be borne if they are to be successful as the last preserves for many endangered species.

The Frozen Zoo

I n the research laboratories of the San Diego Zoo stands a large metal container identified by a brass plate as "The Frozen Zoo." What the frozen zoo holds is material invaluable to today's research and the possible key to reconstructing and bringing back to life animals like the woolly mammoth that have long been extinct.

Straight out of science fiction, the idea of reviving a once extinct species is not as far fetched as it sounds, according to Dr. Kurt Benirschke, director of research at San Diego, formerly chairman of the Department of Pathology for the University of California at San Diego School of Medicine. Recombinant DNA, which would be employed in the process, was itself once only a dream. Now scientists in many laboratories are recombining DNA particles from different animals to create new forms of life and rapidly advancing men's knowledge about the origins and nature of life itself.

Actually, the frozen zoo is a deep freezer—a very deep freeze— that uses liquid nitrogen to maintain constant temperatures around $-122°$ C. $(-250°$ F.). In this extreme cold living cells, including spermatozoa, can be kept alive indefinitely. The principle has been used since the 1950s to keep alive the semen of domestic livestock for artificial insemination—and more recently of human males who pay to commercial sperm banks the money required to get the comforting feeling of immortality that comes from the knowledge that one's stored but still living sperm can make one a father 100 years after death.

The charismatic Dr. Benirschke, a lean, energetic man in his middle fifties, kept his own personal frozen zoo for many years, collecting living cells from a variety of animal species, including such highly endangered creatures as the blue whale, the largest animal on earth. However, containers of this kind, unless carefully safeguarded by alarm signals that will be instantly heeded, sometimes spill the liquid nitrogen. When this happens the living cells stored in them soon die. The thought of a liquid nitrogen spill destroying his previous collection of rare animal cells gnawed at Dr. Benirschke. Moreover, he could never escape the knowledge that he, a mortal man, had no way of insuring that the collection would be faithfully maintained after he died. Loving wives and children might not fully appreciate a bequest left in an otherwise normal will that assigned them a cell bank to be maintained in perpetuity. It would be better, Dr. Benirschke knew, to make his frozen zoo the property of an institution with an existence independent of the life-spans of men. That was achieved when he accepted the position offered by the San Diego Zoo and persuaded its director and trustees that the cell bank, now so big that it requires new containers, would become an invaluable adjunct in any program designed to propagate and preserve rare and endangered animal species.

The process of freezing living tissue at cryogenic temperatures is called "cryonics." Some of the initial impetus in cryonics came from another idea of science fiction that frozen living bodies might remain in a state of suspended animation for indefinite periods, the time, say, it takes a rocket to go from earth to Alpha Centauri. Those who sought ways to trick death also held out the hope that their temporarily deceased bodies, quickly frozen before deterioration had begun, might one day in the future be resurrected by trusted descendants who had learned the techniques of restoring life.

Men had seen, after all, nearly perfect specimens of woolly mammoths, extinct some 10,000 years, that had been taken from nature's deep freeze, ice or frozen tundra in the far north of Siberia. So lifelike were some that it seemed as though they were sleeping and needed hardly more than the injection of some drug and a few moments by a warm fire to come to life. Even more exciting, a kind of amphibian called triton had been found in the permafrost near Yakutsk, Siberia, at a depth of thirty-six feet. This animal was determined by radiocarbon analysis to have been

frozen for 90 years. Yet after it was thawed, it revived and went on to produce healthy offspring during the remaining six months of its life.

It was men like Dr. Benirschke whose primary interest as a scientist is cytogenetics—the study of the nature and constituents of chromosomes—who pointed out that freezing whole bodies was inefficient and space consuming. Instead, these men advised, freeze living cells taken from skin or liver, for in each cell of any living creature is a genetic code carrying the same complex set of instructions that formed and shaped the original body and programed some of its behavior. Theoretically, one could take such a cell from an animal, no matter how large or how small, and recombine the elements to create a fertilized egg which could then be surgically implanted in the womb of a stand-in mother. From that point on nature would take over, from egg to embryo to birth. But no matter from what species the stand-in mother came, provided she was closely enough related, from the same genus, for example, the emerging baby would be the species from which the original cell sample had been taken. In the hearts of most scientists with this knowledge lies the secret hope, sometimes spoken, that one day in Siberia another frozen mammoth will be found with living cells in its body. Then through cloning scientists could produce a fertilized egg, implant it in the womb of an Indian elephant, and there would once again be born a genuine woolly mammoth.[1]

San Diego's frozen zoo already holds living cells from over 400 species representing 15 different classes of animals. These might one day be the last hope of saving such species as douc langurs, orangutans, gorillas, Sumatran rhinos, tan-handed titis, maned wolves, and many more whose cells are included in the bank. If zoos become the final reserves of many species, cryonic banks, the frozen zoos, will represent the last desperate stand.

The frozen zoo does not, however, function solely as a safe-deposit box. Cell samples are used almost daily in the important research on genetics that is part of the San Diego Zoo's total research effort, which gets its thrust from the twin objective of

[1] For those interested in personal immortality cloning offers little hope. Replicated creatures will carry no memories of the body from which the living cells were taken.

improving health and reproduction of captive animals. Much of the genetic study done by Dr. Benirschke and his associates is devoted to chromosomes, specifically to karyotypes, the chromosomal key to an animal species that distinguishes it from all others.

In spite of all the years that have passed since Linnaeus first proposed his method of plant and animal classification, the proper identification of species is far from complete, and much of what has been done is wrong. Spider monkeys, the gangly primates from Mexican, Central and South American jungles, have been jumbled together in zoo exhibits for years on the general assumption that they were all pretty much alike, with perhaps some subspecific variance. Their cell structures, though, reveal that they are not all alike. Differences are sometimes so great that no effective reproduction could be sustained in a mixed captive breeding group, for to achieve sustained propagation, like must be with like. In Hagenbeck's day some zoo men delighted in experimenting with crossbreeding. Lions and tigers produced either tigons or ligers, depending on who the father and the mother were. But the offspring, like mules, have not produced young. The offspring of less obvious crosses or of what have long been incorrectly assumed to be members of the same species, like Galapagos tortoises, may propagate, but in most instances the rate of reproduction slows until finally, one day, it stops—hardly the desirable end of a program designed to save an animal species from extinction.

Studies of chromosomes are also used by San Diego to ferret out animals with genetic "errors," which in otherwise virile or fecund animals cause a high proportion of malformed young or fetal deaths and miscarriages. Jack, a handsome, dominant male douc langur monkey in one San Diego troop, carries rearranged genes. Of the young Jack sires, half will die before or shortly after birth. Armed with this certain knowledge, Mark Bogart, San Diego's young primatologist, can further the amorous case of other male doucs and push Jack into a premature retirement. In the herd of the beautiful Soemmerring's gazelles in Busch Gardens, Tampa, Florida, there was excessive mortality from stillbirth. When San Diego acquired two females from Tampa for its herd at the Wild Animal Park, a study of their chromosomes revealed several anomalies. One female had 35 and the other 36, where both should have had the latter. Moreover, there was a wider difference

in some of the constituents. These anomalies, the San Diego researchers suggest, may help explain the mortality, although their discovery is probably only the first clue in what has to be an intensive job of detection.

Still another objective of genetic studies seems at first blush to be a curious one. Analysis of chromosomes is used to determine the difference between male and female animals. Nature, unfortunately, is not consistent in displaying that difference externally. In some species, called dimorphic, males and females have easily discernible differences in colors, sizes, shapes, or styles of plumage. Other species, called monomorphic, look exactly alike as mature animals. This characteristic, of course, poses serious difficulties for anyone trying to breed them. The breeder must either wait until one of the monomorphic animals gives a clear-cut indication of its sex—by laying an egg, for example—or throw the animals together in the hope that the boys will find their way to the girls, an approach that doesn't always work because some animals will only mate in pairs isolated from others of their kind. The whole process of telling boy from girl can be sped up through a fairly quick analysis of sex chromosomes.[2] In female mammals these chromosomes look like an X. The sex chromosome in males consists of one X and another element designated Y.

However, since chasing after and restraining animals to take, painlessly, the cell samples necessary for analysis of chromosomes may cause traumas, San Diego researchers have turned to other methods of telling the sex of birds that are monomorphic, about 20 to 30 percent of all species. For this breakthrough, another lab came into play. Directed by a young, handsome, curly-headed Ph.D., Bill Lasley, the San Diego endocrinology lab was the first to be established by a zoo. The lab started with urine studies, but as an outgrowth of these got involved in the ambiguous world of telling the sex of birds, which as any fancier knows, do the business of expelling wastes quite efficiently by combining both urine and feces in a single release. Talking about this fact one day, Dr. Lasley and one of his lab technicians, Nancy Czekala, speculated that analysis of the sex hormones discharged with bird droppings might divulge the sex of any given bird. More exactly, they

[2] Sports enthusiasts will recall that officials in the last Olympic Games used analysis of chromosomes to be certain that girl athletes were in fact girls.

posited the theory that a discernible difference between the amount of estrogen (female sex hormone) and testosterone (male sex hormone) would point to gender. Their resultant studies, confirmed by analysis of chromosomes, dissection of birds that had died, and matching results against the known sexes of dimorphic birds, showed that the key to telling male from female bird is a ratio between estrogen and testosterone, since both are present in any bird. Once birds have reached adulthood when sex hormones are present, the male birds have a lower ratio of estrogen to testosterone than the females. The method, which has been proved correct in nearly every case, may eventually be even more valuable to bird breeders by telling them which male birds will become the most potent breeders, for apparently those with the lowest ratio of estrogen to testosterone would, if they were professional football players, talk in the lowest voices, walk with the most suggestive swaggers, and have the most girls clamoring after them.

What Dr. Lasley has found to date is that determination of pregnancy through urinalysis works very much the same on animals as it does on humans, particularly when apes and monkeys are the subjects. By now Dr. Lasley has studied enough species from different animal families—antelope, rhino, giraffe, horses, deer, cats—to convince him that urinalysis will become an indispensable tool in captive breeding programs. The problem lies in telling what changes in urine content signal pregnancy for any given species of animal, for the signals vary from species to species. Having to break new ground each time he does a urinalysis on a previously untested species, and generally from a single sample, Dr. Lasley has to extrapolate from knowledge he has gained on other species. As a result he has become a master of limbsmanship. He does his tests, makes his prognosis, and waits with crossed fingers and silent prayer to see if he was right. Most often he has been.

When Dr. Lasley and his associates first set out to get samples for urinalysis there were occasional misunderstandings with keepers, some of whom tended to view requests that they collect urine from their charges with some distaste. "What am I supposed to do?" asked one frustrated keeper at the Wild Animal Park, "follow that damned rhino around one-hundred acres with a

bucket?" Affable and persuasive, Dr. Lasley soon convinced him that the task was not that difficult. As long as the keeper personally saw the rhino urinate and got there while the ground was still saturated a trowel full of mud would do very nicely.

The degree of sophistication that techniques used in human medicine can bring to veterinary medicine in a zoo was exemplified in 1977 by two cases, both involving Caesarean operations, one to save a mother's life and the other to save a baby.

At the San Diego Zoo a female douc langur, Xuan, was expecting. Among monkey fanciers many believe that the douc langur (douc is Vietnamese for monkey) is the most beautiful of all. Native to Southeast Asia, the doucs are fine featured, with clear skin on their cheeks and slightly up-slanting eyes that impart an Oriental appearance. As doucs sit grooming one another they seem like human primitives gathered at the end of the day. They were among the many victims of the Vietnamese War because of the ceaseless bombing and spraying of chemical defoliants on their native jungles, which also concealed the soldiers, guerrillas, and civilians who sometimes shot them for food.

Few doucs exist in zoos. The largest troops are at Cologne, Basel, Stuttgart, and San Diego. San Diego actually has two troops, thanks in part to the generosity of the Gladys Porter Zoo in Brownsville, Texas, the director and board of which decided that the future of the doucs was more important than keeping their four females after the last male had died. All four went to San Diego, two through outright sale and two on breeding loan against the day when propagation might bring Brownsville another troop with a male.

Viewing their doucs the way a gem dealer would a collection of fine diamonds, the vets and research staff at San Diego, assisted by such civilian experts on the doucs as Dr. Lois Lippold, a professor of anthropology at San Diego State University, carefully monitored the langurs' health and behavior. Keepers regularly collected urine samples from the females, particularly when they were pregnant. It was from a routine urinalysis on the expectant mother, Xuan, that Dr. Lasley found evidence which shook him. It showed that Xuan's unborn infant had died.

If Dr. Lasley had correctly interpreted the evidence in Xuan's urine, and the right actions were taken, then a new dimension would be added to the usefulness of the endocrinology lab. Technicians could provide early warning to vets that would enable them to save precious females with dead fetuses before those females sickened and died. At a hastily assembled conference Dr. Lasley stated his recommendation in a voice he hoped was firmer than his conviction at the time. Xuan's unborn baby is dead. Operate immediately to save the mother. Whether or not the vets were skeptical, they had already seen enough proof of the value of the endocrinology lab to heed Dr. Lasley's advice. Xuan was immediately rushed to surgery and a Caesarean performed which proved that Dr. Lasley had been correct about the dead fetus. Xuan, sick for a while, soon recovered, and a year later gave birth to a healthy baby, again through a Caesarean. In both instances, incidentally, Xuan's mate had been Jack, the male douc with the rearranged genes.

At the Los Angeles Zoo a female gorilla named Ellie was pregnant for the fourth time. Ellie was perfectly capable of giving birth without incident as she had done three times before. What concerned the Los Angeles officials was a nasty habit Ellie had developed. Ordinarily a pleasant-dispositioned, gentle lady, she had developed an attitude toward her offspring that was positively Medean. She regularly gave birth to them, cleaned them, and then killed them rather horribly by mutilating their faces. She was also prone to make the situation more difficult for her handlers by refusing to surrender the corpses. Because one does not try to take anything, including dead babies, away from an alert, female gorilla, she had to be knocked out with drugs before the dead infants could be retrieved from her sleeping quarters.

When Ellie's fourth pregnancy was discovered, the Los Angeles officials, notably Dr. Warren Thomas, the director, and Dr. Gerald N. Esra, the chief of veterinary services, huddled to discuss the alternatives they could use to keep this baby alive. These boiled down to three. They could let Ellie bear the baby, knock her out with a capture gun and take the baby to be hand-raised. They could anesthetize Ellie a few hours before the baby was due and induce labor artificially while she was under. Or they could anesthetize Ellie when birth was imminent and take the baby through a Caesarean.

The first alternative was discarded as being too risky for every-

body, Ellie, the baby, and zoo personnel who would have to enter the sleeping quarters to get the baby while Ellie presumably slept. They knew they would have to wait until the baby was actually expelled before they used the capture gun, which meant that Ellie might have time to injure the baby before she went under. Moreover, as Dr. Sedgwick's experience with the tiger had shown, the depth of an animal's sleep under drugs may vary from time to time, further adding to the risk of having to retrieve the baby before Ellie killed it.

The second alternative was also too uncertain. If labor couldn't be induced rapidly enough, they might have to give Ellie more anesthetic to keep her under (or otherwise have on their hands a dopey, confused, and irritated gorilla awakening to find several men manipulating her abdomen). Moreover, if labor couldn't be induced, they would have to do a Caesarean, only under circumstances that made it an emergency rather than a planned operation.

That left the planned Caesarean as the best alternative. The decision was made easier because Dr. Esra was aware of a new technique of monitoring pregnancies in humans that had been developed by Dr. Louis Gluck, head of the department of neonatology, University of California School of Medicine, San Diego. For obstetrical surgeons a touchy aspect in performing Caesareans had always been timing the operation. Ideally the Caesarean baby should enter the world at the very moment he would in natural childbirth. Dr. Gluck, a pioneer and innovator in designing techniques and equipment to save both human babies and their mothers, had found a way of timing Caesareans so that the operation would coincide with the almost exact time the baby would have arrived naturally. His method, first published in 1971, requires drawing some amniotic fluid from the mother's womb in the period immediately before birth. The fluid is analyzed to determine the amount of phospholipids present. When these lipids show a sharp rise from their normal level, an indication that the baby's lungs are fully expanded, birth is near.

In researching the method Dr. Gluck used rhesus monkeys. Consequently both he and Dr. Esra knew that it stood a good chance of working on other primates, even though it had never been tried on a gorilla. Dr. Esra knew roughly when Ellie had conceived. Counting down and leaving a margin for error he drew amniotic fluid shortly before the baby was due. One day late in Ellie's term, the phospholipids in her amniotic fluid rose sharply, signaling that birth was near. Ellie was drugged, taken to surgery, and a strong, healthy male baby was delivered by Caesarean and immediately taken to the nursery to be hand-raised, receiving, logically enough, the name Caesar. Ellie herself recovered without complication and was allowed to rejoin three other females and two males in one of Los Angeles's two attractive gorilla exhibits. She will, it appears, be able to have at least one more baby.

Contrary to the suspicions of some conservationists and antivivisectionists, who entertain dark thoughts about what happens to the animals in zoo research programs, those few zoos that fund research—notably London, Antwerp, East Berlin, New York, Washington, Philadelphia, Brookfield, Oklahoma City, Portland, and San Diego—are seeking to improve the health, welfare, and reproduction of captive animals. So sensitive are some of the major United States zoos to possible complaints about the use of animals in research that two of them, New York and San Diego, have written policy directives that forbid curators from selling any animal to centers where they might be used in biomedical research.[3]

In the United States the three zoos with the largest research budgets, New York, Washington, and San Diego, have approached research along differing, though complementary lines that reflect the convictions of directors and principal investigators. New York backs an astounding number of field studies, mostly in the tropics of Africa, Asia, and the Americas. It can be said quite truthfully that the sun never sets on New York research. Independent investigators with grants from the New York Zoological Society may be studying crocodiles in Yucatan, buzzards in Tanzania, or swamp deer in India. Many of these studies have achieved a measure of fame. From George Schaller's work on mountain gorillas, lions, and tigers have come both scientific and popular books that markedly expanded human knowledge of everything from food

[3] The same directive also forbids sale of animals to pet dealers or circuses. Recently, the American Association of Zoological Parks and Aquariums dropped the word "research" from its logo and urged all members to do the same.

preferences to sexual antics of animals. Animals were observed over many weeks by this patient investigator willing to undergo dangers and hardships while following animals around in the places where they live. Much of the drive behind New York's sponsorship of field research has stemmed from the zoo's director, William Conway, who was convinced several years ago that field studies of animals should be conducted before wilderness areas were closed out or wild animal populations reduced to the last few survivors. Foreseeing the need for captive breeding to save rare and endangered animals, Conway also foresaw the desirability of learning as much as possible about the natural behavior of creatures that might become the subjects of captive breeding.

Studies of behavior also characterize the research programs of the Washington Zoo and its 4,000-acre breeding reserve at Front Royal, Virginia. At Washington, however, these studies focus on the captive behavior of species the zoo officials are breeding or hope to breed. Drs. Devra Kleiman and John Eisenberg (a husband and wife team) have made considerable progress in adjusting breeding programs to the behavioral requirements of such animals as the lesser panda and golden lion tamarin, both of which have previously bred in zoos, but never with the regularity and predictability that must characterize successful captive propagation.

Although not as spectacular, nor as well publicized, as its bear-sized cousin, the giant panda, the lesser panda is seen by some animal lovers as the more beautiful. Somewhat like a raccoon in size and general appearance, this animal from the lower slopes of the Himalayas is covered with long, fine, auburn-red hair. The bushy tail, as long as the body, is also auburn, but with faint white bands. An inquisitive, foxy face is highlighted by pure white on ears, nose, and a comet-shaped stripe extending back from the eyes. Its poetic Chinese name, fire fox, seems apt and descriptive.

Lesser pandas have been kept in zoos for many years. But no sustained breeding had been achieved until the researchers at Washington found a single idiosyncrasy of female pandas with young. The mother will be frustrated to the point of losing interest in her offspring unless she can move them from one den to another several times between birth and weaning. A female lesser panda can be made content in captivity if she is provided with two or more separate dens, which can be anything from a dog house to a hollow log. The distance between dens need not be great, but their presence apparently gives the female the comforting illusion that she will be able to confound whatever predators are after her young. By periodically moving her cubs, which come one to four in a litter, she plays a shell game that keeps potential enemies guessing which den she is using.

The golden lion tamarin, a tiny monkey from a limited coastal area near Rio de Janeiro, Brazil, is now endangered, largely because its jungle habitats are disappearing to make way for urban development. It was first threatened because fashionable ladies in eighteenth-century France admired its cuteness, the squirrel-sized body covered with luxuriant golden hair and an appealing humanoid face framed by a lion's mane. Madame de Pompadour had one which was referred to as *le petit singe lion*. With such royal patronage to introduce them, the little animals soon became favorites of the pet trade.

Few golden lion tamarins have been successfully bred in zoos. Those that produced offspring either had a large number of abortions and stillbirths or they ignored, abused, or inadvertently killed their young. As a result of this record, and the prohibition against importing them, their numbers in zoos have now dwindled to the point where only the Washington, Brookfield, Oklahoma City, and Los Angeles zoos have groups large enough to have successfully bred them. Of these the largest, some 30 animals, is at Washington. Early in their intensive studies of these tamarins the Washington researchers, led by slender, dark haired Dr. Kleiman, who agonizes over the uncertain future of this species, found that the reason for so many infant deaths was ignorant parents. To become good mothers female golden lion tamarins, before they are sexually mature, must gain experience by caring for younger brothers and sisters. This training, however, cannot be too long protracted. Nature tends to exact penalties from creatures that are reluctant to leave the home fires and go forth into the world. A female golden lion tamarin who stays with her parents and siblings too long— beyond four or five years—will probably never achieve sexual maturity. She is, in short, caught between two stools, the requirement for learning and the necessity to go out and apply that learning if her species is to survive.

The research at Washington also disclosed that diets of fruits

and other carbohydrates which had been fed to golden lion tamarins in zoos were inadequate. Breeding was improved by changing to diets heavy in proteins.

San Diego's current research program was projected in a white paper issued by Dr. Benirschke after several meetings with staff members, trustees, and scientists. During the first year, genetic and endocrinology labs were to be established. These were to be followed by a virology laboratory, all now a reality. Rounding out the research department will be a behavioral lab. Dr. Benirschke is convinced that the identification and control of disease vectors (viruses, bacteria, and parasites) is of critical importance if enlarging populations of captive animals are to be kept healthy in zoos. At best, he points out, zoos and safari parks are crowded places compared to the wild habitats from which the animals originally came, and because every animal that enters a zoo carries some bug, the threat of disease becoming epidemic is constant. Nor do animals have to be in contact with one another to spread diseases. Staff members, particularly keepers, can pick up viruses or bacteria on shoes and clothing and carry them unknowingly from exhibit to exhibit. Moreover, some disease vectors remain present in any enclosure where animals have once been housed. In the wild these vectors could be diffused, suppressed by natural loam, or purged by periodic fires. In zoos they remain a lurking threat, not so much to older animals that have built up immunities, but to the newborn and very young. The San Diego Wild Animal Park lost two slightly premature infant Indian rhinos within two or three days after birth to the omnipresent common bacteria staphylococcus, pseudomonas, and enterobacteria, which obviously had no effect on the rhino parents nor to other adult animals in the same enclosure.

In what seems a contradiction to their professed aims, zoo researchers are now becoming as interested in preventing some animals from being born as they are in finding ways to increase the number of captive births. The plain fact is that given the proper environment and encouragement some animals breed all too readily —and too rapidly—confronting zoo managers with overpopulated enclosures and no market for their surplus because many zoos are having the same success. Curators, desperate to relieve the tensions and reduce the forage bills, telephone one another or advertise surplus animals at sharply discounted prices, even give them away, through announcements in the monthly publication of the American Association of Zoological Parks and Aquariums.

When successful breeding programs bring overwhelming numbers of any particular species into a zoo, officials have only a few courses of action available. One of the most desirable, because it is an announced objective of all captive breeding, is to send surplus animals back to begin restocking their wild habitats. Animals like the North African addax and scimitar horned oryx or the Indian blackbuck, all of which have bred well in captivity, may still be endangered in the wild. But for reasons to be more fully discussed in the chapter "The Way to Ararat," restocking the wilderness is presently difficult and sometimes impossible.

Propagation can be effectively, though unkindly, curtailed by separating males from females for one to two breeding seasons. However, this approach, which is increasingly being resorted to, is both costly and risky. The cost comes from the need to build extra enclosures and buy more food to care for separated animals, and there is risk that when once again males are put with females, changes will have taken place in the group dynamics that will reduce or even halt future propagation. A good breeding male may have passed his prime or become subject to harassment by younger, untested males. Previously fecund females may have entered their equivalent of menopause.

Several years ago virtually every zoo in the United States and several in Europe found itself with a surplus of Siberian tigers, which had enjoyed a period of great popularity with zoo directors, who are often subject to bandwagon psychology. The figures tell the story. In 1970 there were 66 Siberian tigers in American zoos. During the next four years 191 cubs were born, of which 140 survived. By January, 1975, there were 209 Siberian tigers, including 115 females. For a zoo operator a problem of overpopulation in tigers becomes immediately apparent. Besides being the largest of the big cats, Siberian tigers tend to live harmoniously only in small, closely related groups. They are not social animals. In the wilds of Siberia, Northern China, Korea, and Manchuria they lead a solitary existence except when they get together to mate. If too many, especially too many males, are put into one enclosure, they are likely to tear one another to shreds—rather noisily—as the

operator of one safari park found out the hard way. To reduce propagation, therefore, most zoo operators either separated the sexes or performed vasectomies on the males.

Males can be harmlessly deprived of their powers to reproduce through a simple vasectomy operation, which in theory is reversible, but in fact may not be. In using vasectomies, however, zoo operators don't consult with one another beforehand. They tend to view their own collection as an independent unit, without regard to what other zoo operators may be doing to the same species in their zoos. Unless zoo-wide planning for the breeding of endangered animals is introduced, the world may be treated to the amusing, but tragic, possibility that every male of a temporarily overabundant species like the Siberian tigers will end up being vasectomized. Then unless some of the vasectomies can be reversed, panic may ensue as zoo directors frantically telephone one another in their search for an untreated male. In this kind of situation, unlikely as it might be, the master records of zoo animals stored in the computer of the International Species Inventory System (ISIS) are of no help, for they don't describe the sexual abilities, or inabilities, of males. For that information one must go to the stud books maintained on most threatened or endangered species kept in zoos.

Euthanasia is another approach to controlling the growth of zoo populations. The very old, the malformed, the newly born can be killed quickly and painlessly with the type of injection that veterinarians regularly use to put a pet cat or dog to sleep. The method is not, for obvious reasons, publicized or even much discussed among zoo men. One does not find it as an agenda item at AAZPA conferences, even though its use is defensible. The greatest public outcry against it would be raised by those visitors to whom an elderly animal, particularly a favorite like a bear, had become a distinctive personality, but also the thought of harmless little furry creatures being put to death without any chance to live would not sit well with many who are sentimental about animals. Zoo operators who resort to euthanasia also know that they must take care not to be selective in the healthy animals they eliminate, for otherwise they would create new forms that diverged from the original wild species.

The most obvious answer to the problem of curtailing numbers of captive animals has, of course, occurred to zoo researchers: contraception. But the word contraception is easier said than the task accomplished. Some early attempt to use chemical contraception on African lions, another species whose surplus in zoos presents a constant challenge, resulted in animals losing all their hair, scarcely a dignified condition for the king of beasts, whom one can imagine skulking naked in its enclosure to the taunts of visitors.

Dr. Ulysses S. Seal,[4] of the Veterans Administration Hospital in Minneapolis, and the Department of Biochemistry, University of Minnesota, has urged the use of progestins to achieve contraception in exotic animals. These synthetic hormones have proved successful on several species. Implanted surgically under a female's skin in a container the size of a .45 caliber bullet, the progestins are gradually absorbed by the animal's body over a predetermined period of two or three years. While present they prevent conception, but when they are finally absorbed, the female can conceive again. Progestins, however, cannot be used safely on all animals. They appear to be effective in the big cats, but may not be safe for dogs or other animals which have a predisposition toward infection of the uterus.

Painstaking research, species by species, will be required to find safe contraceptives for each. Working in cooperation with Alza Corporation, researchers in San Diego have recently experimented with vaginal rings which hold pure hormone extracts in sufficient amounts to prevent conception while a ring is in place. The first animals on which this was tried, incidentally, were the white rhinos, whose numbers so greatly increased through the labors of Mandhla and his successors.

While contraception has been getting some attention in zoo research programs, its diametric opposite, artificial insemination, has been getting even more. Overabundance through captive breeding has been experienced in only a few species; the need for captive propagation is acute for hundreds. Whenever zoo officials write articles or give talks about what they are doing to propagate endangered species, someone in the audience invariably writes or asks, "But why don't you use artificial insemination?" Those in charge of zoo breeding programs would like nothing more. Sper-

[4] Dr. Seal is also the man most to be credited for establishing the International Species Inventory System (ISIS) program.

matozoa could be shipped from zoo to zoo, thereby eliminating the risk of transporting animals and the burden of preparing the paperwork required to get permits every time an endangered animal is shipped across state lines or from continent to continent. Sperm could be kept alive in frozen zoos against the possibility of males dying out or becoming unobtainable while females still lived. There have been, in fact, one or two instances when females lived in zoos for many years after the last surviving male of their species had died. Martha, a passenger pigeon, was the sole survivor of a North American species so numerous in the early nineteenth century that they literally blotted out the sun during migrations that took several hours to pass a given point. In 1914 Martha died in the Cincinnati Zoo, and with her a species that had actually been hunted to extinction. Had there been live sperm in a sperm bank and the knowledge of how to inseminate passenger pigeons, Martha might have become the means of restoring her species to life.

The rub is knowledge. Zoo research must establish the how and when of insemination for every single species of the thousands kept in zoos. To understand the full extent of the problem one need only imagine the difference between inseminating a hummingbird and inseminating an elephant. Think also about the difficulties likely to be encountered in obtaining the sperm from a bull elephant in the first place. Interestingly, one method has already been tried by researchers at the London Zoo. Working with gamekeepers in Kenya, technicians from London have quickly extracted live sperm from bull elephants killed minutes before to reduce overpopulation in national parks like Tsavo. Frozen and rushed to London by air, the sperm was used to attempt insemination of female elephants in the zoo, so far without success.

The technique of introducing spermatozoa to egg artificially, got its start in 1776 when a priest-scientist, Abbé Lazzaro Spalanzani, successfully inseminated 165 frogs. Fascinated by what he had wrought, Father Spalanzani continued his experiments and four years later inseminated a dog. By the end of that century a British physician named E. Home had artificially inseminated a human female, and a Russian scientist, E. I. Ivanoff, had developed techniques for inseminating horses, cattle, sheep, and a few species of birds. From relatively slow beginnings the use of artificial insemination increased rapidly. In the 1930s it was regularly used by breeders of domestic animals in both the United States and Europe. The early 1950s brought an important refinement, the method of freezing semen in straw containers for later use. Now the semen from prize stock could produce hundreds and thousands of offspring many years after the donor had died. By 1975 an estimated 59 million cows, 47 million ewes, 1 million sows, 125,000 mares, and 56,000 goats were being artificially inseminated in one year. So, for that matter, were nearly 5 million turkeys.

That artificial insemination will one day be widely used in zoos is now taken for granted. Young of several species of birds—hawks, falcons, ocellated turkeys, sandhill cranes—have already been conceived this way. Dr. Stephen Seager, a veterinarian working at the Institute of Comparative Medicine, Baylor University, has demonstrated that semen can be extracted from males of all exotic animals. "Can be," however, is a far cry from actually taking semen as a routine procedure. There are numerous difficulties, not the least of which is an understandable reluctance on the part of male animals to relinquish their seed. Aside from the danger to animals in being captured and restrained so semen can be taken, the actual collection may be difficult. The three principal methods used are hand manipulation, electroejaculation, and artificial vaginas. Hand manipulation is probably the least used. As the name electroejaculation suggests, the male animal is stimulated by low voltage electrical impulses to ejaculate, whether he wants to or not. Artificial vaginas, which have a semen container attached, can be used either to masturbate a male or be so strategically and temptingly placed that he does the job himself. This method poses one risk. A male may get to liking the artificial vagina so much that he loses interest in real females who, after all, are more demanding.

San Diego researchers used electroejaculation on their fine male pygmy chimpanzee, Kakowet, to obtain semen for a mission with far-reaching implications for the zoo world, even though it was unsuccessful. In the Antwerp, Belgium, Zoo languished three female pygmy chimpanzees who had no male companion, in spite of the fact that this zoo still has close ties with Zaire, the former Belgian Congo, the only place in the world where wild pygmy chimpanzees live. A distinct species of great ape, this animal, *Pan*

paniscus, is about two thirds the size of its cousin, the more familiar chimp of circus acts and Jane Goodall's studies, *Pan troglodytes.* How many pygmy chimps there are left in Zaire jungles nobody knows, but their continued existence on earth is threatened most by the fact that local tribesmen like to eat them, an act that smacks of cannibalism to anyone who has studied these primates, for they have a high intelligence and appear almost human.[5]

Unable to obtain a male pygmy chimpanzee, Walter van den Bergh, director of the Antwerp Zoo, was amenable to the suggestion advanced by Dr. Benirschke in San Diego that long-distance artificial insemination be tried, using semen from Kakowet shipped live by air to Antwerp. One of the oldest and most respected of zoo directors, the sardonic van den Bergh is as a kind of Pope in the profession. His pronouncements amount to bulls, originating most often from his large office, a Sistine Chapel of zoos with a skylight of stained glass animal portraits. Here van den Bergh sits behind an enormous desk, wreathed in cigar smoke, listening to Bach and Beethoven as he works. He was an early advocate of the need for captive breeding.

There are few pygmy chimpanzees in zoos. In the United States none save San Diego and the Yerkes Primate Center near Atlanta, Georgia, have them, and in Europe only the Antwerp, Frankfurt, Stuttgart, and Wassenaar zoos. Kakowet had proved himself a good breeder with, for a while, one minor drawback: he produced nothing but female offspring, one a year for several years. Ordinarily this would have delighted the San Diego officials, being preferable to the opposite, but somewhere along the line one or two males would be required if a sustained captive breeding program was to be successful. Finally, after a succession of five female babies, Kakowet and his mate Linda produced two handsome males in 1975 and 1977.

A first attempt to send Kakowet's semen untended through air freight failed. Somewhere along the line the package was shunted

[5] Their similarity to *Homo sapiens* is nowhere more evident than in their blood, which under electrophoresis—a method of separating and highlighting blood constituents—is almost indistinguishable from human blood, to the point where human-pygmy chimpanzee transfusions might be possible under some circumstances.

into the wrong bin for a few days and by the time it reached its destination the spermatozoa had expired. Dr. Benirschke and his staff determined then that the package would have to be taken by courier. The second batch of semen was kept alive in San Diego's cell bank until a responsible person going to Europe could be persuaded to undertake the mission.

That responsible person was a highly respected globetrotting San Diego businessman, Robert F. Smith, then first vice-president of the Zoological Society. Appearing frequently before industrial groups as a lecturer and consultant on management, Smith often went to Europe, and in 1972 was scheduled to conduct a seminar in Brussels, a trip that presented the perfect opportunity for him to act as the emissary carrying Kakowet's sperm.

The semen container which Smith was to carry looked like a miniature milk can. Actually it was a super-thermos filled with liquid nitrogen that would hold the live sperm at cryogenic temperatures for ten to fourteen days.

The scene at Kennedy International Airport on the night Smith was to leave has to be imagined. Here at a fast walk comes a well-dressed American businessman, tall, stout but not fat, and with a pleasant, smiling face. He hurries toward the loading area for Sabena World Airlines. Slung over his shoulder is a flight bag. In one hand he carries a brief case, the badge of his occupation, and a light overcoat. In the other he holds what appears to be a small aluminum milk can. The Sabena lounge is crowded because an earlier flight was canceled and many of its passengers have found space on what is going to be a full Boeing 747 on the flight to Brussels. Many people are already lined up to pass through the airport security check where their hand luggage is inspected. By the time Smith reaches the inspection control there are perhaps 150 impatient people in the line behind him.

As he places his briefcase and the can of semen on the counter Smith smiles at the lovely black girl who, with an air of great efficiency, is going through hand luggage. In telling of his adventure later, Smith described this girl as a twenty-year-old edition of Lena Horne. The girl quickly checks his brief case, and then turns to the can with Kakowet's sperm. "You'll have to open this," she informs Smith. There is a moment's pause as Smith, normally an

articulate man, gropes for the best words to answer her request. "I'm sorry," he finally stutters, "but I can't. I mean it's impossible. Uh, look, I made arrangements ahead of time to take this aboard."

"Well, nobody said anything to me," the girl snapped. "What's in it?"

On his way to the airport Smith had thought about the uniqueness of his mission, and had chuckled a little over it, but he had also faced up to the possibility that he might be asked such a question. He resolved then that his best course was to tell the truth. Now he looks the girl straight in the eye, smiles, and in a voice loud enough for her to hear, but not so loud, he hopes, that people behind him will overhear, he tells her the truth. "That can contains the frozen semen of a pygmy chimpanzee."

For a moment the girl just stares, first at Smith and then at the container. Then the air of efficiency, the brisk, businesslike manner vanishes. Looking up as though appealing to the Deity she slaps one hand to her forehead. "*This* has to happen on *my* shift!" she exclaims in the manner of one much put upon.

Fortunately Smith had prearranged with Sabena's officials to take the can of semen aboard without inspection, so when the girl called her nearby supervisor, he was allowed to go aboard without further question, much to the relief of the restive passengers behind him. For reasons difficult to explain, the container with its unique contents had received enough advance notice to create great curiosity in the airliner's crew. On the flight over the Atlantic every member of the crew, including the Captain, dropped by to look at the container and talk briefly with Smith about it.

It is a comment on the nature of his mission that Smith's troubles were not over when he got to Belgium. In what would normally have been a brisk wave-through at Belgian Customs the semen container again proved to be an obstacle. The customs officer wasn't at all sure he would allow it into the country. Here the problem seemed to turn more on its worth than its contents. "What is its value?" the inspector asked in the best English he could muster. Unfortunately at this point Smith, he admitted later, made a mistake. Instead of saying, "It has no value," or "It's worth ten dollars," or something on that order, he replied, "It's priceless," meaning, of course, beyond mere value. "Priceless," however, is one of those words that can mire one in a semantic bog. To the customs inspector priceless apparently meant value upon which some duty should be levied. Even the curator from the Antwerp Zoo, who had come to meet Smith and take delivery of the container, was unable to break the impasse. Wondering how he could extricate both himself and the container, Smith had an inspiration. Long experience had taught him that in out-of-the-ordinary cases some bureaucrats, particularly in the lower echelons, want most to protect themselves against fault finding by superiors. In these circumstances, the best defense is an authoritative piece of paper which can be shown to explain a decision. This paper Smith now produced was a letter from the San Diego director, Charles Bieler, to Walter van den Bergh, a man well known through Belgium. The letter did it. Happy that he could keep it to justify his action, the inspector waved both Smith and Kakowet's sperm on through.

The end of this story was frustrating. Kakowet's semen was alive when it arrived, but when the Antwerp researchers tried to inseminate the female pygmy chimpanzees with it, it didn't take. Perhaps the problem lay in the coagulation of the natural fluids in which the spermatozoa lived. They were thicker than would have been normal during intercourse, possibly even to the point of imprisoning the individual spermatozoa so they couldn't reach the egg. More likely, though, the problem lay in not fully understanding the females' cycle so that insemination could take place at the best possible time when in nature the female would be most receptive to a male's advances. The lack of knowledge about ovulation time, most researchers in this field believe, is the greatest single obstacle to the use of artificial insemination on exotic animals. Using the San Diego Zoo's endocrinology lab to study blood and vaginal cells, Dr. Lasley and primatologist Mark Bogart were able, after a year's research, to determine the length of cycles between ovulations in both ruffed and black lemurs. The difference was marked. Ruffed lemurs went 40 days between ovulations, while black lemurs ovulated every 33 days. Knowing this, Bogart can now introduce male to female on just the right day, particularly with ruffed lemurs, a rowdy bunch much given to noisy squabbles and domineering females who can make life miserable for a male when they are not interested in sex. More encouraging, Dr. Lasley and Bogart are convinced that successful artificial insemination of

lemurs will be accomplished in a few months and that the long-range transportation of semen for successful artificial insemination will become a reality for which Smith's mission to Antwerp helped pave the way.

The Battle of
Puget Sound

I n the minds of some zoo professionals the ideal zoo would include only plants, animals, keepers, and the scientific staff. It would be a garden without people—no elderly gentlemen climbing in with the alligators, no gray-haired ladies accusing staff members of cruelty to animals, no children littering the grounds with gum and candy wrappers or tossing germ-laden peanuts and popcorn to the monkeys, no people casting their wishes with coins into the seal pool. The zoo would be a fine and quiet place, but then, as the Cavalier poets were fond of pointing out to fair maidens, so is a grave.

Virtually all zoos *are* public institutions. An indispensable element in their mix is people. Whether privately owned, operated as a trust or nonprofit corporation, or run by federal, state, or municipal governments, zoos exist to serve people, and they need visitors to justify and help pay for their existence. True, the new role of zoos in breeding threatened or endangered animals can be undertaken without people looking on—and in fact the most effective programs will be away from public view—but sustained captive breeding by zoos will not succeed without understanding and sympathy from the public who will be asked to provide, directly or indirectly, the necessary funds. Captive breeding programs, in short, have posed a new challenge in public relations for zoos.

The evolution of public relations in zoos has been most influenced by the way people feel about keeping wild animals in captivity. In the early days of modern zoos, particularly during the late nineteenth and early twentieth centuries, zoo visitors were

176

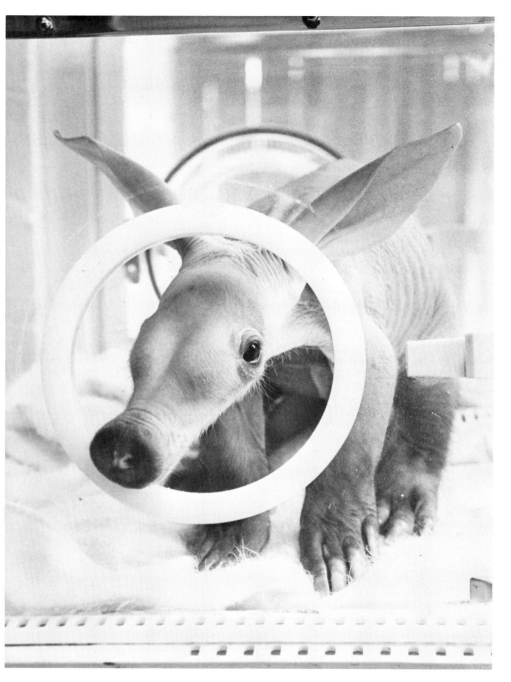

This aardvark, a blue baby, turned a healthy pink in
the oxygen-enriched atmosphere of an incubator.

"Alvila," the only offspring of the San Diego Zoo's silverback "Albert," had to be handraised in a nursery.

This black lemur, "Lazarus," being held by nursery-keeper Sue Schroeder, was twice brought back from the dead.

Infant pigmy chimpanzee in the San Diego Zoo nursery.

As Miss Zoofari, Joan Embery has taken 300 animals, including this white rhino calf, to *The Tonight Show*, where she and Johnny Carson espouse the conservation of wildlife.

OPPOSITE PAGE: Dolly, a gorilla at the San Diego Wild Animal Park was taught how to be a mother by a muscular male college student.

In the long air trip from an elephant orphanage in Sri Lanka, Devi was the pawn in a frustrating game between San Diego Zoo curator Mark Rich and a host of regulators.

By showing killer whales, managers of marine parks like Sea World helped create both sympathy for the whales and an ironic backlash against themselves.

generally insensitive to the methods used in housing and caring for wild animals, except in cases of obvious physical cruelty and not always then. Zoos had no need to justify their existence through planned public relations programs; they were widely accepted as a fact of life, and without criticism. With the exception of those rare instances when zoo people made scientific contributions regarding the classification or anatomical character of animals, or zoos served, perhaps without being conscious of it, as part of the laboratory for a Linnaeus or a Darwin, zoological gardens were superficial places of pure entertainment like the animal fair in these familiar lines:

> I went to the animal fair.
> The birds and the beasts were there.
> The old baboon, by the light of the moon,
> Was combing his auburn hair.

> The monkey he got drunk;
> He sat on the elephant's trunk.
> The elephant sneezed with an awful wheeze,
> And what became of the monk, the monk,
> And what became of the monk?

In the joyous but insensitive world of that verse animals are simply to be enjoyed as playthings, objects to be teased, laughed at, derided. And that was the chief attraction of zoos, that and novelty. To the animal fairs came people who are still a large part of the zoo-going public, young lovers, couples with their children, older gray-headed folks, all out for a Sunday stroll, so to speak, hoping to be amused by animal antics, see delightful animal babies, and view the latest strange or bizarre creatures to arrive from far-off exotic lands.

But there came a time when superficiality wore off and novelty could not always be achieved. Of course, the zoo continued to be a place of entertainment (a word some present-day zoo managers worry about because they fear it connotes the same image as carnival or circus), but it also had to respond to greater public demand for information about the animals people saw. Without foregoing their earlier role, zoos increasingly became educational institutions. In the development of this new mission, however, there was and continues to be a great disparity between the best and the worst. Both in Europe and the United States some zoos do a much better educational job than others. Nor is effectiveness in education a factor of size. The small Arizona-Sonora Desert Museum, on the outskirts of Tucson, is a zoo that does a superb job of public education through graphics and static museum displays, and by the exhibits of live wild animals from the Sonora desert of Arizona and Mexico. Conversely, there are still some major zoos that offer little that can be called educational beyond signs that identify and state one or two facts about the animals on display.

As the social role of zoos was enlarged, so was the need for planned public relations, even though relatively few zoos can even now afford full-time public relations officers. In their new capacity zoos were serving two publics (often, of course, the same): those who wanted to be entertained, and those who wanted to learn, and public relations had to respond to both. To bring in visitors looking for fun the task of public relations was little more than press-agentry—getting newspaper and radio and television editors to accept and run stories and pictures about events at the zoo. Pictures were preferable because seeing the animals often made people want to come to the zoo.

Fortunately for PR people, certain pictures of animals are almost always accepted by the media. Editors are fond of cute baby animals (provided they are not snakes—snakes remain anathema to most editors, who persist in the notion that snake pictures frighten pregnant women) because they know the readers or viewers are. Pictures that combine animals, preferably babies, with children or pretty girls are also staples, for most editors hold to the tested theory that "animals, legs, and children" create the most popular features. So frequently are animal pictures used in the media that many have become stereotyped. They are shown year in and year out with little change except for the specific animals depicted. The poses, the backgrounds remain the same—lions with a majestic mane, preferably showing long fangs in a yawn, but if not, merely looking regal; hippos with wide open mouths; and the inevitable seasonal pictures: at Christmastime an orangutan or chimpanzee (or virtually any other cute primate) wearing a Santa Claus hat and often, but not always, carrying a bag of toys; ani-

mals that appear to be kissing or looking soulfully at one another, or giraffes with necks entwined, on St. Valentine's Day; a ground-hog, if the zoo has one, studying its shadow to see if winter has ended; polar bears swimming, splashing one another, or sitting on ice during the hottest days of summer (if no polar bears are available, tigers will do); a baby ape wearing a people mask, carrying a jack-o-lantern, or playing in a pumpkin around Halloween.

The objective of the press-agentry is simple. Its only relevance is to the zoo as a place of entertainment. It is designed to attract visitors tomorrow, the next day, or the following week. For the long-term interests of the zoo, modern public relations people know they must promote it as an institution that has a loftier purpose than mere entertainment. They want the public to understand that most zoos now enjoy status as educational and scientific institutions. In the jargon of PR, "a perspective in depth" is required. The zoos must be promoted through longer, more thoughtful pieces: articles, books, special publications, and radio and television specials. Such promotional material will help to attract visitors, but its primary purpose is to establish the zoo as a valuable and necessary social institution.

The increasingly important requirement that zoos become life-boats for animal species that are threatened or endangered in the wild has received little attention from public relations people, largely, no doubt, because few zoos have actually established soundly based captive breeding programs.[1] Not that zoo directors and their PR people overlook animal births as a source of publicity. Births are frequently reported, particularly if they have occurred for the first time in captivity to an exhibited species. The history of zoos, however, is replete with recorded first-time births that received widespread publicity but in reality resulted from the natural actions of ripe males and females placed together in circumstances not antithetic to their mating. Perhaps indeed they mated several times and produced several young before one or the other died

[1] The seriousness of many zoos in this regard can be called in question by the fact that the American Association of Zoological Parks and Aquariums has no committee to deal with the important captive breeding function. Captive breeding is lumped with all other aspects of conservation under a Conservation Committee.

and the process ended—scarcely the definition of sustained captive breeding.

It is probable, in fact, that self-congratulatory publicity about births, in which zoo people seek to give the impression that they are making a contribution to wildlife conservation, will backfire as more and more conservationists add their voices to those already questioning the right of zoos to exist. First-time births can provide valuable information if careful notes are kept from the time court-ship begins until the young animals are able to leave their parents. But these scientific records are seldom kept, let alone published, so that each new attempt to breed the same species is like reinventing the wheel. The mere fact that an animal species will breed in cap-tivity is of dubious value, since quite obviously the species breeds somewhere or it wouldn't exist.

Society's need for zoos, which until a few years ago the public accepted with little thought or discussion, is now seriously being questioned by many conservationists in both Europe and the United States. Some of these critics are responsible and rational, others emotional and unthinking to the point of hysteria; yet no matter how reasoned and informed their attacks may be, they tend to tar all zoos with the same brush. The most motley and ill-kept roadside collection of animals is lumped with a New York or San Diego Zoo, and the conclusions reached by the critics tend to be the same as those found in this statement from an "Investigative Report" by a group known as United Action for Animals. Under the alliterative headline "Torment, Torture and Terror Close in on Zoo Animals" the report states: "It's time to phase out zoos. It's time to liberate zoo animals from exploitation by not replacing those that die. It's the only way to save them from being made abnormal by animal behaviorists whose objective is the modifica-tion—the alteration of the animal's natural behavior."

The attacks by people who support conservation groups op-posed to zoos differ in degree, not in kind. These people are, more-over, generally more vocal and literate than the norm, and more likely to state their views collectively and individually to elected representatives. Consequently, their voices have helped shape many of the restrictive laws which now bind zoos in Laocoönian coils of bureaucratic red tape when they try to obtain animals from

the wild or ship endangered animals to one another. Above all, the sharp attacks have underscored the need for zoos to have their own voices through lobbying groups and effective public relations —as the managers of Sea World, Inc., discovered during the agonizing ten days that followed the battle of Puget Sound.

In this drama of a PR officer's nightmare come true, the animal actors were killer whales, sleek black and white, beautifully streamlined members of the whale and dolphin family that can attain a length of 30 feet and weigh up to nine tons. As their common name suggests killer whales were long victims of a bad press. To them the Romans gave the name orca, or sea devil. From the Roman period until very recently no good was said of killer whales in either scientific or popular literature. Now known technically as *Orcinus orca*, over the years they have been tagged with such scientific names as *Tyrannus balaenarum*, *Formidabilis balaenarum*, *Delphinus gladiator*, and *Orca destructor*, all of which suggest an attitude toward them based on something less than sympathy. Scientific writers have described them as killing "from sheer love of slaughter" and delighting in "blood and rapine" (though what they raped the author did not specify), or using their extraordinarily long dorsal fins to "rip up the belly of a whale!"[2] As late as 1959, a French scientist wrote that the killer whale, "a voracious carnivore," was "nearly a cannibal" (because it sometimes ate dolphins), and he characterized killer whales in general as "bloodthirsty beasts"—all of this in a purportedly serious work about the cetaceans. For writers like Jack London killer whales were "sea wolves." Because in London's times humans tended to kill wolves on sight in the mistaken belief that they were evil, ravening creatures that chased sleigh riders in the dead of winter and slaughtered livestock for the fun of it, association with wolves was scarcely conducive to building public support for the whales. The degree to which the orcas were reviled was such that naval vessels used their distinctive fins—and therefore the whales—as targets for gunnery practice with live ammunition, and marksmen along the shore popped at them with rifles. Until 1973, every whale brought into captivity bore the scars of old bullet wounds.

How soon they forget, the managers of Sea World, Inc., could

[2] Untrue, but the fins are useful as a means of differentiating sexes. Males have a straight fin, females a scimitar-shaped one.

have said about the outcry of press and public after the battle of Puget Sound. Starting in the late sixties and early seventies organizations like Sea World, Marineland of the Pacific, and other marine parks captured and trained killer whales for acts that soon made them featured players and public favorites. During this period there was a dramatic change in the way people viewed killer whales. The millions who watched Shamu, the first trained killer whale, and others that followed her, no longer perceived the orcas as bloodthirsty beasts. Instead, the killer whales joined other whales and dolphins as beings only slightly inferior to men. They were "minds upon the waters," intelligent, playful creatures that kissed young ladies on the cheek and allowed trainers to put head and shoulders in their toothy jaws.[3]

Operators of marine parks have not claimed that they were the only medium responsible for bringing about this remarkable turnabout in public attitudes. Objective field studies of killer whales resulted in scientific books and articles that depicted them not as heartless killers bent on blood and rapine, but as highly organized predators that lived and hunted in packs called pods. They killed, yes, quite skillfully, striking their prey swiftly at speeds of twenty-five to thirty miles an hour. Sometimes, it is true, they played cat and mouse with prey animals, but like all carnivores their modes of killing were the results of millions of years of evolution and could no more be disparaged by reasonable men than the rise and fall of the tides.

One irony in the changed view toward killer whales is that the old stereotype of them as terrible sea beasts probably started because they hunt and kill warm-blooded animals like seals and dolphins with which people can easily identify and sympathize—when they are not killing the same animals themselves. No one would have called killer whales bloodthirsty had they eaten only shark, which is also a regular part of their diet. Baleen whales, after all, are also predators, but since they scoop up millions of crustaceans called krill for which humans have no feelings, nobody has accused baleen whales of being heartless killers, though presumably

[3] However, Annette Eckis, a secretary at Sea World, San Diego, volunteered to ride Shamu, fell off, tried to swim away, and was severely bitten on her leg—probably because Shamu mistook the leg for a baton that the whale was trained to retrieve as part of her act.

the krill all die. Nor has the sperm whale, a toothed carnivore that may rip giant squid apart while eating them, been heaped with opprobrium, except by Captain Ahab, and he dumped it all on one whale.

It was a combination of objective scientific studies filtering through to the popular press, movies, and television; changing attitudes toward the conservation of whales in general; and the opportunity to see live killer whales perform intelligently and gently in marine parks that closed the circle of irony on Sea World at the battle of Puget Sound. If the events in that battle were depicted in a play, it would have a prologue and two acts, with a rousing first-act curtain.

Foremost among the characters in the drama was a man named Don Goldsberry, a student and capturer of killer whales. Goldsberry, who had collected the original Shamu,[4] was associated with Ted Griffin in rescuing Namu, the first killer whale to be captured when in 1965 she was accidentally snared in gill nets belonging to a Canadian fisherman, William Lochkobit, near Namu, British Columbia. At the time of Namu's capture, incidentally, just six years after the French scientist had characterized killer whales as bloodthirsty beasts, Griffin and his associates had been portrayed by the media as admirable, and a mediocre movie about their exploit made heroes of the captors and helped change the attitudes toward killer whales by portraying Namu sympathetically.

By 1976, and the battle of Puget Sound, however, Goldsberry had lost the hero's cloak and was cast by large segments of press and public around the Seattle area as a villain of the deepest stripe. It must be understood that Goldsberry is a man whose volatile personality is attached to a very short fuse. His public-relations profile is like that of many professional people, particularly those who fear their work may be misinterpreted in the mass media, or for one reason or another believe they have been shabbily handled by the media.

A tough, muscular outdoorsman and former fullback who stands nearly five feet, ten inches and weighs around 190, Goldsberry states his opinions with a no-nonsense directness that sometimes rubs people the wrong way. While engaged in the work of

[4] Shamu has since become a stage name for several of Sea World's trained killer whales.

whale catching, which he has made his profession, he wants no strangers around. For one thing, he believes amateurs in small boats are likely to get in the way, creating dangers for themselves, the whale collectors, and the whales. Later events on another whale hunt in another place were to prove this belief correct.

In addition to Goldsberry, on whom fell the villain's cape, the other characters in the drama at Puget Sound were an aide to the Governor of Washington State, a newsman named Dan McGaffin from KING-TV Seattle, an NBC affiliate, and six killer whales. The aide becomes a messenger to the gods at Olympia; McGaffin and the news people at KING-TV are an angry chorus; and the whales will occupy the collective roles of Helen being kidnapped by Paris and the Trojans.

The prologue, featuring Goldsberry, McGaffin, and a different group of whales, took place in 1971 at a place called Penn Cove on Puget Sound, but the events at Penn Cove created a dark glass through which Goldsberry's future actions would be seen. Goldsberry and his whale collectors working on their own had surrounded thirty-three whales with their nets and were in the process of selecting those that would go into captivity and those that would be released. Not all were intended for marine parks. Over the years several whales, studied largely through telemetry, provided information on sonar, underwater communication, and navigation for organizations like the University of Washington, Stanford University, the Boeing Airplane Company and the United States Navy.

A year before this time a tragedy had occurred which stirred many of the residents around Penn Cove to anger, for by 1970 killer whales were a welcome addition to the local scenery, coming as they did around the same time every year, generally in August, remaining awhile, and then departing on what happened to be an annual migration. In 1970 some the the visiting whales had been left behind dead, their corpses washing up along the shore. Several had had their bellies slit and rocks, concrete, and old chunks of iron placed inside. Because whale collectors had been in the vicinity before the deaths, some residents blamed them.[5] The State of Washington passed a Marine Mammal Protection Act re-

[5] Nothing was proved, but accidents do occur in animal collecting, particularly in the earlier stages of developing collecting techniques.

quiring that an observer from the State's Fish and Game department be aboard any boats collecting whales in Puget Sound.

Against the grisly backdrop of 1970 the netting of thirty-three whales in 1971 became a newsworthy event. Reporters and cameramen from most major newspapers and TV stations were dispatched to the scene. Don McGaffin, called away from vacation at his new place on the shore of the cove, came with a news team from KING-TV. Goldsberry received the media people courteously, if not with great enthusiasm, aboard his large floating capture dock, which is shaped like a square U. Most of the media representatives held their interviews, took their pictures and left, but McGaffin and crew stayed on to the point that Goldsberry asked him what he was doing. "Getting pictures for the news," McGaffin replied. One of the people McGaffin chatted with on the dock was the state inspector, who freely discussed why he was aboard. That night when the news story on the whales was beamed from KING-TV, it concluded with McGaffin speaking directly into the camera relating factually what the state inspector had said about the 1970 deaths. Goldsberry interpreted the broadcast as a deliberate blast of him and his crew.

The following day, still assigned to the story, McGaffin and his cameraman rented a boat operated by a local fisherman and his eight-year-old son. As they were getting ready to cast off, an associate from KING-TV who had just returned from the whale collectors' dock, warned McGaffin that Goldsberry had threatened to throw him and his cameras into the water. McGaffin scoffed at the threat and set out. When the fisherman's boat, really a large rowboat powered by an outboard motor, was still some distance from the floating dock, McGaffin and his companions noticed that five power boats, one a thirty-footer, were lined up abreast facing them. As the gap between them and the dock narrowed these boats started up and moved toward them like a squadron of torpedo boats. Then came what McGaffin, a former Marine pilot, described as the most frightening experience of his life. It appeared that the five boats were deliberately trying to scuttle the rowboat. Like buzzing fighter planes they charged in from every side. When it appeared that collision was inevitable, they peeled off, creating waves that caused McGaffin's boat to pitch and rock violently and take water over its gunwales. Daunted, but cool,

McGaffin directed the cameraman to get pictures of the attack as they maneuvered to escape. The entire scene appeared that night on KING-TV, and later in McGaffin's award-winning TV special "Catch 33" which dealt with the capture of the thirty-three whales. Although Goldsberry conceded later that he had "lost his temper" in the attack on McGaffin's rowboat, he began to believe that McGaffin had it in for him.

During the years between the Penn Cove affair and the battle of Puget Sound, Goldsberry continued his work and studies with the killer whales. Long before the Federal Government, he helped set standards for keeping the whales in captivity, including such life-and-death matters as tank size and water quality. His knowledge of whale acoustics and anatomy were brought to bear in the rescue of Sandy, a killer whale that had beached itself. Ordinarily, beached whales die, and when found, Sandy's condition was pitiful. The animal had lost around 1,500 pounds, had cracked ribs and an impacted tooth, and worst of all, lacked sonar, probably the reason it had run ashore to begin with. Rescued and nursed back to health, but still lacking the sonar it needed to survive in the wild, Sandy lived four years in a Sea World tank at an outright cost of many thousands—an unsung deed of altruism for which neither Goldsberry nor Sea World received much credit after the battle of Puget Sound.

The battle itself was spread over three days of March, 1976, with most of the significant action taking place on the third day, a Sunday morning. Sea World had authorized Goldsberry to collect four whales needed to back up four already captive at the firm's three marine parks in San Diego, California, Cleveland, Ohio, and Orlando, Florida. The collecting expedition was perfectly legal, for permits had been issued under the United States Marine Mammal Protection Act of 1972, legislation primarily designed to protect dolphins from tuna fishermen, but applicable also to the capture by United States citizens of seals, sea lions, sea otters, polar bears, and all whales and dolphins anywhere in the world.

Bona fide as the permits were, press reaction after the hearing at which they were granted should have tipped the Sea World managers off to the possibility of stormy weather ahead. At the hearing three spokesmen for conservation groups opposed issuance of the permits. No dramatics were involved, no shouting, gestur-

ing, and threats of mob violence; the naysayers simply said their piece, were listened to politely, and the permits duly issued. However, from some of the press reports next day a casual reader might have gained the impression that the hearing room had been crowded with angry citizens, shouting and waving their fists in opposition to the permits—or as one newspaper put it, there was a "public outcry" against collecting the four whales. Acting logically and legally, Sea World managers overlooked the seething psychological forces ready to explode.

The whale hunt itself took place in the cold waters of Budd Inlet, south toward Olympia, capital of Washington State. The site was not of Goldsberry's choosing, but he had few alternatives under the requirements laid down by his permits. The conditions and areas allowed for collecting the whales were so restrictive, in fact, that Goldsberry and his men rather bitterly joked that they could catch killer whales "as long as they weren't black and white and were taken within two square miles centered on Mt. Rushmore."

Friday and Saturday were occupied with preliminaries, locating and beginning the roundup of a small pod of whales. The hard work involved little drama, save for one element. A spotter plane was used to keep track of the six whales in the pod as they moved down the Sound. From the shore many eyes saw the plane as it flew back and forth across the whales, dipping down every so often so that the pilot could get a closer look, for some of Goldsberry's many calculations during the roundup would be based on the composition of the pod. If, for example, it was only a segment from a larger pod, but without the pod bull—the male leader—the whales would react differently in the final stages of the roundup than they would if the pod bull were directing them. From the shore, however, the watching eyes saw only the plane and the whales.

Sunday morning. With first light on a clear day Goldsberry and his men were readying gear and nets for the final stage of the hunt. Three boats would be used, two high speed chasers of 19 and 30 feet and a larger boat of 56 feet. As admiral of this small flotilla, Goldsberry would direct the final roundup, dispatching his boats to headings based on the actions of the whales. Secure in the knowledge that his actions were legal under the United States

Marine Mammal Protection Act, and with a government inspector aboard, Goldsberry paid no particular attention to the fact that the final chase would take place within clear sight of the shore, literally under the windows of the state capital buildings, close to where, on the same weekend, by an excruciating turn of the screw, was being held a conference on the conservation of whales.

One wonders at this point how many cards have to be stacked against a public-relations officer—an attempt to capture whales where numerous people have made the whales a cause; within sight of the shore near a capital where a conference on whale conservation is taking place; and in the background press and television people who hold no brief for whale collectors in general and Goldsberry in particular. The answer is—one more card. Out for a race in a friend's sailboat, one of several on those same waters, was a top aid to Daniel Evans, governor of Washington State.

It would be obvious to any audience now that Goldsberry was racing to meet his nemesis. The time had come. The day was clear. The whales were there. The chase began. For hundreds of on-lookers the effect was apparently that of a small naval engagement. Goldsberry's flotilla surged forward with engines roaring against a backdrop of racing sailboats. Sighting on the long fins of the killer whales whenever the animals broke water, Goldsberry and his crew were ocean-going cowboys moving the herd toward the corral, a point in the inlet selected as the best place to encircle the whales with nets. The faster boats moved in and out, back and forth, nudging the whales along, sometimes moving in to drop seal controls, small underwater explosives like firecrackers, originally developed to frighten seals and sea lions away from fishermen's nets, but useful too in capturing whales. The noise and force of these popping explosions helped keep individual whales with the pod on the course Goldsberry had selected, but they were perfectly harmless to the animals. To some who watched from the shore that day, however, the use of these "torpedoes" seemed a heinous act. Others, including the Governor's aide and his wife, maintained that the spotter plane dropped explosives, although Goldsberry denied using the plane during the final chase.

At the chosen location, some five hundred yards off shore, selected with such precision in relation to tidal movement that an error of a hundred yards might have meant death by drowning for

some or all of the whales, Goldsberry and his crew dropped the nets and closed them around the pod of whales. From their point of view, the chase was over. Now all that remained was to transfer the whales to the holding pen 70 by 70 feet in width and 30 feet deep, from which, one by one the animals could be lifted in slings, laid on foam rubber cushions, given blood tests, and the selection of four animals for Sea World made.

Except for putting the whales into the holding pen, the final steps were never taken. Within hours the battle of Puget Sound shifted from Budd Inlet to the press, TV, and courts of Washington State. Everything came together now to spring the ironical trap. Goldsberry and Sea World had helped mold the public attitude toward killer whales which, amplified many decibels by a generally critical press and TV, threatened Sea World's continued right to train and exhibit the orcas. Finally, indeed, the hullabaloo threatened all United States zoos.

The chase that Sunday had been seen by many people, some watching from dining rooms where they were breakfasting or reading Sunday comics, others from the shore; several, those who were literally on the scene, from racing sailboats. Many, including the Governor's aide and his wife, were highly incensed. The aide set into motion the machinery which would bring an injunction against removing the whales from Puget Sound. Claims were made that the whales had been torpedoed and that the spotter plane had dive-bombed them. What had started out as a local story became a snowball that grew into an avalanche. From KING-TV the news went out over the entire NBC network. McGaffin, though, scrupulously refused to rerun the 1971 footage of the attack on his boat. He believed that would be hitting below the belt.

Within the next three days reports of the battle of Puget Sound had appeared in newspapers, on radio, and on TV throughout the United States, and for that matter wherever in the world whale conservationists exist. While the reporting was largely objective, except for some accompanying editorials, its very intensity penetrated the consciousness of people who had taken up the saving of whales as a grand cause and were now used to casting the killer whales as good and decent creatures. Few noted that the killer whales, neither threatened nor endangered in the wild, may have increased in number because fewer hands are now turned against them. In the storm of protests the assertions by Sea World's managers that they were acting within their legal rights achieved all the impact of whispers in a hurricane. Among many residents of Washington State, particularly those near Puget Sound, the frenzy reached near tar-and-feather proportions. Sea World was viewed, without foundation, as a wealthy out-of-state corporation bent on plundering Washington State's territorial waters. Five death threats were sent to various Sea World managers.

Called from a corporation meeting on public relations in Florida and told to get on top of the matter (which was to prove to be like getting on top of an erupting volcano) William Seaton, Sea World's director of public relations, hurried to Seattle and for ten days spent the most harrowing period of a life that had already included a stint as a starving author on the island of Majorca. On his second day in Seattle a salty female taxi driver asked him point blank if he were "one of those God damned whale catchers?" Nonplussed, Seaton was tempted to say no, but pride and calling required that he tell the truth. "I'm from Sea World, if that's what you mean," he answered. The woman then pulled the taxi over to the curb and spent several minutes lecturing him in colorful language on the evils of catching whales.

More serious than stern lectures, general opprobrium, and death threats (which the executives who had received them nervously discounted) was the real threat of precipitous legislation that would inhibit, if not stop, future exhibition of killer whales. Senator Warren Magnuson of Washington State immediately drafted a bill prohibiting the future capture of killer whales for purposes of exhibition and rushed it through the United States Senate on a voice vote prompted by the first great wave of emotional reaction to the stories about the battle of Puget Sound. This bill caused shudders in all United States zoos, for it would have established the precedent of selecting particular species for special protection simply because they were popular. For eager politicians such emotion-based conservation might prove a good way to garner votes from animal lovers in their constituencies. By establishing a political rather than a scientific basis for protecting wildlife, popular animals get attention while lesser-known or unpopular animals were neglected. Snakes, for example, would not fare well if people

voted on which animal species deserved to be protected. Worried about these and other implications of the Magnuson bill, directors of the major zoos moved, through lobbying groups, to oppose it. In the House of Representatives the calming effects of time and the lobbying of zoos effectively stifled the legislation.

At the front in Seattle the Sea World people mounted a counter-attack that took two forms. The public relations staff led by Seaton sought to place stories and quotes about the good treatment of killer whales in captivity and the role that captive whales had already played in changing the killer whale's image from ravening beast to intelligent, admirable, marine animal. Lawyers, meantime, were seeking to lift Washington State's now firm injunction against taking the whales from Puget Sound. This courtroom battle was a war of nerves for each side. The Washington officials wanted to keep the injunction in force beyond the expiration date of Sea World's permit to capture whales, at which time their injunction would be academic, while Sea World fought to have the injunction lifted so they would not have to go through the expensive process of getting more permits and capturing more whales.

In the end the managers of Sea World recognized the truth of an old public relations adage: You generally make a bad story worse by fighting back, which is another way of saying that efforts to rebut adverse publicity are generally like throwing gasoline on a fire. In a compromise settlement Sea World agreed to send the two remaining whales (the others had escaped) to the University of Washington and help the scientists there put radio transmitter packs on the animals so that their movements could be monitored after they were released. Moreover, Sea World agreed that in the future they would refrain from capturing whales in Puget Sound. Shortly after, when the affair was no longer big news, the United States permits were extended and Goldsberry captured four whales in an undisclosed area away from Puget Sound. These animals were flown to Sea World's parks without public notice—an accomplishment really, considering the size of killer whales.

In reviewing the lessons to be learned from the Battle of Puget Sound thoughtful zoo managers recognized that a blow had been struck against one of their cherished notions, notably, that they had the responsibility to exhibit some animals—like killer whales—

in order to enlist greater public understanding of the need to conserve wildlife threatened mostly by man. No one suggested that killer whales could be bred on a sustained basis in captivity, although a birth (followed shortly by death) occurred at Marineland of the Pacific and Sea World has a tank designed for breeding whales at San Diego. But killer whales are one of several species whose continued survival on earth depends largely on the goodwill of men. To achieve goodwill people must first be educated. Some knowledge, it is true, can come from articles, books, movies, and television, but none of these is a substitute for the real animal—the living, breathing three-dimensional creature. It is the animal itself that speaks best for itself, as the hue and cry raised against Goldsberry and Sea World had ironically proved.

Some public relations people might argue that Goldsberry and Sea World made a mistake by not allowing media people to participate from the beginning in the capture of the whales. This cooperative approach was precisely the one chosen by managers of the Minnesota Zoological Gardens when that zoo mounted an expedition to capture beluga whales in the waters near Churchill, Canada, on the southwest edge of Hudson Bay.

In August of 1977, the new Minnesota Zoo, a state-sponsored entity, had not opened. Because the zoo's management, led by Donald Bridgewater, the director, hoped to attract two million viewers a year to a well-designed park that will specialize in animals from the northern temperate and arctic zones (but will include some tropical species as well), they thought it would be desirable to generate as much advance publicity as possible to let the world know they were coming. The hunt for the beluga whales seemed to offer the opportunity for a public-relations coup, especially since the media people invited were happy, even eager to pay their own expenses on the ten-day expedition. If the idea was good, the result didn't show it. According to columnist Jim Klobuchar of the Minnesota *Star*, the expedition to Churchill "scored the same kind of public relations 10-strike achieved years before by Heinrich Himmler and the Gestapo."

The quest for these white whales, 10- to 15-foot denizens of arctic oceans, was an object lesson in the truism that plans for public-relations programs should include worst-case scenarios, so that initial enthusiasm for what seems a good idea does not blind

one to the dragon's teeth, barbed-wire thickets, and mine fields that may lie ahead. The fiasco at Churchill developed naturally—like poison ivy in a field of clover.

Five groups of people, each with its own objective, congregated in Churchill to take part in capturing the belugas. The zoo managers wanted to generate advance publicity (which of course required that some whales be caught); the zoo scientists, assisted by professional whale hunters, wanted to capture whales; a legislator from the state was an interested observer of how the state's money was being spent; the media people were out for a good story; and the townfolk of Churchill saw a chance to reap some economic gains. Given this variance in motivation, the bomb was ready to explode if a detonator was inserted. At Churchill the detonator was alcohol.

No one can chase whales unless the whales are there. The absence of whales during the first few days at Churchill led bored zoo managers, whale hunters, reporters, and photographers, and the legislator to look for other diversions. But a glance at the map reveals that Churchill is isolated. It is a town with no place to go, no roads leading out, no amusement centers, no cities nearby, nothing but two bars stocked with LaBatt's beer and Canadian Club whiskey. Let another writer for the *Star*, reporter David Peterson, detail what happened: "It was a trip that saw the leader of the expedition, associate zoo director H. Brad House, loudly chewing out a Minnesota legislator in public. It was a trip that saw several confrontations between members of the press corps and zoo officials over what the press regarded as a sweetheart deal between the zoo and WCCO-TV. And it was a trip in which reporters were told point-blank by two staff scientists that the reporters—who had been invited along but paid all of their own expenses—had 'no business being there.' "

Peterson goes on to report that everyone, including the news media representatives, did some drinking but, he adds, "a few zoo officials drank heavily, often beginning in the morning, and became obviously drunk on occasion."

It soon became apparent that alcohol and whale hunting didn't mix. On the first attempt to capture whales the confusion was so great, with numerous small boats milling about and crashing into one another, that the chief whale hunter, a Canadian, called the hunt off when, according to Peterson, "he saw one of his drivers engaging in a serious discussion with an outboard motor." Upholding Goldsberry's contention that capture boats and press boats shouldn't be involved together in a whale hunt, the presence of 14 news media representatives on the expedition put as many as 10 boats into the water that frequently got into one another's way. The result, as Goldsberry would have predicted, was that no whales were caught while media people were along. One beluga had been captured before the main body of the expedition arrived and a second was caught after zoo officials reluctantly banned press boats from the area.

John Fletcher, director of the small Como Zoo in St. Paul, understandably concerned about the competition offered by the much larger Minnesota Zoological Gardens, took advantage of the unfavorable press his rival received because of the disastrous beluga hunt. Fletcher put out his own release notifying media editors that the Como Zoo was going to conduct an intensive hunt for giant carp on the Mississippi. Noting that the expedition to capture the beluga whales had included a four-hundred-dollar-a-day expert on whale sex, Fletcher proudly claimed that his expert on the sex of carp was a local fisherman who had agreed to come along at $3.50 an hour plus the exclusive right to print a picture of the capture in the *Skyway News*. He added that the Como Zoo's expedition would be based at Homer, Minnesota, because "they have an early curfew there and so far as I know our people will not be threatened by large supplies of LaBatt's beer and Canadian Club whiskey."

The occasional tactlessness that zoo professionals display in dealing with media representatives is seldom the outgrowth of a truculent nature. Often it arises either from lack of training in the niceties of public relations or from previous experiences as a source for printed or televised stories that have left scars—incorrect or out of context quotes, facts distorted or wrong, editorial emphasis on elements of a story that the professional thought were trivial and not worth recording. And media people themselves are not always tactful or gifted in human relations. They sometimes infuriate zoo professionals by asking questions that display a profound ignorance of zoos and wildlife, and they sometimes make demands that cause even patient zoo professionals to look grimly at one another. One

producer, phoning from Hollywood, couldn't understand the reluctance of zoo officials in San Diego to let him borrow one of their two precious Indian rhinos so he could film it walking down Wilshire Boulevard for a promotional stunt. The costume designer responsible for the gorilla suit to be used in the remake of *King Kong* asked the Public Relations Manager at the San Diego Zoo to send him a lock of real hair from a male gorilla. The PR manager lauded his efforts to achieve realism in the role, but pointed out that nobody took a lock of hair from an active male gorilla, and to render him inactive for such a purpose entailed too great a risk. Not uncommonly also when film crews are on zoo grounds they assume somehow that all the animals have been trained to respond on command. "Get that rooster to crow," one director demanded of a keeper in the San Diego Zoo. "He has to crow in this scene."

Publicity stunts or events connected with television or motion picture filming in zoos can result in unplanned comedy or near tragedy. For several years the San Diego Zoo scored a public relations triumph with a half-hour television program called *Zoorama* which started as a local show, was later picked up by the CBS network and telecast nationally, and ended as most TV shows do by being syndicated. In the days before the new portable TV cameras the filming of one episode a week posed many problems of preparation for the zoo staff. On one memorable day the script called for a segment about Kodiak bears, largest of the terrestrial carnivores (actually a subspecies of the widespread brown bear that is confined to Kodiak Island of Alaska), an animal that can tower an awe-inspiring ten feet high if it chooses to stand on its hind legs. The producers of *Zoorama* were eager to show the immensity of the Kodiak bear in relation to a man, but since the live bears wouldn't stand on cue and few men could be found that would be willing to stand beside one if it did, zoo staffers cast about for another way to show the comparison. Somebody remembered that the zoo had been given a stuffed Kodiak bear many years before, a prime example of the taxidermist's art that stood a magnificent ten feet, had one paw raised in a threatening manner, and displayed an angry snarl that revealed long white teeth. Perfect. The bear was duly located in a storage room, dusted off and taken late in the afternoon to a spot near the Kodiak exhibit where the next day the filming was to be done. The construction and maintenance personnel who moved the bear stood it in a grove of eucalyptus trees where it would be out of the way until needed.

There was, however, one trivial oversight. Nobody had bothered to notify the bear keeper, Ken Willingham, who had already left for the day. Just at first light the next morning Willingham started to make his rounds. He walked cheerfully down the service road behind the bear exhibits when to his consternation he saw near the Kodiak grotto a full-grown bear, obviously angry, for it was standing full height, one paw raised menacingly, an angry snarl on its face. And it appeared to be looking at him. The light was still dim enough so that Willingham didn't see the glass eyes, nor notice that the bear was not moving. His first thought, a reasonable one under the circumstances, was that one of the two bears in the exhibit had somehow escaped. His responsibility, he knew, was to sound the alarm so that the bear could either be recaptured or destroyed, for within three hours the zoo would open. Turning quickly he raced to the nearest phone, pausing once to ascertain whether or not the bear was following him. He called the security office, informed them of the escape, and asked that the curator and vets be notified so they could assemble a capture team. "I'll keep track of the bear," he informed them.

Instead of going back down the service road, he skirted the canyon and took a position on a vantage point that overlooked the bear grottos but with a nearly unscalable hillside between him and the menacing Kodiak. When he reached the vantage point and saw that the bear was standing in exactly the same position, he had his first real doubts. However, because he did not know that the zoo owned a stuffed bear, let alone planned to use it for a television film, he had to play it safe. Perhaps he was confronted by an unusually immobile bear. To think otherwise was to believe that some prankster had during the night scaled the zoo fence with the stuffed bear and then dragged it several hundred yards to the Kodiak grotto.

When another two minutes had passed and the bear still hadn't changed position, Willingham cautiously moved in for a closer look. By now the daylight was bright enough so he could see the glass eyes and the pedestal on which the bear stood. Feeling a little foolish he hastened to call the security office back and tell them

to notify the curator and vets that, er ah, he had seen a stuffed bear, not a real one. Later there was some laughter at his expense, but it tended to be lost in caustic remarks about the ancestry of public relations people—and their failure to communicate.

A second breakdown in communications several years later created the kind of situation that demonstrates the hairsbreadth distance between tragedy and comedy. To generate some advance publicity for the remake of *King Kong* the studio's public relations department dreamed up the idea of confronting real gorillas with Kong, or in this case, the man-sized Kong suit with a stunt man inside. Arrangements were made with the San Diego Zoo's PR people, after their initial reluctance was overcome. Curators, vets, and keepers agreed that the experience would probably not bother the two gorillas, a much admired silverback named Albert and his consort, Bouba. Memos were sent to every department notifying them of the stunt. One security guard, however, did not get the message.

At this time security guards in the zoo's sizable force habitually carried pistols. The guns were seldom used, but most of the guards were retired from the armed services and they knew how to shoot. Two or three years before, in fact, a guard had become a hero because he used his pistol to kill a wolf. The animal was attacking a boy who had with great effort scaled an eight-foot wall and tried to take a short cut through the wolf exhibit. All security guards clearly understood that their first responsibility was to save the lives of people if ever those lives were threatened in the zoo.

On the appointed day, a busy one during the Christmas holidays, the stunt man showed up at the public relations office, put on his Kong suit, and was then conducted by PR people through the zoo to the gorilla exhibit. The sight of the stunt man walking along in what was a highly realistic gorilla suit was more than enough to attract a large following. By the time the party reached the exhibit the crowd was immense. A press of people surrounded the stunt man as he began to play his part, encouraged no doubt by the delighted looks on the faces of his audience. Safely separated by a moat, hedge, and guardrail from Albert and Bouba, the stunt man went through what he imagined to be gorilla motions, pounding his chest, swinging his arms, and shuffling along on all fours.

The two gorillas, Albert especially, evinced some mild interest, and Albert, a fine-looking animal, although he has been a disappointment as a breeding male, did charge back and forth across the front of the grotto giving the kind of grimacing, chest-beating display that zoo visitors love to watch.

The gorilla exhibit at the San Diego Zoo is one of several ape grottos that form a semicircle on a slope just over the edge of a mesa. Visitors can see the animals close up or from a higher vantage point some fifteen or twenty yards above the exhibits. The stunt man-Kong was putting on his act in the area between the higher vantage point and the front of the grotto. He experienced some difficulty because the press of people around him was so thick. Consequently he and the zoo PR people asked the crowd to stand back while the stunt man, continuing to pretend he was a gorilla, could rush through the crowd and climb part way up the stairs leading to the vantage point.

The timing couldn't have been more perfect. At the very instant the stunt man-gorilla charged through the crowd, which rapidly parted in front of him, the zoo's security officer who hadn't gotten the message arrived at the vantage point to see what was causing all the commotion. The first image to strike his eye was an escaping gorilla that posed an obvious threat to a large number of zoo visitors. Beating its chest, this gorilla charged through fleeing people and started up the steps toward him. Wyatt Earp could not have slapped leather faster. Mindful of the previous incident with the wolf, the officer had his gun halfway out, ready to use it on what he saw as an escaping gorilla.

Inside his mask, one fancies, the gorilla turned absolutely white. But he was a lucky stunt man. Out of the corner of his eye the security officer noted that both Albert and Bouba were in their grotto. More to the point, the zoo visitors, after parting to let the stunt man through, were not reacting as they would have in the vicinity of a real escaped gorilla. Some of them, in fact, were laughing at all the good fun. Moreover, a second glance at the phony gorilla was enough to distinguish it from the real thing. So the security officer did not pull his gun, and the fake gorilla lived to perform other and probably less dangerous stunts, like falling off of horses and being set on fire.

In the television age a supreme achievement in public relations

is exposure on one of the nationally televised talk shows like Merv Griffin, Mike Douglas, Dick Cavett, Dinah Shore, and Johnny Carson. The late night Johnny Carson show beams out to approximately six million homes night after night, so that stars or authors can be made by one long exposure on the show, and a regular that appears many times achieves the kind of fame that causes the public to recognize that person on the street.

It was through the Johnny Carson show that Joan Embery, a strong, hearty, outdoors girl with Scandinavian good looks and figure, enhanced her role as emissary for the San Diego Zoo and Wild Animal Park and their animals. Miss Zoofari, as Joan is called, was the creation of the same William Seaton who later became corporate Public Relations Director for Sea World when he was public relations manager for the San Diego Zoo. Miss Zoofari was not born out of pure inspiration. She started as a kind of necessity. Zoos are constantly asked to send speakers—"and be sure to bring some animals"—for schools, service clubs, women's clubs, supermarket openings, and many more. In addition local television stations like to have zoo people and animals appear on live local shows.[6] In many instances, of course, these events are good public relations, but they do represent a drain on the energies of zoo curators and others whose main tasks are not public relations, and who, for that matter, are often ineffectual public speakers or TV performers.

Seaton's conception, therefore, grew out of a growing need that couldn't be supplied through the Zoo's regular channels. Miss Zoofari would become the zoo's principal emissary on the public-speaking and TV circuit. Her first embodiment was a budding starlet with a pom-pom girl's figure who left after a year because she never quite got the hang of working with animals. Seaton looked for a replacement, and as is so often the case, found the right girl right under his nose. Joan Embery had already been working at the zoo for two years as an attendant in the Children's

---

[6] Many states now have regulations designed to assure humane treatment of animals and protect the public. These laws restrict or prohibit wild animals being displayed in public places outside of zoos. For the same reason many zoos won't allow animals to be taken out for any but strictly educational purposes, and not even then if the animals are dangerous or from threatened or endangered species.

Zoo. Not only was she fond of animals (save for snakes and crawly things like tarantulas and millipedes), she had a zoo of her own—a collection of animals she later expanded to include a Shetland pony, thoroughbred Arabian horse, ferret, pig, pygmy goat, and cockatiel. She had, moreover, the kind of radiant personality that attracted people, and if she felt any fear in front of audiences, she didn't display it.

Joan's early months as Miss Zoofari conditioned her to the kind of problems she was to encounter later on the Johnny Carson show. Before becoming Miss Zoofari, while she was an attendant in the Children's Zoo, she trained a young elephant, Carol, to paint canvases by swabbing them with a large brush held in her trunk. (Joan's initiative with Carol first brought her to Seaton's attention.) The canvases were laid flat on the ground, Joan scattered pigments of harmless finger paints on them, but from that point until she pressed her trunk against a canvas or stepped on it to make her signature, Carol was the artist, creating highly impressionistic works that were later given titles like "Peanut Explosion" and "Twilight in India." Carol's works, no more than 40 canvases, sold for an average of $100 each and are hung as far away as New Jersey, and as a result of her relationship with Joan, Carol became a regular on the round of public appearances. A special trailer was built so she could travel in comfort.

But Carol had about her some elements of a free spirit who was not always docile and easily led, and sometimes elected to give unplanned performances of her own. Just before a television appearance when a freshly dressed and made-up Joan bent over to unfasten a chain on Carol's hind leg before unloading her from the trailer, Carol, accidentally or deliberately, chose exactly that moment to release a liberal load of dung squarely on top of Joan's head with but twenty minutes to go before Joan was due to be seated, smiling prettily, on the inevitable studio couch. Carol's aim was so perfect that Joan could only suspect that the elephant had acted less from need than mischief.

Carol's most memorable performance, however, came at a civic luncheon given to honor the zoo and its outgoing director Dr. Charles R. Schroeder. The mayor, councilmen, and three hundred other dignitaries were present in a large banquet room of a leading downtown hotel. Joan and Carol were there as greeters, after

Seaton in a talk with the hotel's manager had assured the man that Carol was "trained." The mayor had just been introduced and was rising to make his comments when Carol began to urinate on the carpet in one corner of the banquet hall. A urinating elephant is not delicate about it. Carol let go a cascade that seemed to splash down like a small unceasing waterfall. The mayor paused, guests tittered, and the hotel manager looked apprehensively at the puddle which grew, as he watched, into a small pond on the new, patterned carpet. Even Joan, who would normally accept such elemental manifestations of nature as forest fires, hurricanes, and peeing elephants, was embarrassed by her protégé. At the end of the banquet, amusing and effective as some of the speeches had been, there was little doubt that Carol's contribution would be the most remembered.

When at last Joan's round of public appearances with animals—and Seaton's perseverance—brought her to the summit, a chance to be on the Johnny Carson show, it looked for a while as though she would never make it. Due at the Burbank studios of NBC in time to start shooting at 5:30 in the evening, Joan, two keepers, a wombat, a koala, and elephant Carol in her trailer, got lost on the Los Angeles freeways and barely made it to the studios with five minutes to spare. Of the animals, Carol was the only proven performer (Joan was saying silent prayers that her performance that evening would not include any exhibition like the one at the banquet), but Carol was immediately unsettled by the multitude of mirrors backstage. Wherever she looked there were elephants, and she wasn't quite sure how to act. That Joan's first appearance was a success is a tribute to her grit and Johnny Carson's showmanship. On stage in front of the cameras, for the first time facing a national instead of a local audience, Joan was understandably nervous, but apart from a slight catch in her voice once or twice it didn't show. Carson demonstrated an ability to extract laughs from at least one of the animal guests that he later displayed in every one of the shows that featured Joan and some 300 animals ranging in size from a tiny poison-arrow frog to a horse, small rhino, and elephant Carol. Considering the unpredictability of wild animals there have been few hitches. When Dudley-Duplex, a two-headed California king snake, crawled up Johnny Carson's sleeve, it was not according to the script, but Carson's reactions provided one of the funniest episodes. A full-grown cheetah which as a cub had licked Carson's face came back as a full-grown animal, jumped at Carson, who ducked, and landed in Ed McMahon's lap. Krinkles the aardvark, who had also appeared as a baby, stubbornly refused to be led off stage as an adult and when he proved too much for Joan to carry by herself, Carson had to help. A spectacled cobra, which at the zoo could be counted on to spread its hood in the typical warning posture of the species, refused to spread it in front of a national audience, but spent its allotted time trying to escape. And Howard, a normally garrulous mynah bird, who delights audiences at the Wild Animal Park's bird show, froze under the bright lights and wouldn't say his usual "My name is Howard," or give his derisive "Ha. Ha. Ha." Taken backstage, he commenced his act so that he could be plainly heard through the rest of Joan's appearance. Given a second chance Howard performed like a seasoned actor. And just to demonstrate that Carol wasn't the only one who could make puddles, a baby water buffalo puddled while waiting to go on, creating enough water that Joan slipped and fell when she went backstage to get the animal, so that she had to come back onto the set in wet clothes.

It might be assumed that Joan's appearances on the Johnny Carson show, and later on other national talk shows, represented no more than the most superficial type of public relations, designed to impress people who were looking only to be entertained. Certainly the shows are entertaining, for when Joan's appearance is announced there is a noticeable quickening of applause. However, because of Joan's deeply held convictions about the worth of animals, she has given many viewers reasons why wildlife should be preserved. In telling about the animals her comments, while they echo the sentiments of many zoo professionals, are not the parrot responses of rote learning. They stem from personal research, some eight hours' worth before each appearance, in her own and the zoo's library, and through questioning keepers, curators, and veterinarians. As she commences her studies about any animal that is to be shown, she keeps uppermost in her mind one question: "What makes this animal unique?" (She is also driven by worry that the day will come when Johnny Carson or somebody else will ask her a question she cannot answer.)

Because Joan's appearances have made her a national figure, she

receives around fifty fan letters a month, most of them coming within a week or so after an appearance. As might be expected some of these contain various propositions and proposals of marriage, and a few, fortunately not many, are downright unkind. One lady, for example, asked how such an obviously nice girl could work for an organization that cut up little animals. The reference startled Joan, who wondered what she had said to give the woman that impression. After reviewing a tape of the previous show, she concluded that the lady probably had reacted to the word "research" when Joan had talked about the zoo's research program, for in the minds of a few animal lovers research always means vivisection.

The greatest number of Joan's fan letters, however, are from young people who want to pursue a career like hers—difficult because her position is unique in the zoo world. Assuming that these fans are really interested in any zoo career, Joan, who answers all letters, has written a short booklet about zoo jobs.

It would be hyperbolic to claim that Joan's appearances on national television stifled the voices of people who want to do away with zoos. It is no exaggeration, however, to say that Joan and her animals, and Johnny Carson's reactions and comments, have helped still these voices, for many of those opposed to zoos have discovered that zoos cannot all be lumped together and that animals are accorded decent, humane treatment in most zoos. Most important, these people have benefited by seeing the animals, and listening to both Joan's and Johnny's fervent espousal of the idea that unique animal forms are worth preserving. One cannot ask much more of public relations.

The Way to
Ararat

Within the past few years the monks of Mariastein in Switzerland ate the last European otter in their area during Lent, when the consumption of meat from warm-blooded animals was forbidden. The monks' argument for including otter in the Lenten diet was a model of syllogistic reasoning. Otters, they explained, spend most of their time in the water. So do fish. Therefore, otters are fish, which *can* be eaten during Lent.

The extinction of wildlife at the hands of men, whether of individual populations or entire species, has frequently been just that casual. The dodo, the great auk, and many others bear mute testimony to that. Fortunately for the world the European otter, once found everywhere on the continent, still exists in some areas, mostly in Russia. One doubts, however, that the monks of Mariastein knew the status of the species when they chewed on the last local otter. As their desire to observe the rules of Lent indicates, they were serious about their religion. Their meditation and prayers showed, no doubt, great concern for people. About the extinction of human beings, particularly unsaved or unregenerate ones, these monks cared. About the extinction of otters, quite obviously, they cared very little, although perhaps they later had some regrets that future Lenten dinners would not include this warm-blooded "fish."

For many people the concept of extinction itself is difficult to understand, let alone care about. Not long ago the education department of the San Diego Zoo received a letter from a high school boy who needed material for a term paper. His assignment was to write about an animal which he had personally observed over a period of time at the zoo. But, he added by way of clarification,

he wasn't interested in just any animal. He wanted to observe "one of the really extinct ones."

Possibly the reason people have difficulty grasping the idea of extinction is that it wasn't born until the early nineteenth century, although by then the process of man-created extinction was already well under way. The European wild ox, that legendary aurochs, for example, became extinct in 1627. But before the time of the French scientist Baron Georges Cuvier (1769–1832) there was utterly no way in western thought to comprehend extinction as a natural process. Religious thought, which dominated all thinking up to Charles Darwin, would not allow it. Evolution had not been promulgated as a theory, and knowledge of evolution is necessary to grasp fully the idea of extinction. Those fossil remains, the old bones, leaves, and shells that had been found before Cuvier's time were explained away either as accidental and interesting mineral formations that looked like plants and animals, or as the bones of creatures that still existed somewhere on earth. Such ignorance is not strange. Much of the earth remained unopened to the eyes of western science. The headwaters of the Nile had not been found; most of Africa, in fact, was still the dark continent. South America had been touched only around the fringes, and many islands of Indonesia and the South Pacific remained a mystery. It was widely assumed that all present animal forms were descendants of those that had landed on Ararat with Noah and that they all continued to exist somewhere. Extinction, therefore, did not exist until Cuvier cautiously introduced the idea to science by concluding that the enormous bones of some dinosaurs were indeed of animals that no longer existed. He stayed within the bounds prescribed by religion, however, by theorizing that these extinct animals had been wiped out fairly recently by such natural catastrophes as fire, flood, and earthquake. No one at the time would dare suggest that some of the discovered fossils were of animals that died out millions of years in the past.

In many parts of the modern world the idea of extinction—the complete obliteration, the passing into nothingness of entire animal species—is still not widely understood. This is especially true among less sophisticated, developing peoples, who are often most concerned with preventing their personal extinction, but even among some citizens of highly developed nations the concept has no reality. For others, who may comprehend extinction well enough, the disappearance from earth of "lesser" animals is a matter of no more consequence than eating the last otter at Mariastein. Consequently, before zoos can fully succeed in captive breeding, they will have to increase the number and kinds of their educational efforts to impress on the public the moral outrage of man-created extinction, and more important, the reasons why endangered animals should be preserved.

The way to Ararat, in other words, begins with understanding, and ends with caring. There must come a general shift in attitudes comparable to that which brought the killer whale from reviled to admired creature, worthy of people's energies and efforts to save it from harm. Zoos will have to teach their public that the masterpieces of nature are every bit as deserving of preservation as the masterworks of man—that a gold and brown Rodrigues Island fruit bat is the moral equivalent of a painting by Rubens or a statue by Michelangelo.

Educating the public to be concerned about the possible extinction of many animal forms, however, is only one of the responsibilities that zoos will have to assume if captive breeding is to be a success. Before the public can care, zoos will have to care. No activity by zoos has received more lip service and been less seriously undertaken than captive breeding. All zoos subscribe to the idea, but few are really doing much about it. This failure is not a factor of size. Gerald Durrell's Jersey Zoo is small, but no zoo in the world is more truly dedicated to captive breeding (including, by the way, breeding the Rodrigues Island fruit bat whose numbers in the wild may be no more than 150). The Arizona-Sonora desert museum is also small, but it devotes part of its budget and the energies of its professional staff to a program to breed the margay. A beautiful spotted cat, smaller than the ocelot, the margay formerly ranged in forested areas from the American Southwest to Argentina. Because of the fur and pet trades, it has become threatened or extinct over much of that range. The Tacoma Zoo in Washington is undertaking the captive propagation of the highly endangered red wolf, a canid that has been killed off principally by ranchers and is now threatened by genetic swamping through interbreeding with coyotes on the fringes of its restricted

range in the American Southeast. The Portland, Oregon, Zoo has ambitiously undertaken the breeding of Asian elephants.

These programs in small institutions demonstrate that any zoo can breed at least one species. There are, however, genuine difficulties that many zoos face. Some lack the space to keep the numbers of animals that captive breeding requires. The superb Basel Zoo occupies only some thirty acres in the heart of a city. The large and magnificent West Berlin Zoo, one of the world's greatest in number of animals exhibited, has no room for enlargement in its island city. Working with the animals already there, the West Berlin staff under Director Dr. Heinz-Georg Klös achieve good breeding results, but deaths exceed births and the staff can do little with many of the young but sell them to other zoos. One captive breeding program, of Argentine pampas deer, may be sustained.

Quite a few zoos lack the money to establish captive breeding programs. As a rule of thumb, with some exceptions like the National Zoo and several state-owned zoos in Eastern Europe, privately operated zoos are better financed than those run by governments, particularly city governments. Hard pressed cities find it easier to cut the zoo's budget than to reduce police and fire protection or other community services. Moreover, the city-operated zoo most often occupies a low position in the city's administrative hierarchy. Zoo directors, often subordinated to park commissioners, must operate through cumbersome chains of command which place a number of uncomprehending bureaucrats between the director and the mayor. Budgets have to be approved at several stops by people who don't know the difference between an aardvark and a jaguarundi and may sharply question any funds allocated for captive breeding. Even brooms and buckets may have to be requisitioned in a process that often takes weeks between order and delivery, if in fact the order is approved. Moreover, the selection of zoo employees through civil service may create difficulties when keepers who don't properly care for their animals can't be fired without a lengthy and frustrating procedure. As a result, zoos run by governments are often the poor relatives of the zoo world. Many barely scrape by in day-to-day operations, let alone have extra funds for education, research, or captive breeding.

The size of a city has no bearing on the way its zoo is administered, although civic pride often does. If a Martian were to judge the relative sizes of San Diego and San Francisco by their zoos, he might assume that San Francisco was a village and San Diego an enormous city, whereas both places have roughly the same population and there is more wealth in San Francisco. The principal difference between the two zoos lies in the fact that San Diego's is operated by an independent, nonprofit zoological society on city land and San Francisco's is administered by a city government that appears indifferent to its zoo. The San Diego Society's budget for public relations and advertising alone is roughly the same as the entire budget for the San Francisco zoo. Yet there is no discernible reason why San Francisco's zoo should not be organized the same way as San Diego's. It is a credit to a hard-working director, Saul Kitchener, and his professional staff that San Francisco has established captive breeding programs with lowland gorillas, East African colobus monkeys, spider monkeys, and musk ox.

In some instances city-operated zoos prosper because of civic pride or for a short time they catch the interest of mayors or councilmen. Sometimes effective auxiliary organizations like the Greater Los Angeles Zoological Association (GLAZA) give strong financial and moral assistance as GLAZA has done for the city-operated Los Angeles Zoo. There are instances also when a highly gifted and persuasive director can push measures through a reluctant bureaucracy.

While shortages of space, funds, or both are serious obstacles to the establishment of captive breeding programs by some zoos, no obstacle is more serious than the inability or downright reluctance of some zoo managements to accept the responsibility that is being handed them. The sad fact is that some zoo operators simply do not want to bother with the increased load that captive breeding brings: the burden of housing, husbandry, feeding, research, and compliance with numerous laws and regulations pertaining to endangered animal species. Content with the old, comfortable niche in which all they have to do is exhibit animals and tell the public a little about them, these zoo managers take shelter under an umbrella held over them by the zoos that are engaged in captive breeding.

Most advocates of captive breeding agree that there is room in the world for what might be called the satellite zoo, a smaller organization that swings in the orbit of a major zoo in its area. Satellite

zoos can provide homes for surplus animals that might otherwise have to be destroyed (for one of the ironies of successful propagation is that animal populations may increase beyond the carrying capacity of the space allotted to them). In some instances satellite zoos can establish second or third herds, and breed them with the guidance of the larger organization. Some such diversification will be required to protect captive-bred animals from contagious disease or catastrophe. Nonetheless, every zoo management that honestly wants to can start at least one captive breeding program of its own, selecting perhaps a seriously threatened or endangered species from its own area, as the Philadelphia Zoo has done with the bog turtle. Whether newt, vole, lizard, or warbler, as Gerald Durrell has observed, the small, little-known, or "ugly" animals deserve to exist just as much as the larger, more exotic ones.

Some zoo managers with the best of intentions about captive breeding do not comprehend that a program involves more than throwing one or two pairs of animals together in the hopes that they will produce offspring, which, of course, they often do. To be self sustaining, geneticists claim, each captive breeding program should have the equivalent of eight pairs and preferably more to form the nucleus—the founder group. Geneticists doubt that Noah's Ark could have accomplished its mission with founder groups of only one pair each. What often occurs when the founder animals are too few is what geneticists call "inbreeding depression." Over a few generations the animals may breed, but then comes a marked decline in their fitness; a word that encompasses vitality, vigor, fecundity, and fertility. Finally the breeding ceases altogether.

The cause of inbreeding depression is excessive matings of closely related animals. Fitness is maintained in large breeding groups because the couplings of unrelated animals produce fewer combinations of deleterious recessive genes. Deleterious genes are those that replicate malformations like cataracts and cleft palates, or pass along hereditary diseases like hemophilia and sickle cell anemia. The larger the original number of genes, called the gene pool, the less chance there is that deleterious genes will find one another to produce the unfit, ill, and malformed offspring.

In the wild, gene pools are constantly refreshed in various ways. A young male baboon will be cast out from his home troop and by necessity have to gain acceptance in another unrelated troop. Silverback gorillas regularly kidnap females from a rival band.[1] Young hawks and eagles are pushed into territories far removed from their parents. And in the great Medusa-head mating balls of garter snakes near Manitoba, Canada, chance, if nothing else, dictates more frequent encounters of unrelated snakes. Among many animal species father-daughter, mother-son, brother-sister incest is rare (although not unheard of); there appear, in fact, to be scent signals that warn animals when they approach a close relative.

It can be argued, and examples given, that some large animal populations have grown from remarkably small founder groups. All of the golden hamsters alive in the world are descendants of one male and two females who were litter-mates. The European wisent (bison) went through a genetic bottleneck of 17 animals, all that were left on the continent before captive breeding brought the species back from the brink of extinction. The revival of the wisent provided, in fact, a fascinating irony which shows that the introduction of new genes into a breeding group is not always beneficial, and causes a cytogeneticist like Dr. Benirschke to argue that chromosomes should be studied for possible deleterious features before animals are mated. Sixteen of the wisent in the genetic bottleneck were closely related members of one subspecies. The seventeenth wisent, sole survivor of a second subspecies, was added to give the breeding group new blood. This animal, it developed, was loaded with deleterious genes, more indeed than those found in the remaining 16 animals. His contribution, in other words, tended to muddy the gene pool.

Those who advocate large captive breeding groups argue that exceptions like the golden hamster and wisent do not alter the fact that inbreeding is likely to bring loss of fitness and eventual extinction of the breeding group. What the exceptions do demonstrate is that hope should never be lost. If the world population of

---

[1] Early explorers like the Frenchman Paul du Chaillu (who knew better) took back to Europe stories about gorillas that kidnapped black women. These stories, in turn, led to the popular portrayal of gorillas as monstrous rapists, giving them the kind of bad press that culminated in the original version of *King Kong*. It was all very titillating in the Victorian age, but the deflating truth is that male gorillas are anything but oversexed, and possess barely discernible reproductive organs.

a species is reduced to two, provided they are male and female of the right age, the effort should be made to breed them. The Mauritius kestrel (hawk), whose wild population was reduced to seven, may yet be brought back through captive breeding. So may the California condor, a species which now numbers no more than forty birds. The fitness of small founder groups such as these can frequently be resumed if they are bred to sufficient numbers after passing through a genetic bottleneck. Zoo managers, unfortunately, are too often prone to sell surplus animals before the group reaches a large enough size.

As breeders of domestic animals are aware, the bad effects of inbreeding can be offset to a small degree by the judicious selection of strong characteristics in animals to be mated. However, while this kind of interference with natural selection may be desirable in breeding cattle and horses, it is not in keeping with the effort to preserve wild species. According to Dr. Michael Soule, a population biologist at the University of California, San Diego, fitness involves much more than the continued ability to propagate. When animals live for several generations in a zoo, with every physical want cared for, they are likely to lose the ability to survive in the natural world outside the welfare state, in intense competition for food, territories, and mates.

Wild mice, for example, build snug nests which protect their naked newborn from the elements. When the same species of mouse is propagated for several generations in the laboratory, the group may continue to reproduce well, but provided with food in a sheltered environment, the mice no longer have to build snug nests. In one study researcher Carol B. Lynch discovered that some laboratory-bred mice change their nest-building habits within a few generations. Of six strains she observed, one started building extra large nests (which might in the wild be the equivalent of drafty, unheated houses for the mouse babies), and two strains built nests much smaller than those used by wild mice.

Brown rats studied by S.A. Barnett and R.C. Stoddart changed their territorial and aggressive behavior within six generations. Fed and kept warm in the easy conditions of captivity under the benign rule of their human laboratory masters, the rats became notably less aggressive than their wild brethren. Where a wild male rat would have attacked and tried to drive off any males that intruded on his territory, the sixth-generation laboratory-bred males greeted intruders as members of the family. Within the restricted space of the laboratory cage this friendly behavior was adaptive. It served the rats well because it reduced the tensions which would have made life in the crowded environment virtually unbearable. However, left to shift for themselves in the wild, the hand-shaking male rats would most likely be chopped down or run off by any wild males they tried to greet as long-lost brothers.[2]

Knowing that zoos do become welfare states, those zoo professionals that want to retain fitness in their captive-bred animals try to simulate conditions of a wild environment. Such an approach is difficult, if not impossible, when exhibits or breeding compounds do not have the space animals need to establish territories, keep a safe flight distance from potential enemies, or escape from a rival after the combat between males that may precede mating.

When natural conditions cannot be achieved or closely simulated some zoo scientists have tried to use behavior modification to teach animals techniques that, it is hoped, will help retain their fitness.

For a period some of the most advanced work in behavioral modification was being done by Dr. Michael J. Schmidt, a veterinarian, and Dr. Hal Markowitz, a psychologist, at the research center of the Portland Zoo. The objective of this program, according to its authors, was to encourage "resident animals to exercise in ways that emphasize their species specific capabilities," a psychologist's way of saying to help animals be themselves.

Schmidt and Markowitz and their associates used the familiar conditioning made famous by Ivan Petrovich Pavlov, who demonstrated that dogs taught to associate a bell with their feeding soon salivate every time the bell is rung, whether or not they are fed. In the experiments at Portland animals were taught to respond to signals which told them that if they performed certain tasks they could get food. In the Diana monkey cage, for example, the mon-

---

[2] It should be noted, however, that the dynamics of some wild populations are subject to abrupt changes. Dr. Shirley Strum of the University of California, San Diego, found that within one generation baboons of a troop she studied in Kenya progressed from infrequent opportunistic predation on Thompson's gazelles to deliberate hunting, first by single males and later by cooperating males.

keys had to go through four steps to get their reward. When a light flashed on, a monkey pulled a chain which turned on a second light. The chain beneath this light had to be pulled in turn before the monkey would receive, in the best Rube Goldberg fashion, a single poker chip. This chip was the money which the monkey who worked for it could spend for food by dropping it into a slot that triggered the release of a food pellet. If the monkey wasn't hungry, he could save his chip and spend it later, running the risk that it might be stolen by a cage mate.

Advocates of free enterprise and all those opposed to the welfare state may take heart by learning that the Diana monkeys apparently favored working for their feed instead of receiving it as a daily handout, for if they didn't play the game to get food, they were fed anyway. Some monkeys earned their entire daily intake of 25 pieces of monkey chow and 10 of fruit by earning chips one at a time to pay for them. In the process, the experimenters claimed, the monkeys received much more exercise than they otherwise would. The experimenters did not claim, though perhaps they might have, that the monkeys may also have enjoyed being busy—as opposed, say, to sitting around all day with nothing to do but pick their fur and watch the passing visitors.

Many zoo professionals, including Warren Iliff, director of the Portland Zoo, are opposed to behavioral modification of the type used on the Diana monkey. The Portland Zoo has, in fact, stopped experiments of this nature. Iliff (and others who feel as he does) believe that the learned behavior is unnatural, and may actually do more harm than good by creating stereotyped responses, giving the animals a false impression of the foraging process, and possibly inducing the wrong kind of exercise. As Iliff points out, "We don't really know enough about the natural behavior of most zoo animals, so in using behavior modification we may be creating abnormal behavior instead of inducing natural." Others opposed to behavioral modification fear also that it may be used to please the public by setting up what are essenitally carnival acts similar to those that feature piano-playing chickens that peck out simple tunes for a few grains of corn.

Another obstacle to large-scale captive breeding by zoos arises from the fact that zoo professionals have either ignored or not understood the amount of cooperation that will be necessary among their institutions. Ancient traditions are hard to break, and many zoo directors (or their boards) persist in the old ways that were common when animals were plentiful and inexpensive. They try to excel one another, hoard single rare animals as a miser hoards gold, cling chauvinistically to labels and claims that in the past brought renown to their zoo, or cooperate only on their own terms.

Fortunately, spurred by a dawning if too-long-delayed recognition that business can no longer be done at the same old stand, many zoo managers are now giving evidence of a desire to cooperate in breeding efforts. The most frequent manifestation is the "breeding loan," whereby one zoo sends an animal to another for purposes of propagation without relinquishing ownership. If the loaned animal actually helps to produce babies, the two participating zoos assume ownership of the offspring in accordance with an agreed upon sequence, perhaps with the zoo that made the loan getting every other youngster beginning with the first.

There are a few instances, too, when one zoo may provide free stud service for another. In the Phoenix Zoo languished Hazel, a gorilla, whose mate, Casey, had died of valley fever—a shame really, because Casey was a gorilla of distinction. He had come to Phoenix originally aboard Hugh Hefner's *Playmate* jet, that solid black plane with the bunny ears painted on its tail. A drugged and snoozing Casey spent the entire flight from his original home in Omaha stretched out in the enormous, round bed in Hefner's airborne bedroom—a picture that conjures up all kinds of interesting possibilities. What if Casey had awakened and gone forward to the pilot's cabin? What if there had been a playmate aboard who didn't realize who was in the master bedroom? What if . . . At any rate, not long after his flight Casey died, and the Phoenix officials, unable to get a breeding male, looked around for some way to have Hazel serviced so that she could at least be provided with the solace of a youngster. San Diego Wild Animal Park officials offered the services of Trib who had recently fathered Jim. So Hazel came to the Park, spent some time in quarantine where she was tested for communicable diseases like valley fever, and then put with Trib. After some courtship preliminaries, the two got down to serious business. In no time Hazel was pregnant. It was then mutually agreed that Hazel would return to Phoenix

to have her baby. Otherwise, the two institutions found, they would have to apply for a permit to ship the baby across state lines. Fetuses, fortunately, can travel without permission (unless they are in the eggs of birds being shipped in from overseas).

A breeding loan that set the pattern, because it received so much publicity, came with the famous trip in 1966 by the London Zoo's female giant panda Chi Chi. The object of Chi Chi's travels, made aboard a specially modified British European Airways Vanguard propjet, was to provide her with a mate, An An, at the Moscow Zoo. Put together, the two animals displayed some initial interest in one another, but soon fell to fighting (which, who knows, may be one of the giant panda's courtship rituals) and were separated by nervous handlers. The same pattern was repeated each time Chi Chi and An An met thereafter, so their marriage was never consummated.[3] The zoo world, however, took notice and the loaning of animals by one zoo to another increased, more in England and America than on the continent, where fierce rivalries remained.

Advocates of captive breeding emphasize that more than breeding loans will be required if a large number of species are to be propagated in zoos. Some breeding groups, they say, will have to be administered cooperatively by several participating zoos. A model for this approach, called a breeding consortium, has been provided by the trustee administrators who direct the destiny of the world herd of Arabian oryx. Desires and needs of the participating zoos in San Diego, Phoenix, and Brownsville, Texas, are second to the best interests of the oryx. Animals can neither be sold nor traded without the trustees' consent.

There are presently numerous instances in which several zoos may possess one, two, or a few of an animal species like the okapi which may all but be impossible to replace from the wild. Common sense would then seem to dictate that these zoos agree on a plan to breed the animals as though they were one herd, communally owned, at a site with the most space, best climate, and best support services. The only American zoos which currently have okapis have begun discussions about forming a consortium,

[3] Giant pandas hail from China and to date the only successful captive births have occurred in Chinese zoos. However, the National Zoo has two which researchers believe may breed and, if this zoo's success with lesser pandas is any indication, they will.

and recognizing that virtually no orangutans, chimpanzees, or gorillas will be imported from the wild, zoo directors in the British
Isles have agreed to form consortia for each of these species, starting with the gorilla. A general willingness to participate in joint
breeding efforts, however, has not as yet permeated the zoo world.

Related to the call for greater cooperation among zoos in the
formation of jointly administered breeding groups is a request by
zoo researchers that communications about breeding plans, research, husbandry techniques, and results be speeded up. There
are now only five principal sources of information about captive
breeding programs, the *International Zoo Year Book*, the Annual
Report of the Jersey Wildlife Trust, the East German publication
Der Zoologische Garten (printed in German), International Zoo
News, and the proceedings of one international conference on captive breeding. The problem, researchers point out, is that over a
year elapses between the time a manuscript is received and its publication, but the need for information about research findings and
results of established breeding programs accelerates each passing
hour.

The introduction of a computerized International Species Inventory System (ISIS), sponsored through the AAZPA, has already helped speed up the process of locating potential mates
among the mammals, birds, and reptiles in participating zoos, but
so far only slightly over a hundred of some 600 zoos in the world,
with only three in Europe, have paid the fees and had their in-
ventories programed into the computer. Moreover, computer runs
give only vital statistics like the parentage, age, and sex of animals.
A member director cannot communicate his intentions through
ISIS—tell other zoos, for example, that he is going to contraceive
breeding in one species, stop breeding altogether in another, or
commence a research program on a third. Invaluable information
of this nature is seldom published. Instead it is released in a hap-
hazard manner through personal conversations, letters, or sometimes inadvertently in talks given at periodic conferences.

While zoo people themselves are much to blame for the obstacles that hinder progress toward the widespread installation of sustained captive breeding, they by no means create the only snags.
Much of the interference with zoos making a greater contribution
to the conservation of wildlife is caused by local, state, and fed-

eral governments, particularly the latter, and by the often con-
flicting and intimidating rules and regulations of transportation
companies, with airlines being the worst offenders. Over the past
few years laws and regulations about the taking, shipping, and
housing of animals by zoos have proliferated like weeds in an un-
kept garden, and with them a greater burden of paperwork and
need for administrative personnel, including legal staff, for law
violations can result in substantial penalties. These days, zoo directors joke, they can tell when an endangered animal is ready to be
shipped because the weight of the required paperwork equals the
weight of the animal. One story tells it all.

When Mark S. Rich, Associate Curator of Mammals for the
San Diego Zoo, landed in Colombo, Sri Lanka, on the first of December 1977, he anticipated no difficulty in accomplishing his
mission. He was to pick up and fly back to the United States by
commercial jet a tiny orphaned wild Ceylonese elephant called
Devi, who would live first in the Children's Zoo and later join
other Asian elephants in the main collection at San Diego. All
necessary arrangements had been made, including reservations on
the airlines—Swissair from Colombo to Singapore; Pan Am from
Singapore to Los Angeles. Aside from having to take care of the
elephant, Rich concluded he was really getting a short vacation.

Behind Rich lay all the paperwork that had been necessary to
procure Devi in the first place. Because the Asian elephant is an
endangered species, and the Ceylonese subspecies the most endangered of all, Rich had completed the required questionnaires
and forms and undergone the other rigors of getting an export
permit from Sri Lanka and an import permit from the United
States, both required under the Convention on International Trade
in Endangered Species.

In justifying the international shipment of an endangered species
a zoo must among other things show that the animal can be used
for breeding. If the animal is a female like Devi, a prerequisite, of
course, is that the zoo either have a male of the same species or
show clearly how it proposes to breed the animal without one. At
its Wild Animal Park, San Diego already had an Asian male who
would mature only a few years before Devi. This male, however,
was not Ceylonese. If it were thought desirable to preserve the
purity of the subspecies—a question much debated among captive

breeders—then Devi could eventually be shipped off on breeding loan to the Calgary Zoo, which owns a bull Ceylonese elephant. In any event Devi could be bred, so one requirement was satisfied.

There were, however, several others. With the burden of proof on him (and the zoo) Rich had to show that the removal of Devi from Sri Lanka would not work against the survival of her species in the wild; that she had not been captured illegally (like the snakes and lizards brought in by the Philadelphia Reptile Exchange); and that she would be shipped in a way that would reduce or eliminate risk of injury, damage to health, or inhumane treatment enroute. Finally, he had to show that the San Diego Zoo had the stature, resources, and experience to keep a Ceylonese elephant.

Rich and the zoo had met all these routine, and generally desirable, requirements. In addition they had sweated out the thirty-day period that is allowed for public comment after the zoo's application for a permit has been published in the *Federal Register* of the United States. During this interval individuals or groups can oppose the issuance of the permit or request that certain restrictions be placed on a zoo before it gets the animal. The result is that permits are sometimes denied or have to be modified.

In thinking back over what he had already gone through to get Devi—who was now bought and paid for—Rich felt a warm sense of relief as the jet touched down at Colombo. He even had in his briefcase the papers required by the State of California. These had to be attached to Devi's shipping crate to show that the San Diego Zoo was duly licensed in California and was allowed to import animals. For the next few days, Rich thought, he could relax a little, get to know the local zoo people, visit some of the game reserves and ancient ruins, maybe get in a little skin diving in the warm coastal waters before his scheduled departure on the eleventh. It was good, also, to know that he would be home in time for Christmas with his wife and newborn son, their first child.

There is a line in Marc Connelly's play *Green Pastures* when de Lawd says, "Everything dat's fastened down is comin' loose" (He is, by the way, speaking to Noah before the flood). The line perfectly describes what happened to Rich over the next ten days. What he confidently thought was arranged, fixed, confirmed, set,

secured, nailed to the floor, fastened down, started comin' loose faster than a ball of yarn in a room full of kittens.

On the day he arrived Rich, accompanied by Chandi de Alwis of the Colombo Zoo, visited the local cargo office of Swissair to confirm the December 11 departure. In an indifferent manner the Swissair agent informed them that the flight to Singapore was confirmed all right, but there was a slight problem after that. He produced a telex which stated that Pan Am no longer held space for the elephant on the flight from Singapore to Los Angeles. In that instant Rich's comfortable world began to crumble. While his brain scan conjured the image of him and a baby elephant sitting mournfully on the tarmac at Singapore trying to hitch a ride out, he asked the agent, in a voice that was reasonably calm given the circumstances, if Swissair, which had received the advance payment, had tried to find alternate routing. The agent hemmed a little and hawed a little more, but finally he looked Rich in the eye, shrugged, and owned that he was a businessman whose best interests in the name of profit were not served by shipping an elephant and its keeper across the Pacific, since Swissair did not fly the Pacific to the United States. Now if Rich were willing to return by way of Europe and the Atlantic, that was a different matter. He would have to wait a month or so, of course, and he (the agent) could not confirm space beyond Frankfurt or Amsterdam, so possibly there would be further delay in Europe, but everything considered. . . .

In tones of icy restraint Rich interrupted. Shipment by way of Europe was out. The weather there was too cold; there would be too many takeoffs and landings and numerous possibilities of long waits and delays, all of which would threaten the health and well-being of Devi that he was pledged to preserve. In addition it would place additional strain on him, for Devi was supposed to be fed every four hours day and night, which meant that he had to sterilize the utensils and boil the water for her formulas. The dialogue in the Swissair office ended.

Rich knew that he faced a critical choice. He could fly back to the United States without Devi, who was being well cared for at the Sri Lankan elephant orphanage, but unless he transported Devi within a reasonable time, the zoo's import permits would expire.

Then they would have to go through the tedious process of re-
applying. That approach seemed needless and costly. Besides—his
dander was up. A deceptively mild-mannered man in his early
thirties, slender, about five feet eight inches tall, with reddish
sandy hair and a mustache, Rich does not enter a room as an overpowering figure, but he has in him the kind of strength that enabled
him to become a captain in the Green Berets during the Viet-
nam War, learn the Vietnamese language, and after the war to go
back and earn an M.S. in Zoology at the University of Connecti-
cut. The tougher side of his nature now took hold. He resolved
as he walked away from the Swissair office that he and Devi were
going to get to the United States as originally scheduled if he had
to devise a way of smuggling her back on a seat in the passenger
compartment. Possibly, he chuckled bitterly to himself, he could
introduce her as a rotund, long-nosed, but very wealthy aunt.

Because the root of his problem lay with Pam Am, Rich called
the next day at the local Pam Am office. The agent there knew
nothing about the original confirmation, let alone the cancellation.
Rich forgave his ignorance, for the original ticketing had been
done in Singapore, but he found it hard to forgive the man's
brusque, unhelpful manner. At his next stop, the office of Cathay
Pacific Airlines, the agent was a complete contrast. A model of
courtesy and helpfulness, he checked through the Air Cargo guide
and found that Japan Airlines had a schedule which might enable
them to fly Rich and Devi from Hong Kong with a change of
planes at Tokyo, thence to Los Angeles. Rich asked him to reserve space if he could, so the agent dispatched telexes requesting
space on JAL and suggesting that Cathay Pacific bump cargo to fly
Rich and Devi from Singapore to Hong Kong in time to make connections with JAL. As Rich left the office he felt a surge of hope.

On the fourth, after several hours of skin diving off the coast,
Rich found that his situation had improved. Both Cathay Pacific
and JAL had confirmed space. Because Hong Kong had not been
included in the original flight plan, Rich sent a telegram requesting
that the Crown Colony's Department of Agriculture and Fisheries
grant him permission to pass through with an elephant. That night
when he returned to his hotel, Rich was downright jubilant. It
looked now as though he would be home for Christmas.

A minor hitch developed two days later when the Cathay Pa-

cific agent informed Rich that they couldn't move the elephant from Singapore to Hong Kong on the twelfth but were certain they could squeeze Devi in on the next day's cargo flight. It would be close, he admitted, but an on-time flight would give Rich an hour to make connections with JAL. Not much time to move an elephant, Rich thought, but having no other alternative, he agreed. As he turned to leave the office, the agent held up a restraining hand. "Before we can ship the elephant you must give me copies of all the necessary documents."

Rich had been expecting this, so the next day he spent his time getting the Sri Lankan export permit (which meant paying for the export license); a certificate of origin that would be required before Devi could legally be brought into the United States; and a certificate of health that Singapore, Hong Kong, Japan, and the United States would require to prove that Devi had no communicable diseases. The weight of the paper now very nearly equalled the weight of the elephant. Believing now that all was once more in order, Rich spent the next two days visiting some of Sri Lanka's wildlife preserves.

On the ninth the wheels fell off the smoothly running machine. When Rich visited the Cathay Pacific office to see if anything more would be required, the courteous, helpful agent had undergone a Jekyll-Hyde transformation. The same man that had persuaded Cathay Pacific to bump cargo for the elephant and to pay Rich's hotel tab in Singapore coldly informed Rich that since Swissair had received prepayment for the trip, they should make out the bill of lading. Moreover, he added, Cathay Pacific no longer intended to pay Rich's hotel bill in Singapore. Because Rich had not asked to have the bill paid in the first place, this last barb seemed the unkindest of all.

Murphy's Law, it soon became apparent, had been working overtime. What Rich had patiently glued together began to come unstuck. At the Swissair office the still less-than-helpful agent produced a telex from their Singapore office which stated flatly that Devi could not—repeat, could not—be landed there. The health authorities, it seemed, were afraid that the little orphaned elephant might carry hoof-and-mouth disease. After a pause to absorb this amazing information, Rich explained that the decision by the Singapore authorities was—ah—somewhat curious (words like ridiculous, outrageous, dumb, stupid, had first crowded into his brain). Did they know that Devi's certificate of health showed she was free of infectious diseases? Moreover, hoof-and-mouth disease was normally a problem with hoofed animals, not elephants. The agent said that these matters were not his concern. He motioned again to the telex as if to say, there it is . . .

Discouraged, but still resolute, Rich and the helpful Chandi went to Rich's hotel, and after several long waits while connections were being made, finally got through by telephone to the health authorities in Singapore. Relieved that his contact spoke perfect English, Rich tried to persuade him in a torrent of words that Devi was a perfectly healthy baby elephant that would in no way threaten the nation of Singapore if she were allowed to pass briefly through. At first the contact wasn't quite sure what Rich was talking about, but when Rich in somewhat calmer tones told him about the Swissair telex, the contact said there must have been some mistake, promised to look into the matter, and hung up. Rich spent a restless night.

Early on the morning of the tenth the Swissair agent informed Rich that Devi could be landed in Singapore after all provided that Rich procure a special certificate stating that she was free of hoof-and-mouth disease. He seemed relieved that he was going to be free of both Rich and the elephant. It appeared that the last barrier had fallen.

Over the past few days, however, Rich had gained several years' worth of experience. He now asked the Swissair agent if any more documents would be required. No, the agent replied, he already had the papers that Rich had supplied to Cathay Pacific, and he was sure that these and the others Rich had on his person would suffice. Convinced at last that he and Devi were outward bound, Rich asked Chandi to have the elephant brought the 65 miles from the orphanage to the Deliwala Zoo so she could be crated and loaded onto the Swissair cargo pallet early in the morning.

Before departure time the next day Devi was in her crate on the cargo pallet, which had been placed in the shade of a tree near the airport tarmac. After a last check to see if the elephant was all right, and certain that she would soon be loaded into the cargo hold of the waiting jet, Rich went through customs and security

at the passenger terminal and took his seat in the passenger compartment of the plane. Devi was still under the tree.

Minutes passed. No activity indicated Devi was going to be loaded. Flight time came nearer. Still Devi sat. No forklifts, no porters, nothing hinted that she was ever going to be moved from her place under the tree. Rich was about to get off to see what had happened when a harassed Swissair agent came aboard and hurried down the aisle to his seat. He asked to see Rich's documents, which were immediately produced. The agent scanned each one carefully then, as though he had exhausted his patience, informed Rich that more documents would be required before Devi could be loaded. It was now two minutes before takeoff. Devi still sat under the tree. What documents, asked Rich. The agent produced some forms that Rich had never seen before. "Oh, those documents," Rich said. He then proceeded to sign his name in letters large and bold as he could make on each of the forms (the purpose of which he hadn't the foggiest notion). For an instant the agent acted as though he wouldn't accept Rich's signature, but then, thinking perhaps that he would be stuck with this persistent American and his elephant for the rest of his life, he nodded, picked up the papers and departed. Apparently he gave the right orders, for the takeoff was delayed twenty minutes so Devi could be loaded aboard. From the cargo hold for most of the four-hour flight the baby elephant's wails came loud and clear to everyone aboard. Certain that the other passengers would peg him as the culprit, Rich buried his face in a book.

At Singapore a few minutes after Devi was unloaded a government veterinarian arrived to inspect her for hoof-and-mouth disease. Then he informed Rich that the elephant could remain in Singapore no longer than 24 hours and that a keeper from the Singapore Zoo would have to tend her the entire time. "There's one problem," Rich told him. "Our flight to Hong Kong leaves 31 hours from now." Faced with this challenge to an official ruling, the vet, Rich guessed, considered sending both him and Devi back to Sri Lanka, but since that solution didn't seem any more practical than letting them stay in Singapore for an additional seven hours, the man relented, acting, however, like someone who had been tricked.

Having learned from the Swissair agent that Japan Airlines required a different type of cargo pallet from that used by Swissair, Rich decided to make the change, if he could, in Singapore, for with only an hour between planes in Hong Kong, he wouldn't have the time otherwise. The people at Cathay Pacific were not particular about whose pallet they carried, so they gave him permission. They also informed him that Devi would be moved to the tarmac at ten the next morning. If Rich wanted to feed her between ten and three he would have to get permission from the airport police.

Thinking that such permission would be readily granted, Rich went to the police office. Absolutely not, he was emphatically told. We will not grant permission. Hadn't Rich heard that terrorists had bombed a jet at an airport in Malaysia a few days before? Over a hundred people had been killed and from India to Japan extra precautions were being taken. A little shaken that the police saw in his earnest American face even the slightest sign of a mad bomber, Rich trudged back to the Cathay Pacific office and got them to make the transfer to the tarmac after noon the next day so he could feed Devi before the flight.

When the Cathay Pacific pilots learned that Rich and Devi had only an hour to change planes at Hong Kong, they shoved in the throttles and burned extra fuel to get there twenty minutes early. For the first time, also, officialdom was gracious and smiling. The Hong Kong Department of Agriculture representative acted as though elephants came through every day. He supervised the unloading, chatted for a few minutes with Rich, then departed. Without any problem Devi was loaded into the cargo hold of the Japan Airlines 747 for the flight to Tokyo. As Rich leaned back in the passenger seat knowing that Devi was safely stowed in the pressurized hold beneath him, he breathed his first sigh of relief in a long time.

Then an ugly thought intruded on his complacency. The Japanese flight crew had come aboard just before takeoff. Had anyone mentioned to the pilot that he had an elephant in the hold? If not, and no other cargo demanded it, the pilot might not turn up the heat. Devi, used to humid temperatures in the 80s, would freeze if the thermometer dropped to 40 degrees or below. There was no question, Rich decided, he would have to tell the pilot.

Unbuckling his seat belt he made his way forward to a point where a petite Japanese stewardess was standing. Only one thought was on his mind—the possible threat to Devi's health. He forgot for a moment the recent bombing in Malaysia. He forgot also his own disheveled appearance, the three days stubble of beard, unkempt hair, dirty blue jeans, and the souvenir T-shirt emblazoned with a dragon and the word Singapore across the front. Moreover he had about him the slightly wild look of a person that hadn't slept for 36 hours.

Even so, he was a little puzzled when the doll-like stewardess turned pale after he told her that he had to see the captain. Then his numbed brain began to make the right connections. She thought he was a hijacker. Quickly he tried to explain that he wanted to tell the captain there was an elephant in the cargo hold. He jabbed his finger toward the floor to illustrate. The girl, unfortunately, understood just enough English to realize from his words and gestures that he had *something* in the cargo hold, and having reached the tentative conclusion Rich was a hijacker, she could easily imagine what. Her visible agitation was now so great that Rich feared other passengers might conclude the same. Realizing that she didn't know he was talking about an elephant, in fact didn't understand the word, Rich tried to say elephant in halting Vietnamese, but this seemed only to make matters worse. Next he tried sign language, pointing to his nose and then pretending to draw it out to a great length. Into the girl's eyes came an expression which indicated she thought she was not only dealing with a hijacker but a mad hijacker at that. Finally, because some passengers were beginning to watch him, Rich decided he would have to risk being thought a complete idiot if he were ever to find his way out of this morass. Motivated by a vision of Devi taking off from Tokyo while he languished in jail as a hijacker, he dangled one arm down from his head as though it were a trunk and walked back and forth in the aisle like an elephant, pausing every so often to point to the hold.

The pantomime would have won no Oscars, but it served. The correct light went on in the stewardess's mind. She motioned Rich to sit down, went forward, and shortly after brought back an English-speaking copilot. When Rich explained about Devi, he was assured that the cargo hold would be heated to a comfortable

80 degrees. The rest of the long trip to Los Angeles was uneventful. A small endangered elephant finally made it to her new home.

Years will elapse before Devi matures, but the ultimate object of her trip from Sri Lanka will be motherhood. Her flight from wild to zoo, without, it is to be hoped, the thickets of red tape and official obtuseness that she and Rich encountered, will be repeated by representatives, male and female, of many other threatened or endangered species brought from the wild to participate in captive breeding. Within the next few years such programs will greatly increase in numbers.

Many conservationists oppose captive breeding as a way of preserving animal species, arguing that conservation can best be served if wild animals are left in protected reserves. No advocates of captive breeding disagree with the desirability of leaving wild animals where they are supposed to be, but these advocates point out that the history of wildlife management, particularly in undeveloped countries where most of the remaining wild species are, gives little reason for optimism. Any perusal of conservation journals published over the past ten years shows that they are repositories of unfounded optimism and unfulfilled hopes. Expressed time and again are the hopes that the establishment of a new reserve—in a country about to be ravaged by war—will save an endangered species; that poverty-ridden farmers will not kill predators that take their cattle and goats; that people hungry for protein will not poach for meat; that vain women will no longer wear the skins of spotted cats; that a newly installed government brought to power by revolution will honor the commitments of its predecessor.

Separated from the hopes, the realities of wildlife conservation are clear. In any struggle between economic interests and the preservation of wildlife, the wildlife almost invariably goes. Poachers in most protected reserves of Asia, the Pacific Islands, and Africa, seeking everything from meat to aphrodisiacs, often outnumber and outgun the game wardens. On the fringes of many reserves pastoralists and farmers crowd the land. Their sheep, goats, and cattle compete with wild ungulates for the grasses; their poisons, deliberately spread, kill the predators. Throughout tropical nations the great trees of the primary rain forests, home for most of the

world's wildlife, are going down under the chain saws of lumbermen, farmers, and developers at a rate, estimates the World Bank, that will exhaust them within 60 years.

There is also a little-noted aspect of the arms race. More and more people throughout the world, many in undeveloped countries, are getting their hands on guns and ammunition. These may be used primarily by armies and guerrillas against one another, but a substantial number are also turned on wildlife—for sport, for target practice, for food. And most guns remain when people stop fighting. Where tribesmen once carried spears many now tote automatic rifles that are often used for poaching by people who view their local wildlife as the monks of Mariastein viewed the otter.

Reserves are a thin red line that in many places is beginning to crumble before the final assault on wildlife. This is the reality. Consequently, the reserves must be backed up with another reserve, the last—captive breeding in zoos. Nothing will be lost, and possibly much will be gained.

An irony remains. The aim of preserving wildlife species through captive breeding is to return their progeny to wilderness or game reserves. There have, in fact, already been several reintroductions. The wisent, bred back, is now once again in reserves. In Europe several zoos regularly breed European eagle owls, which are then trained in hunting techniques and returned to the wild. The San Diego Wild Animal Park housed, fed, and bred a group of California Tule elk for several years until a herd augmented by many young could be put into a new reserve. The first captive-bred Arabian oryx have been returned to a reserve in Jordan.

But this illustrates the irony. The trustees of the Arabian oryx herd determined that only extra males would be sent back first, for unless local attitudes toward the oryx have changed, they may soon be killed by hunters. In short, what has to change most, if Ararat is to be reached, is a state of mind. The monks of Mariastein must be willing to live with and respect the local otters.

The probability, then, is that zoos will hold many captive-bred species far into the foreseeable future, and, possibly, some forever. Most captive breeders doubt, for example, that big predators like lions and tigers can ever be returned to the wild. So while the primary objective of captive breeding will be the reintroduction of wildlife to wilderness, many species will be kept and bred for their own sake, because they deserve to exist, and future generations of people deserve to know them as worthy fellow creatures on a crowded planet.

If all else fails, if zoos don't respond to the challenge of captive breeding, if the attitude of the monks of Mariastein remains pervasive throughout the world and the accelerating decline in wildlife continues unabated—there remains one slim hope. Not long ago the San Diego Zoo received a letter, dated March 27, 1977, from Imperial, Missouri. It read

Dear Sir,

I am planning to take a voyage in the near future with a ship full of animals. I am trying to get a male and female of all animals. I am having good luck so far, except cannot seem to find a male and female ocelot and a male echidna. I am writing your zoo because of the thousands of different animals you have. All of these animals will be used for breeding purposes only. Could you please notify as to wheather [sic] or not you can help me?

The letter was signed—Noah.

Index